Research Methodology

Research Methodology

K.K. Garg

OMEGA PUBLICATIONS

NEW DELHI — 110 002

OMEGA PUBLICATIONS
4378/4-B JMD House, Ansari Road,
Daryaganj, New Delhi – 110 002
Phone: 65901906, 23278062 (Off.)
E-mail : omega_publications@yahoo.com

Head Office:
79/23, Laxmi Garden,
Near Satya Jyoti School,
Gurgaon (Haryana)

Edition : 2020

ISBN :- 81-89612-43-3

PRINTED IN INDIA

Published by Mahendra Garg for Omega Publications, New Delhi -110 002 and Printed at Suman Printers, New Delhi - 110 093

Research Methodology By K.K. Garg

Preface

Research Methodology is defined as "a body of methods, rules, and postulates employed by a discipline", "a particular procedure or set of procedures", or "the analysis of the principles or procedures of inquiry in a particular field". The common idea here is the collection, the comparative study, and the critique of the individual methods that are used in a given discipline or field of inquiry.

Research methodology is the attempt to validate the rationale behind the selected research design and provide justification of why it is appropriate in solving the selected research problem. It is the process by which we evaluate tools that produce knowledge.

The term is also used in the humanities; in literary criticism, a methodology refers to the critical approach, theoretical heuristics, and assumptions about the relationship with the historical and literary context with which a critic analyzes a particular text.

Most sciences have their own specific methods, which are supported by methodologies (i.e., rationale that support the method's validity).

In software engineering and project management, 'methodology' is often used to refer to a codified set of recommended practices, sometimes accompanied by training materials, formal educational programs, worksheets, and diagramming tools. While these would be more accurately referred to as methods, the word methodology is more grandiloquent.

The basic purpose of writing this book is to give to the reader a sound introduction to Research Methodology. It is designed as a College and University reference book for students of Arts, Science, Management and Commerce. The book is also intended as a study and reference for executives in all the functional areas: educational, financial, engineering, administrative, operative, planning, manufacturing, marketing, purchasing and so on. The book's aim and scope can be readily understood by tracing the historical development of the subject. In this book, standard material has been presented in simple language and easy to grasp style so that students may follow the subject-matter and also learn the method of writing answer.

Contents

1

Research Methodology: Foundational Concept

Introduction

Instructors, from elementary schools to graduate and professional schools, are turning to the community as a laboratory to strengthen students' citizenship preparation and academic learning. With student partners, communities are solving individual and community-wide resource and advocacy problems. At the same time, researchers have been studying the effects of this pedagogical model on the multiple constituencies of service-learning students, instructors, educational institutions, and communities and have been publishing their findings.

Some recent markers lend credibility to this burgeoning interest in servicelearning. In 1984, the Campus Outreach Opportunity League was formed to encourage student leadership in community service on college campuses across the nation. In 1985, Campus Compact was established as a national organization with a similar mission and has grown to more than 750 college and university presidents whose membership implicitly declared their commitment to involving students in community work at their respective colleges. In 1990, the National Youth Leadership Council began offering an annual national conference on K12 service-learning. In 1994, the peer-reviewed Michigan Journal of Community Service Learning began to publish articles devoted to research, theory, pedagogy, and practice of service-learning. In that same year, a special issue of the Journal of Adolescence was devoted to service-learning, followed by Education and Urban Society also devoting an entire issue to servicelearning. In 1995 Campus Compact's Invisible College held its first National Gathering on service-learning in higher education. In 1997, a series of 18 monographs devoted to service-learning in the academic disciplines was spawned by the American Association of Higher Education. Today, students of all ages are participating in service-learning at their schools and colleges. The National Center for Education Statistics estimates that more than half of all public high schools engage in some form of service-learning. Increased participation rates, national organization memberships, and scholarly publications reflect the growth of service-learning in America today.

As the field of service-learning continues to flourish, it is essential to develop a knowledge base for, and evidence of, the outcomes and impacts of service-learning. Every field and every educational innovation is bolstered by research and evaluation.

Nature of Service-Learning

What exactly is service-learning? Although there has been a plethora of interest in and development of service-learning opportunities across the country in the last decade, there is, nevertheless, a great deal of misinterpretation about it. Jane Kendall's introduction to the three-volume set, Combining Service and Learning: A Resource Book for Community and Public Service, provided more than 140 terms used in the literature to describe and define activities that involve service and learning. Although it is beyond the scope of this chapter to review or evaluate existing definitions, it is imperative to be clear about how the authors in this book understand the practice of service-learning.

There is broad-based agreement that service-learning is a form of the broader model of experiential education, with community service as the fulcrum. There is general agreement that what distinguishes service-learning from other experiential education efforts, such as internships, practica, simulations, and the like, is its focus on community efforts, which makes a difference for individuals in the community and for students' commitment to the general welfare of society.

Beyond that, there is considerable disparity in people's understanding about this pedagogy. Is service-learning any combination of community service and some kind of learning or does it entail more? Real examples can inform the search for clarity. For example, week-long alternative spring-break programs invariably involve students in daytime service to the community and in evening reflection. College courses across academic departments at universities around the nation involve students in service to the community an d requirement or option. Are these examples of service-learning?

To reduce the confusion about the conceptualization of service-learning, it has become useful to make a distinction between co-curricular service-learning and academic service-learning. The aforementioned alternative spring break trip exemplifies co-curricular service-learning, that is the combining of service and learning outside the formal school curriculum. In this prototype, the student learning that results from the community service is outside what is traditionally thought of as the province of the academy. In contrast, academic service-learning is bound to the curriculum, so that the service is connected to an academic course. The learning in the community and the learning in the classroom are complementary.

Although there is growing agreement about this conceptualization, there remains a wide range of academic service-learning practice. Although all servicelearning courses require community service, some instructors intentionally integrate the learning from the community with the learning in the classroom, whereas others do not. The latter practice is a compromised interpretation of academic service-learning, largely because the community service and academic learning of the course function as parallel, rather than integrated, activities. High quality, academic service-learning initiatives in which the learning informs the service and the service informs the learning create a reciprocal and synergistic relationship between the two.

Perhaps the best way to think about academic service-learning is to identify its necessary defining or essential features. A review of definitions and conceptualizations finds three essential elements of servicelearning: First, there is a service provided in the community, one that responds to a need that originates in the community; second, students' academic learning is strengthened and third, students' commitment to civic participation, active democratic citizenship, and/or social responsibility is advanced.

Having identified these three essential elements, it becomes apparent that service-learning stands in stark contrast to more traditional forms of pedagogy. It is different from traditional pedagogy in many ways, including the role of the student, the role of the instructor, the kind of learning that is valued, and the emphasis on social rather than individual responsibility. This nontraditional nature of service-learning makes not only the practice of servicelearning, but also the study of service-learning, that much more subtle and complex.

Service-Learning Research

A range of positive outcomes has been attributed to service-learning, including gains in self-esteem, career knowledge, social responsibility, and academic performance. The last five years in particular have seen a substantial increase in research on service-learning.

Years ago, much of the data about outcomes, particularly student outcomes, was anecdotal. Anecdotes would come from students, teachers, administrators, and community members, and these respondents served as the sole sources of data. However, in research circles, anecdotal evidence on its own is considered inherently subjective and subject to severe threats to validity and reliability.

In the 1980s, researchers primarily studied outcomes from community service for pre-college students. Conrad and Hedin, the most cited of the pioneering researchers, found that students engaged in community service demonstrated gains in social and personal responsibility as well as in academic performance. Newmann and Rutter, Calabrese and Schumer and others found additional positive results from their studies of student participation in the community.

In 1991, the Research Agenda for Combining Service and Learning in the 1990s ignited service-learning research, primarily the study of single courses at the higher education level. Additionally, the Corporation for National Service and Community Service and its predecessor, the Commission on National and Community Service, began multisite evaluations of the programs they were funding. This flurry of research was followed by a top ten set of questions in academic service-learning; a comprehensive, national study and the development of a national strategic platform for service-learning research.

Knowledge from Past Study

Although a comprehensive literature review is beyond the scope of this chapter, a few snapshots of recent research may be illustrative. Regarding subject matter learning, most studies have used student self-reports, that, although assailable, have demonstrated some positive correlations between the use of servicelearning and students' acquisition of academic knowledge and skills. Research has also clearly demonstrated that service-learning has a strong effect on students' personal development, including self-esteem, confidence in political and social skills, and building relationships with others. Service-learning research also demonstrated that participating students' had an increased sense of social responsibility, expressed as feeling connected to their community. Students were found to have greater racial tolerance, value the role of service in communities, and perceive communities as having capacity for solving their problems. There is also some evidence that service-learning positively affects cognitive moral development, which is related to complexity of thinking about social issues.

Eyler and Giles demonstrated that certain service-learning program characteristics, including quality of the service placement, structured reflection opportunities, and intensity and duration of the community service component, can affect the student outcomes. Finally, a small number of studies has shown that faculty's primary motivation for using service-learning is related to pedagogical improvement, that institutional support facilitates utilization and that, in most cases, resistance is related to problems with implementation. To date, unfortunately and ironically, researchers have only scratched the surface about the impact of students' service on local communities.

Conduct Service-Learning Research

The inevitable question related to service-learning research is, "Why conduct research about this educational practice?" Three purposes are typically cited for conducting research around service-learning, most of which are pertinent to any educational innovation.

The most important reason to conduct research is to improve practice. Researchers are in a position to collect and analyze data that can help shape both existing and new service-learning courses and initiatives. Examples of practice questions that research can answer include: What kinds of service-learning placements are developmentally most appropriate for K-12 and college students? What are the best reflection methods for strengthening academic learning? What are the best ways to crystallize students' lifelong commitment to civic participation? Whereas evaluation can be helpful in answering these questions for specific programs, research can provide generalizable conclusions that can inform the development and implementation of all service-learning courses and initiatives. Research can determine if service-learning benefits students and communities, in what ways, under what conditions, and for how long.

A second reason that is frequently cited for conducting research about service-learning is to develop a knowledge base about this educational practice. A knowledge base not only contributes to the improvement of practice, but it also confers a perception of scholarliness and therefore has a legitimizing function. A knowledge base commands respect and is more likely to draw others to it, either as practitioners or researchers.

A third reason for conducting service-learning research is advocacy. Largely due to widespread confusion of academic service-learning with voluntarism and community service, the latter of which is generally perceived as outside the academy's domain, academic service-learning seeks legitimacy in the academy. Research, as the currency of the realm in higher education, enables advocates to provide acceptable forms of evidence about service-learning's benefits. Positive outcomes from a well conducted research study can turn skeptics into champions.

Problems for Research about Service-Learning

Most studies of service-learning, as well as those of any educational innovation, attempt to discern cause and effect (i.e., whether a treatment, in this case service-learning, leads to changes, however that may be defined, and if so, to what degree). The methodology usually employed for such experimental or quasi-experimental studies is the treatment/control group design. A simplified description of this traditional methodology lays the groundwork for identifying the limitations of this design for service-learning research.

In this experimental research methodology, the treatment group is subjected to an intervention that is absent or withheld from the control group. All members of the treatment group receive the same treatment. The use of random selection maximizes the chances that the groups are equivalent at the beginning of the process, vis-a-vis extraneous factors that may influence outcomes, and minimizes the chances that any changes can be attributable to the differences in the groups. The control group can then be used as a benchmark for determining whether the treatment has led to change, and if so, by how much. If two groups start out as comparable on potentially influencing factors (e.g., gender, race, academic achievement), and if the post-tests reveal differences between the treatment and control groups in favor of the former, then one can conclude with some degree of confidence that the differences may be attributable to the treatment.

According to social science research standards, this traditional research design is sound. Service-learning as a subject of study, however, poses multiple challenges for researchers who would like to undertake this approach to the research. The most significant threat is that this research design relies on equal treatment across individuals in the treatment group, and in service-learning there are many variables beyond the control of the researcher that can compromise this need for treatment equalization. Whereas a study about a new classroom intervention purported to encourage student learning collaboration could introduce some control because the classroom intervention can be planned by the researcher, service-learning students are involved in community experiences that are sometimes beyond the control of the researcher.

For example, in his study on students' perceptions of power and efficacy as a result of participation in service-learning, Miller said, "Reviewing the findings on differential student characteristics and experiences not only deepens our understanding of the students' changed perception of the power of people, but also significantly supports the importance of attending to these variables as mediators of service-learning outcomes". He goes on to say, "In the research area, this study reinforces the need to continue to empirically evaluate these experiences in light of their vast complexity," and that "whole group comparisons, across diverse sets of students and experiences, are likely to obscure important impacts on particular students, and lead to misunderstandings of the service-learning enterprise". Because the experimental research design necessitates a constancy of experience within the treatment group, and because this is beyond the control of the service-learning researcher, it is problematic to generalize cause and effect.

In addition to the methodological problem of lack of control over students' community-based experiences, other challenges to service-learning research abound. For example, most past studies have focused on a limited number of student outcomes. One study might look at academic issues as the dependent variable, while another may look at personal development issues. Furco, for example, has found there are six educational domains that past studies have shown to be positively correlated with participation in service-learning: academic, career, social, personal, ethical, and civic responsibility. But most studies have not attempted such a comprehensive assessment covering all domains. Therefore, the limited selection of outcomes variables in past research has short-changed the study of service-learning.

Another confounding issue for service-learning research is that most past studies have examined very specific courses or programs. This creates questions about generalizability. Even one of the most widely cited service-learning studies has questionable generalizability. In that study, students in a political science class at a large, Midwestern public university were divided into two groups, using random selection: one that was required to perform 20 hours of community service related to the course of study and one that was required to do a time-comparable library research assignment. The students in the community service group reported greater academic gains, received higher grades, and demonstrated stronger social responsibility gains from the beginning to the end of the class than their library research counterparts. The degree to which researchers can generalize findings from this study is not clear. Do the results generalize to all political science classes, or is there something special about the study of Contemporary Political Issues that enables community service to serve a strong academic and social responsibility function? Do the study results generalize to other academic disciplines, such as history or engineering, or were the results influenced by the compatibility of community service with the study of political science? Perhaps it worked with this set of instructors, or this set of students at a large public university, but might not work with other instructors, students, or at other kinds of higher education institutions. It is difficult to generalize from this study due to the limitations of academic discipline, instructor, student, and institution samples. This study's weak generalizability is common to many past studies of servicelearning.

Other problems for service-learning research are discussed in this volume. These include the lack of agreement on a definition of service-learning; the inherent variability among courses and initiatives; the lack of representative sampling of programs; problems with sample selection, randomization, and control groups; failure to investigate impacts subsequent to the service-learning experience; and inconsistent findings across studies for some of the dependent variables.

Beyond the idiosyncratic issues, service-learning research suffers from many of the same limitations as other educational research. For example, naturally occurring conditions, such as length of the semester; variability in the students' personal interests, abilities, and values; and variability in the site placements (individual vs. group activity, high vs. low intensity of the community work, etc.), can each have a dramatic effect on outcomes, thereby limiting the generalizability of any single-site study.

New Research Paradigmm

Given the problems with, and limitations of, past studies and the use of traditional research methods to study service-learning, the authors in this book raise the question about appropriate research methodology for the study of this educational practice. Some have argued that the use of traditional quantitative methods alone underachieves in its discernment of service-learning outcomes; that pencil-andpaper measures are insufficient for capturing the depth and subtlety of outcomes from service-learning experiences.

Some researchers have insisted that quantitative methods should be supplemented with qualitative efforts, such as personal interviews or focus groups, in order to adequately study service-learning. Others have gone further, arguing that the inherent nature of service-learning challenges traditional social science research. They assert that service-learning values learning beyond the classroom and ways of knowing that go beyond textbook and teacher expertise, and that the study of service-learning must use methodologies that are epistemologically consistent with its subjectivistic orientation.

Study of Service-Learning

What directions should future efforts take in studying service-learning? Researchers currently know the most about the effects of service-learning on students, a bit less about service-learning's effect on faculty, less still about its effect on schools, colleges, and universities, and virtually nothing about the effects of students' service-learning efforts on communities and community members. Furthermore, researchers know a fair amount about the effects of service-learning on students during their period of participation, but much less about the long-term impacts of participation. Do students become lifelong civic participants as a result of their involvement in service-learning? How else are they influenced over the long run?

Beyond these kinds of specific research questions, what are the unanswered questions about the study of service-learning? One question has to do with the relationship between K-12 and higher education. Service-learning has penetrated both sets of institutions, and therefore, has begged the question about the relationship between these two sets of institutions, especially around their servicelearning initiatives. Further, can service-learning function as a catalyst for discussions about creating seamlessness between K-12 and post-secondary education?

Another matter pertinent to service-learning research has to do with ensuring the continuation of research in this field. If researchers seek to improve practice, build the knowledge base, and extend the capacity to advocate, then it is important to cultivate the base of new researchers and to encourage further work by current researchers. At least three contributing strategies have been identified. First, cognitive and learning scientists must be enlisted to strengthen the direction of current efforts. Second, because practitioners far outnumber researchers in the service-learning community, one strategy would be to build the capacity of practitioners for conducting research. This might be accomplished, for example, via regional technical assistance centers. Third, current researchers' practice can be encouraged by making available funding opportunities and publication outlets. If research is to continue to flourish, then intentional efforts must be made to build capacity.

Another issue has to do with insuring that the findings of research and evaluation studies are disseminated widely. Because improvement of practice and strengthening of advocacy are primary reasons for conducting research, it is imperative that findings be disseminated throughout the service-learning community, both on campuses and in K-l 2 schools, as well as in local communities. When the dissemination of research or evaluation has only a limited reach, the field of service-learning suffers. How can results from research and evaluation studies be certain to be disseminated? Perhaps an accessible clearinghouse could serve as a repository for all research pertinent to service-learning.

Finally, how can communities contribute to the generation of knowledge about service-learning? This is a call for co-generative scholarship. After all, since the community is involved in the practice of service-learning, shouldn't the community play a role in the development of knowledge about service-learning? Of course, this too, like the pedagogy of service-learning, would be nontraditional, and a stretch for those who argue that only those credentialized can conduct quality research.

As interest in service-learning continues, there is likely to be a concomitant demand in understanding its potential impact on students, teachers, schools and colleges, and communities. More research is needed to understand the power of service-learning.

2

Research Methodology and Statistical Analysis

Introduction

The focus is on methodology rather than results and on student outcomes rather than school, site, or community outcomes. Studying an educational program such as service-learning is difficult, especially when one tries to apply traditional methodologies. Unlike many educational innovations or reform programs, service-learning is not a specific program with identifiable characteristics. Rather, service-learning is an approach to teaching and learning that is given meaning by the school or organization where it is based. It is this challenge that faces researchers: to develop studies that account for the tremendous variability across and even within programs.

As is noted elsewhere in this volume, there is great diversity among service-learning programs. A student's service experience can include a wide range of activities, and even within a given activity, a wide variety of tasks can be performed. Visits to service-learning placement sites can be daily, weekly, or only occasionally, and preparation and reflection can occur in a large number of ways. In fact, it is often difficult to determine what actually constitutes servicelearning. For example, some consider a one-time volunteer experience at a soup kitchen service-learning, whereas others believe service-learning must occur over an extended period of time. The Alliance for Service-Learning in Education Reform developed a list of essential elements or requirements for service-learning, but even these are not presented in terms that are easily operationalized.

This chapter assumes the researcher has established a definition of servicelearning and clearly communicates this definition when discussing the research. Even with the definition problem addressed, researchers face a multitude of meaningful and extraneous variance that can complicate the study and affect the results. The chapter begins with an overview of how empirical studies of service-learning have been conducted, followed by a brief discussion of their limitations. It then presents some recommendations for further development of this work.

Characteristics of Empirical Studies

Most studies of service-learning attempt to identify areas where students experience growth, development, change, and so forth. After participating in service-learning. Pre-testand post-test designs are often used, with the data consisting of quantitative and qualitative responses from and about students. For the purposes of this discussion, it is assumed that all qualitative responses are converted into quantitative indicators. The length of time between pre- and post-administrations varies depending on the service-learning programs being studied. Analyses usually consist of measuring change from pre-test to post-test, and attributing that change, hopefully an improvement of some kind, to participation in a service-learning program.

Comparison data are frequently obtained from students who did not participate in service-learning. They are often selected based on their similarity to the service-learning students on select demographic variables, such as age, race and ethnicity, gender, or socioeconomic status. Using comparison data allows the researcher to explore whether group differences are most likely due to initial differences, maturation, or participation in the program. Although the use of a preand post-design with a comparison group assessed at the same points in time is considered a strong methodological design, the strength of this design is somewhat weakened when students are not matched or are not randomly assigned to groups.

Studies of servicelearning are usually conducted with existing programs and rarely use random assignment for both financial and educational reasons.

One alternative to using a nonrandom comparison group would be to compare service-learning students to national norms on standardized tests and attitude measures. Saying that service-learning students of a given community perform better than the national average on given tests after participating in a program can be a powerful statement, but unless the measure is appropriate for a given program, this strategy becomes problematic as well.

Types of Programs Studied

Because service-learning programs vary widely, it is difficult to assess the effectiveness of service-learning as a whole. Some researchers have examined the effectiveness of specific types of programs. For example, Switzer, Simmons, Dew, Regalski, and Wang assessed the effects participation in the Helper Program had on self-image, attitudes, and behaviors of junior high school students. Youniss, McLellan, and Yates studied a particular type of high school class. Because the within-sample variability is reduced, the results of these types of studies can be powerful in determining the effects of a certain type of program. However, the results are often not generalizable to other types of programs.

Another approach has been to study exemplary service-learning programs or as Conrad and Hedin described, programs that have a "reputation for excellence and as representative of the major variables" of interest in the research. Thus, only programs that "presumably maximize their impact on students" are included. In the tradition of case study research, this is commonly called "information rich sampling". With this approach some of the variability among programs is eliminated and the differences with comparison students are maximized. One drawback of this type of study, again, is that the results may not generalize to programs in which the implementation is less than exemplary. Moreover, problems can arise in operationalizing exemplary programs and assuring they meet these criteria.

Still other studies attempt to evaluate service-learning as a whole, including a wide range of program types in their analyses.

Nationally or state commissioned studies and meta-analyses fall within this category. Significant findings are considered meaningful since they emerge in spite of program and student differences. However, when a diversity of servicelearning programs are aggregated for data analyses, less successful programs may increase the variance within the service-learning group and limit the overall effects of participating in service-learning. Real differences that are related to specific program features may not be identified. Furthermore, by not controlling for variables like program type, these large-scale studies may not have direct relevance for individual programs.

Most studies of service-learning select a sample based on data about the program. Information is usually reported concerning at least some student demographics and some program and site characteristics such as program length, frequency of service, and method of reflection. Although these variables are not usually fully included in the quantitative analyses, they do allow for some comparison of variables across studies.

Constructs and Statistics

Studies that assess the impact of participating in service-learning usually focus on one or more student characteristics or constructs, such as, self-efficacy, selfconfidence, academic achievement, and academic involvement. These constructs are often assessed using some form of scaled scores or by collecting data from student records. In most cases, assessment tools have been reported to have adequate reliability coefficients. The actual measures are often included in the research reports allowing the reader to evaluate the appropriateness of the items.

Studies of service-learning generally look for student level differences using a variety of descriptive and inferential statistical procedures, with statistical significance established at the .05 level. Pre- and post-differences are typically examined using paired t-tests or analyses of covariance. Some researchers have developed innovative methods. For example, Newmann and Rutter created a ranking procedure to identify program or student characteristics from distinguished schools that appear to have a greater impact from lower ranking schools. Although newer methodologies like

Hierarchical Linear Modeling are available to study multilevel data, most studies have relied on more traditional approaches which are often more interpretable to the general reader.

Current Empirical Approaches

Researchers of service-learning have struggled to find ways to document the unique characteristics of the service-learning experience. One problem that tends to limit the generalizability of studies is that the criteria for selecting programs to be studied are often unclear. In some cases it appears programs were selected based on convenience or a willingness to participate in all the required activities. Although a program's willingness to participate is an important concern, most researchers select a sample based in part on information about the servicelearning program. A single school staff member, without additional confirmation and documentation, often provides information about the program. However, these reports are frequently inaccurate. Even when schools are carefully selected, it is possible that the types of schools that support service-learning, especially an exemplary example, may be different from schools that do not. An exemplary service-learning program may be one component of an exemplary school. Thus, the findings are more about the school than service-learning as a separate program.

Another important issue when studying service-learning is choosing the proper construct to measure and the proper tool with which to measure it. Often, researchers attempt to make strong statements about service-learning by measuring its effect on a construct such as academic achievement or selfefficacy, using standardized measures. One problem with this kind of study, of course, is that such constructs may be fairly stable over a short period of time. It might be questioned whether an intervention such as service-learning, without additional support, even should be expected to produce measurable change in such broad areas. When service-learning is embedded within a larger program designed to produce change, these confounding factors may be responsible for any observed changes in students. Furthermore, the effect of service-learning is sometimes more subtle, or does not appear in students until some time after participation in a program.

Selecting or developing appropriate assessment tools is one of the greatest challenges to service-learning researchers. Most studies of service-learning have relied on paper and pencil measures, which are very different from the experiential approach of service-learning. During service-learning students are expected to reflect on their actions, consider different options, and learn from their choices. Students are often confronted with situations that do not have one right or best solution. In contrast, most surveys require students to provide a single answer. Even when students are encouraged to write about their experiences, responses are often categorized into discrete categories for purposes of analysis. It may be speculated that many students who would thrive with experiential, hands-on learning, such as service-learning, would find traditional paper and pencil surveys difficult to complete. Although the reported reliability coefficients for most assessments are generally adequate, few measures have been validated with service-learning students.

With pre-test and post-test designs, a problem that sometimes arises is that pre-test scores are assumed to reliably represent what students were like before they had any exposure to service-learning. However, pre-tests are subject to bias, particularly in cases where students have high expectations for the servicelearning experience. Teachers often present service-learning to students as a powerful, life changing activity, creating high expectations for the program. The experience itself, although enjoyable and educational, is often a great deal of work. Because students learn through realworld activities, the experiences can be frustrating and students do not always see that they have had a positive impact at the site. When post-tests are administered immediately after the last site visit, students may focus more on the struggles than the positive learning that occurred.

For example, if a pre-test asks students about their level of civic engagement, students who have participated in an orientation may portray themselves as more enthusiastic about civic involvement than students who have not participated in an orientation or who have never heard of service-learning. The result, of course, would be that the service-learning students statistically exhibit less or no growth in civic engagement than comparison students, evidenced by smaller pre/post differences. Furthermore, if the service experience was an intense activity, and students complete the surveys immediately following a great deal of hard work, their responses may be confounded by students being tired. Even if data from the service-learning and comparison groups were statistically equated, the service-learning group would show less growth.

A student's previous history can also be problematic for the researcher. Students who have prior volunteer experience or come from a family that values volunteerism, for example, are likely to have different outcomes than other students. And although age is usually controlled for investigations of servicelearning, maturity is not. Even when a study includes children of the same age or grade-level, there are apt to be differences in effectiveness of program that are related to maturity or readiness for the service-learning experience. Another concern with the sample is that few studies have focused on service-learning with young children, particularly kindergarten through fifth grade. Studies of this age would most likely require new methodologies and different assessment tools.

Finally, service-learning programs are continually changing, and data collected about a program today may not be accurate in two months. Staff changes, schedule changes, the addition or elimination of sites, funding shifts, and so on can have a tremendous impact or very little impact, yet studies rarely account for these changes. Particularly exemplary programs may be adept at adjusting to the changing needs of the school and program.

Data Analyses

Data from studies of service-learning are usually analyzed using traditional statistical tests such as t-tests and analysis of covariance. Frequently multiple analyses are preformed, and all statistically significant results at the .05 level are reported. Although such an approach is useful for exploratory analyses, its general use can lead to erroneous conclusions since chance differences may be considered significant. The general rule, to divide the acceptable level of significance, such as .05, by the number of comparisons performed to obtain the level of statistical significance that differences need to exceed to be considered significant, is rarely followed. Furthermore, if the sample size is large, very small differences can reach statistical significance, despite small effect sizes. For example, a threepoint difference might be statistically significant, but if the scale ranges from 0 to 200, it may not be a meaningful difference. The statistical significance of the result needs to be considered in the context of the meaningfulness of the findings.

Finally, a word of caution needs to be made about the general way statistics have been used in service-learning research. Many studies have reported gain scores (post-score minus pre-score) as evidence of student change. Yet, there is a great deal of literature that addresses the problems with using gain scores. Unreliability of the prescores, variance of post-test scores that are smaller than the variance of pre-test scores, ceiling and floor effects, and regression toward the mean are but a few of the problems that can bias the results.

Although data from studies of service-learning could be considered hierarchical, and statistical methods are available to handle these types of data, most studies rely on traditional methodologies such as t-tests and analyses of covariance. These analyses may be more easily understood, but the meaningfulness of their findings is often questionable given the large number of analyses that are typically performed and small effect sizes. Furthermore the assumptions which underlie these analyses are rarely met. Among these assumptions are that the covariate (typically the pre-test score) is free of measurement error and that subjects have been randomly assigned to groups.

Violation of these assumptions may result in an over, under, or correct estimation of group differences. Although the dependent measure is also usually fallible, this measurement error rarely biases estimated group differences, although it may reduce the power of the statistical test and lead to failure to detect statistically significant group differences.

Recommendationn

The need to carefully document school, program, and site characteristics has been stressed. Not only does this help anyone who wants to use the findings clearly understand who participated in the study, but it also provides a framework for interpreting statistically significant student change and findings that fail to reach significant levels.

Selecting the Service-Learning Programs to Study

Whether studying exemplary service-learning programs, a specific type of service-learning, or a broad range of programs, the researcher must carefully define what is and is not service-learning and these definitions should guide the sample selection. If comparison data will be collected, the definition should indicate what student or school characteristics are considered important for selecting the comparison group. If data will be combined from several servicelearning programs, it is important to assure that each program is actually doing service-learning as defined by the researcher. When the study focuses on exemplary programs, the factors that make the program or programs exemplary need to be clearly described. Even if judges are used to rate programs, care must be taken that the judges work from the same definition, and interrater reliability should be established.

The process of sample selection should involve the collection and evaluation of information about potential programs for study. Too often, data about service-learning programs are collected using a simple multiple-choice survey or brief interview asking administrators or teachers about the presence of key features of service-learning at the school. These kinds of probes rarely allow researchers to see what is really happening at a school. The individuals providing information about the program, moreover, should be those individuals who are actively involved in service-learning and who are likely to know the details of a given program. Administrators who are not actively involved with students are likely to know what should be happening in the school, but not what actually is happening. For example, suppose that an elementary school requires 15-minutes of reflection about service each week, but in reality, only five minutes per week are spent on the activity. An administrator would be likely to report the 15-minute rule, but by speaking to a teacher or observing a class, one would establish a more accurate understanding of the program. Researchers need to know what occurs, not simply what is supposed to occur before selecting a program for inclusion in a study.

Program implementation should be monitored throughout the duration of the study. A single survey at the outset is hardly enough.

It is advisable to collect data often, and from multiple sources, including observations, interviews, and reviews of school materials such as press releases, course listings, and awards. This type of information can provide important information about the maintenance of the program over the duration of the study. It can also be quantified and included as background information (covariates) during the analyses.

Furthermoie, if several programs from within a school or school district are selected for participation in a study, it should not be assumed all have simılar service-learning programs. As Sanders noted, "failure to check the accuracy of the obtained description of the program through direct examination or observation, or by confirmation by program personnel" is a common error. He continues by warning that one should not fall into the trap of "assuming that the program was uniformly implemented as intended". Service-learning is especially likely to be subject to variability across programs. Even when schools have participated in the same service-learning training programs, the implementation is likely to vary as service-learning is incorporated into that particular school's culture and classroom.

Collection of ongoing program data will help the researcher remain alert to the types of changes that can impact a study and affect the results. Observational and survey data from and about sites, student activities, reflection, and planning activities will to help assure the program is operating as expected. Development of systematic recording procedures can be used to help quantify the service experience. For example, researchers might record students' preparation activities, such as research, interviews, or group discussion, and whether these activities are teacher or student directed, done alone or in a group, involve outside participants or just the class, and so on. The specific characteristics that are examined will depend on the researcher's design and study goals.

Knowledge of the school's mission and curriculum are important for understanding a program, helping assure the results are generalizable, and putting the data into context, especially when making comparisons across schools. For example, suppose as part of two service-learning programs, students keep journals during reflection. Students in Program A also study poetry, although it is not part of service-learning. Students in Program B have an empirical writing class. Even if the same instructions are given for journal writing, it is likely that student journal entries will reflect these different curriculum experiences. Unless the researcher is aware of the different writing programs, differences in the journals might mistakenly be attributed to the service-learning experience.

Teachers also bring their own differences to service-learning that can have an impact on students' experiences and on the research results. Teachers who report service-learning is "how they always teach" are likely to have a different level of engagement to the task than teachers who found they "were assigned to service-learning." Teachers vary in their experience and comfort working as a facilitator with service-learning. Knowledge of these differences can provide important information for both sample selection and data interpretation and can highlight differences among service-learning programs or even classes within the same school.

It is important to continually assess how a program is being implemented if the program is included in a study. Occasionally, a program will experience changes that have a profound impact on how servicelearning is implemented. For example, if statewide test scores drop, the school may focus more on other pedagogies for master of standards rather than servicelearning. There are several ways to handle data that indicate there have been significant changes within the sample. Minimally, this information should be included in the research report to help the reader evaluate the sample. If a program no longer includes all the key elements of service-learning as defined in the study, the program might be dropped from the study. Alternatively, the researcher may decide to use this information as another type of comparison group. Finally, examination of how the program changed might suggest key variables for further study. For example, if the amount of administrator support decreased at the program that was dropped, amount of administrative involvement might be a variable to include in a follow up study.

Finally, besides collecting information from the sample, it is often informative to examine characteristics of programs not selected or not willing to participate. This might involve interviewing teachers, administrators, or other key personnel, and reviewing the school's mission statement and class curriculum. These data can provide insights for understanding service-learning. Programs may decline to participate for reasons ranging from the time burden to reluctance to be evaluated. Knowledge of the reasons can help guide future sampler recruitment efforts and may help the researcher rethink aspects of the design.

The Design

The pre-test and post-test design provides a way to examine change on the variables of interest and to assess whether there are initial differences between the service-learning and comparison students. Pre-test scores are assumed to be indicators of what students are like before they have any exposure to a treatment (i.e., service-learning in this case). However, in studies of service-learning, this is rarely the case, and student expectations may have an impact on the findings. Student responses on the pre-test can be confounded by knowledge about the program, what is discussed during the service-learning orientation, or prior experiences participating in service-learning. Furthermore, as previously noted, a school that supports service-learning may have a culture that is different from a school that does not. Hecht found that teachers often present servicelearning very positively and suggest that the experience will be life changing. If these experiences result in more positive pre-scores, the post- minus predifferences will be reduced, suggesting service-learning had minimal impact. Therefore, the timing of administration of pre-tests, whether during the first class meeting, after or before the orientation, and so on, may be an important question to consider.

One possible solution is to collect data throughout the service experience. For example, if the service experience will last 15 weeks, students could complete brief surveys four times: at the beginning, twice in the middle, and again at the end. Student journals can provide another method to track changes over time.

Constructs and Assessment

Research about service-learning needs to begin with a strong theory about the areas in which student change might be expected. As noted earlier, studies often focus on traits that may be fairly stable over a short period of time. Even if one assumes that constructs could exhibit change within a short period, the theoretical framework must suggest that it is reasonable to see the hypothesized changes given the program characteristics. The areas in which student change is expected should reflect the study schools' objectives for service-learning.

Service-learning can be introduced for many different reasons, such as creating a safe environment, providing career skills, or creating real world links to the curriculum. The goals may be to address a specific problem, such as an increase in school violence, or a very broad one, such as to enrich and expand the school's mission. Researchers should look for student outcomes in areas where change would be expected given the program goals and activities. For example, to expect positive growth in literacy skills when students have been engaged in environmental testing of water or park clean-up may not make sense. However, simply knowing the goals for a service-learning program is not enough information.

Programs with very different goals may provide similar experiences for students, whereas programs with similar goals may provide very different experiences. Student outcomes depend on the activities and experiences at the site, during reflection and during planning, as well as how service-learning is infused into the curriculum. For example it might be hypothesized that students will have increased literacy skills, if as part of the water testing, students prepare reports about the findings for the community, write press releases, teach other students about water testing, and develop a booklet that will be distributed through City Hall. In another program, the focus might be on developing a scientific understanding of the characteristics of the water, chemicals that are present, and being able to create a graphic presentation of the findings. Accurate knowledge of what students are doing would help a researcher identify constructs to be investigated and to understand the results.

Talking with the students and teachers as well as reviewing school materials such as the mission statement, curriculum, and lesson plans can help researchers develop program specific hypotheses. A grid can be developed that identifies service-learning program goals and activities and links these with expected student outcomes. It often helps to have individuals not connected with the service-learning programs or the research review these grids and rate the likelihood that the expected student outcomes will be found given the design of the program. These ratings could be as simple as a five-point scale, with 1 indicating very unlikely to 5 indicating very likely. When a study includes numerous programs with different learning goals, ratings for different student outcomes are likely to vary across the different programs in the study. Data analyses could examine student outcomes aggregated across all programs, for individual programs and using the ratings as a variable in the analyses. For example, schools might differ in their rating of improved academic achievement as a student outcome variable. Rather than look for global improvement in academic achievement, a researcher could explore student achievement only among programs where it is likely and compare these students with the comparison students.

Studies of service-learning need to use multiple modes of assessing student outcomes. As discussed previously, use of paper and pencil surveys may not be the most appropriate approach. If the researcher uses an established assessment tool, it is important to assure the assessment is appropriate for the given population being studied. For discussion of this topic, see texts such as Nunnally or Thorndike, Cunningham, Thorndike, and Hagen. An assessment that is highly reliable with urban high school students may not be as reliable with rural middle school students. Asking a small representative group of students to discuss the questions before administering it to the entire sample can be very informative. It is also important that the terminology of the assessment be understandable to students. For example, although the study is about service-learning, it is possible students in a given school call "servicelearning" by a different name, such as home and careers, community service, community action, or simply mathematics or science. Although reflection may be a critical part of the program, it might not be identified as a separate component. Instead it may be necessary to prompt students when they talk about what they do in the community or when they write in their journals. Often it is valuable to adapt assessment tools to reflect these changes.

Methods for examining student change after participating in servicelearning might explore how the assessment can be made more realistic. Students, who have successfully worked cooperatively on a service-learning project, may find answering a survey without consulting with peers at odds with the design of the service experience itself. Furthermore, it might be questioned whether some students for whom service-learning is a meaningful experience, and where the greatest change might be observed, are the same students who have a difficult time completing a survey that requires reading and writing proficiency.

For areas such as career awareness, students could be asked to demonstrate their learning through a self-developed project. This type of approach would focus the assessment on the program goals and emphasize tasks that are related to a student's service experience. A public presentation of what is learned through service-learning could take many forms. If service-learning occurs as part of an academic class, and the academic goals are clearly defined, students could be asked to share what they learned with another class, the community, parents, and the like. When researchers study a small number of classroombased service-learning programs, they can help teachers develop assessments that directly link the assessment with the content and performance knowledge students are expected to gain. If the sample is too large to allow this type of individualized assessment, development of a service learning rubric that is reviewed by teachers, could be used to collect similar data across classes, while allowing teachers to rate students relative to their individual lessons. A rubric can be developed and used to assess student learning in numerous dimensions, such as academic knowledge, understanding of others as reflected in choice of presentation materials, preparation, alignment with other knowledge, or real world applications.

Student portfolios that include student work related to the service experience are another method used to assess student change. Students or teachers could select work that demonstrates growth in the areas of interest. For example, the instructions could ask for inclusion of a piece of work that shows how the student demonstrated problem solving skills or how academics were enriched. The types of work that students select would provide another indicator of what students feel they have learned and what they value from servicelearning. If student portfolios can be maintained over several years, this data could provide the basis for a longitudinal study of the impact of servicelearning. The use of portfolio assessment in education can be found in De Fina or Grace and Shores.

Student records can provide data concerning attendance, disciplinary incidents, awards, and choice of courses or extra-curricular activities. Examined over time these data can provide information about how service-learning has impacted a student in specific areas. Report cards, especially with younger children, frequently include narrative sections that can be analyzed. Finally, third party reports from other participants such as teachers and site coordinators can provide additional valuable behavioral indicators.

Data Analyses

Whether a researcher relies on a traditional paper and pencil survey or creates scores from other forms of assessment, data analysis must begin with a careful review of student responses. Missing data must be examined and a decision made whether to eliminate the student from the entire study, drop the student from some analyses, or estimate the missing responses. When a large number of students leave particular questions blank, it may suggest a problem with the assessment question or task; for example, students did not have enough time, the reading or task was too difficult, or the instructions were confusing.

Item analysis for questions with a specific percentage of missing responses (e.g., items that more than 20% of the students do not answer) can be performed to determine whether a specific subgroup of the sample found the question or task difficult. Breakdowns could compare the number of students who did and did not answer the question on variables such as type of site, program, type of reflection, dates the survey was completed, gender, age, or grade. To accomplish this, a dichotomous variable is created for each question (answered: 1; not answered: 0), and the number of students with a -1 or 0 falling into each category is compared using Chi Squares. If significant and meaningful differences are found, follow up interviews can provide insight into why questions were not answered. A decision must then be made concerning whether to retain the question or drop it from further analyses. This type of analysis may suggest groups that should be analyzed separately for particular constructs, such as looking at responses from males and females individually. The results can be used in later studies to help revise the assessment questions.

If the number of missing responses is small and appears to be randomly missing, researchers may decide to estimate the missing responses using one of several options. The missing response can be replaced with the overall mean for that item. However, if site, program, or other differences are suspected, a more appropriate choice may be to substitute the mean for that group. For example, the mean of students at a given site on an item can be substituted for the missing response rather than the overall mean. Another option is to estimate the scale using responses, given by the student, to other items on the same scale. A criterion, such as 90% of the scale items are answered, is established, and a scale score is estimated by averaging the other items. It is important that scale scores for all students be calculated as averages or that the average be converted to the same scale as other students. There are excellent resources for directing the researcher in ways to handle missing data, such as Allison, Cohen and Cohen or Little and Rubin.

Another issue related to data analysis is that many variables function as both independent and dependent variables. For example, student achievement might be an outcome variable for some analyses and a control variable in others. This suggests a modeling design, such as path analysis or structural equation modeling, is appropriate. It is important however to remember that these approaches require a strong theoretical model about the causal relations among the variables before testing the data. Although different hypotheses can be tested, these analyses are not used for exploratory purposes. For information about these approaches, see texts such as Pedhazuar and Schmelkin.

Another option is to treat the data as multilevel data; that is, students are thought of as nested within sites and sites are nested within schools. A statistical technique called Hierarchical Linear Models (HLM) can be used to examine multilevel data of this type and will allow for the examination of both site and student characteristics. Although HLM builds on a linear model, it extends the analyses far beyond the traditional analysis of variance, analysis of covariance, and regression designs. Using this approach, it is possible to explore "relations occurring at each level and across levels and also assess the amount of variance at each level". HLM also allows for control variables, similar to the control variables in an ANCOVA design. However, an advantage of HLM is that the problems of inadequate sample sizes that arise when conventional linear modeling is used are greatly reduced. Furthermore, aggregation bias and problems with the unit of analysis are lessened.

Data from studies of service-learning fall naturally into this model. With students serving as the unit of analysis, each student is then attached to a site. Site variables can include a range of variables such as type of service site, teacher experience, or how often students visit the site. Student characteristics might include gender, age, or prior family experience. The dependent variables can include the constructs of interest in the study and different models can be tested for different outcome variables.

HLM will work efficiently with 22 to 27 sites, allowing for variability at the site level to be evidenced as well as variability at the student level. Although problems of small sample sizes are reduced using an HLM approach, they are not eliminated and add to the complexity of the analyses. Based on both theory and an examination of the data, it may be possible to combine sites. Careful examination of the data may reveal that meaningful groupings are not the most obvious ones. For example, groups might be formed based on the type of contact students have with others at the site, such as direct contact with the same individuals each visit, direct contact with different individuals each visit, occasional contact, or no direct contact.

HLM allows for background variables such as socioeconomic status and achievement to serve as control variables and to be included for individual students and as a school average. Pre-scores can also be entered into the analyses as control variables. In many ways, HLM allows for data exploration by using different control variables and various characteristics of the site. Control variables can be selected after examining student responses and variability across schools.

A simple example of how this procedure might be applied follows. Selfefficacy might be predicted within each of 25 service sites from a pre-score and socioeconomic status. HLM then allows for examination of how the regression weights for the 25 equations function as characteristics of sites. These data provide indications of differences across sites while considering relations within sites. By varying the control variables it is possible to examine how impact varies according to site and program characteristics (e.g., intensity and nature of interpersonal contact at sites, the degree to which a collegia] relation with adults is encouraged, opportunities to engage in autonomous behaviors, and characteristics of the reflection). Student pre-test data, student and program leader interviews, site questionnaires, and observation data can be as create control variables for the HLM analyses.

In summary, the types of data analyses and ways in which the information is used depend on the research questions and theoretical framework for the study. It should not occur outside of the context of the service-learning programs. As Cohen stated, "the informed judgement of the investigator is the crucial element in the interpretation of data, and that things take time".

Conclusion

The purpose of this chapter is to consider approaches that have been used in empirical studies of service-learning and to present recommendations for new ways. The findings and approaches of earlier studies provide a useful guide for future research. Educational researchers confront many challenges as the demand increases for outcome-based evidence to support or refute the value of programs such as service-learning. The issues raised in this chapter are not unlike those confronted by researchers of other broad-based educational movements such as charter schools, progressive education, home-schooling, Head Start, and literacy. Like service-learning, each represents an approach to education designed to provide students with learning opportunities. Each is larger than a single program or series of textbooks. Instead, they are ways educators, students, parents, and the community think about learning and try to create learning environments for their students. The task of the researcher, therefore, becomes that of pulling together meaningful information from a wide range of programs and then developing some general conclusions. Because these programs are so different, this pulling together is often very difficult. This chapter briefly examined some of the challenges that researchers face and some of the decisions that may need to be made. Although it does not provide an indepth discussion of the ways to address these problems, it presents some recommendations and ideas for further exploring these issues.

3

Service Learning Research Methodology

Introduction

The purpose of this chapter is to identify some general themes and issues raised regarding research in service-learning, and place these within perhaps a more global context about how a better common understanding of the methodological vocabulary for research on service and experiential education might be developed. It is not the purpose to of this chapter to enter the philosophy of science debate represented by the exchange between Liu and Richman, for example, except as it relates explicitly to research methods pertinent to service-learning.

The typology adopted here is to consider the language used to express one's understanding of service-learning research within two contexts. The first is defined as an internal context of which the focal point is on multidisciplinary research about service-learning. The second is described as an external context of which the focal point is disciplinary methodology that may be brought to bear out service-learning.

Even a cursory review of the literature indicates the existence of a significant amount of research on service and its relationship to patterns of behavior, mostly in young adults and adolescents. The extant research is generally unconstrained by a disciplinary convention that is both a strength and a weakness. It is a strength in that the research is enriched by the exchange of ideas from a broad range of disciplines that is the hallmark of interdisciplinary study. It is a weakness in that it lacks the formal conventions that help define research within the confines of the traditional academic disciplines. Thus, there are relatively few parameters to help guide the researcher in the quest to link his or her research to that of previous studies, which gives it a coherence and anchors it in the body of literature. It is somewhat analogous to gardening. Cross-pollination and fertilization enriches the environment, which creates an explosion of growth. But if left unchecked that growth itself can limit the garden's ability to bear fruit. The garden must be pruned back to maximize its productivity.

Public Debatt

Demands for research are driven by political agendas that are diametrically opposed to one another. On the one hand, there are those who believe service has no place in the academic curriculum and that it detracts from the basic, traditional educational curriculum (the "3 Rs"), which society needs and from which it has strayed. On the other hand, those who support the service-learning and experiential education pedagogy believe it has the potential to offer a means to encourage students to take ownership of their education and connect them to civic life in a manner that enhances values that define a democratic society.

The research agenda seems quite straightforward. Either service-learning works to meet its objectives or it does not. Both camps expect evidence that will settle the issue in their favor. Indeed, a body of empirical evidence is being built as this volume demonstrates. But the lens through which that evidence is measured has too often been ground to fit the ideological orientation of those doing the looking. Both camps are guilty of this error, oftentimes with the best of intentions. Those committed to empirical research realize the evidence is unlikely to be so clear cut. Because the stakes are high and the focus of attention is on the results of research, those engaged in research must be especially diligent about how they conduct it and how they present it. Like it or not, the pedagogy of service in the curriculum has become politicized in a way that requires those engaged in research to be clear about the research methodologies employed and the results they deliver.

Methodological Issues

There are at least three points that may serve to aid one's understanding of the general problems associated with comparing the traditional academic pedagogy with that which incorporates service into the curriculum. First, what one is trying to measure may be very different. In the traditional pedagogy the researcher normally measures outcomes based on a given set of responses to questions. The SAT and ACT tests are archetypal examples. These tests place premium value on their capacity to capture an individual's aptitude for a given knowledge domain. How that aptitude is developed is of little consequence within the context of the test. There is virtually no value associated with the process of learning, only the outcomes.

There is a very long track record associated with these kinds of measurements that allow them to inherit the mantle of credibility by default: "It's the way we've always done it," mentality. Experiential education, on the other hand, places a great deal of value on the process of learning. However, because there are few accepted standards for how one measures the process of education, evaluation tends to fall back on instruments designed for an entirely different (and in some ways antithetical) set of criteria. They are different because what one is trying to measure is fundamentally different. They are antithetical in the sense that to the extent the process of learning is ignored, its value is discounted by default. There are plausible reasons for this. For instance, educators generally have less confidence in the ability to measure the effectiveness of the process for acquiring knowledge than in the ability to measure the knowledge acquired. Indeed, the means through which individuals acquire knowledge and the value of knowledge based on the means of acquisition is a debate as old as philosophy itself. It is certainly a debate with which social scientists are familiar.

Second, the demand that research prove or disprove the utility of service in the curriculum is misplaced and is counterintuitive to the principles of the scientific method, which is so misunderstood by friend and foe alike of service in the curriculum. The Falsifiability Principle, articulated by Karl Popper, for example, helps one appreciate that, according to the rules of formal logic, definitive proof through empirical research is impossible. What is needed is to engage continually in research that is replicable within the limits of the social sciences so that over time confidence in expressed hypotheses is based on the accumulated preponderance of the evidence provided by research that tests the hypotheses.

Third, social scientific research in a democratic society, by its nature, is challenged by the problems associated with cause and effect and the ability to use instruments to disaggregate the two. Is the dependent variable really dependent? Can one control for sufficient variance to gauge the effect of the independent variables? Replication of previous studies is especially challenging in the social sciences where individuals with complex, ever-changing personalities are involved in the experimentation. Comparative methodology offers hope for addressing these questions.

Methodological Issues within the Research Community

Many of the chapters in this volume identify certain methodological weaknesses within the research literature, and the contributors have offered their respective insights about how these might be addressed. However, before this is possible two issues must be addressed that, in many ways, are mirror opposites of one another, but which are equally frustrating. Both issues will be addressed throughout the chapter within the context of specific methodological concerns, but a general statement about each may help the reader better appreciate the need for balance between the two.

The first of these is the "splitting of hairs" phenomenon, one that is omnipresent in the broad arena that defines the service-learning literature. Here the dilemma is one of trying to be unnecessarily narrow in the definition of terms. Terms such as research, evaluation, and assessment are sometimes treated as if they should be mutually exclusive of one another. Although one must applaud the interest of scholars to make necessary distinctions among terms for the sake of clarity of meaning, it is also true that one ought not ignore or discount among terms the penumbra of ambiguity that is often present. For example, if researchers want to conduct an assessment of a given servicelearning project, they may very well expect to engage in research toward that end, and continually evaluate whether the research meets the objectives of the assessment. Thus, research, evaluation, and assessment are all part of the same enterprise to enhance one's knowledge about a given set of activities. A number of other permutations could be offered to make the same point. The point is this: It is important not to choke the life out of terminology by putting it in such a confining straight jacket that either it is irrelevant or cadaverous. For language to be useful, it must exhibit properties of shared understanding and be adaptable enough to be useful in a variety of contexts. The apparently endless effort to distinguish among service-learning, community service, and experiential education is perhaps the best example of questionable hair splitting. Even if the scholarly literature could come to consensus about distinctions among the three, it is doubtful that it would translate very well to many of the practitioners in the field who, more often than not, are teachers at various levels simply trying to find ways to stimulate their students to learn more through a variety of pedagogical techniques. Teachers, for example, are less concerned about the conflicting definitions used by academics to describe specific patterns of behavior than they are about what stimulates their students to learn in the particular environments in which they find themselves. Indeed, some of the hair splitting can seem pedantic and be intimidating to those who might otherwise experiment with a pedagogy that employs resources beyond the traditional classroom. This is not to minimize the value of using terms precisely.

The second phenomenon is quite the opposite but in some ways more problematic and prevalent. Here it is referred to as the undefined term phenomenon. It is perhaps most often observed in reviews of the literature where various types of data analysis are compared. Examples that fall into this category include such terminology as hard data and rigorous methods as if these words had some self-evident, intrinsic meaning, which of course, they do not. Often implicit in the use of such terminology is that empirical information that is subject to statistical analysis is on its face more legitimate than information collected and analyzed by other means.

A corollary of this phenomenon is the overt use of terminology in highly idiosyncratic ways. For example, the term empirical research has been defined as research that is quantifiable and subject to statistical analysis. This is a gross misrepresentation of the concept of empirical research as commonly understood. This topic is addressed in more detail later in this chapter.

A second corollary is the use of language that is meaningless either because it is undefined, or because it is part of the jargon of a particular discipline, or both. Such language usage is confusing and trivializes accepted norms to the detriment of interdisciplinary collaboration in the building of a useful corpus of literature on which researchers and practitioners can build and use. The exhibition of these phenomena does not render valueless the analysis undertaken or the conclusions drawn, but they do compromise the utility of the value the studies may have.

A third corollary presents perhaps the greatest obstacle of all because it transcends the capacity of the individual researcher to address the problem. That is the evolution of different meaning for the same word across disciplines. For example, the term normative is used in the service-learning literature, but it is a term that has different meanings in different disciplines. Indeed, psychology and sociology have relied heavily on the descriptive mode of analysis and use the term normative in that context. But economists and political scientists have used the term in a different way, as a theoretical point of reference for understanding how people behave or should behave. The intent of the descriptive model used by psychologists is different than the intent of the normative model used by political scientists. The different intention has implications for the consequences of how each is used and understood. This is not to say that psychologists use the term in a more appropriate manner than political scientists or vice versa. The point is simply that researchers cannot take for granted the language of discourse used in service-learning research.

The line between the splitting hairs phenomenon and the undefined term phenomenon can be rather thin. One person's splitting of hairs may be another person's attempt to define terminology adequately. The purpose here is not to determine where that line should be drawn in some categorical sense. Rather, the purpose is to remind the researcher to be conscious of the pitfalls inherent in each and take them into account.

Data sets and Comparative Methodology

Empiricism as a modern epistemological reference has its roots in the philosophical work of John Locke and David Hume. It means, quite simply, that the sole source of human knowledge is derived from the senses. In the 20th century the Logical Positivists of the Wiener Kreis reformulated the empirical criterion of meaning to its logical conclusion: the method of verifying a proposition is the meaning of that proposition. Although this definition was not universally accepted, it gave broad latitude to the meaning of empiricism and did not limit the definition only to quantitative data, which lends itself to statistical analysis. Perhaps the greatest empiricist of the 19th century was Charles Darwin. His acute observations and analysis of life on the Galapagos Islands and elsewhere, which culminated in the publication of On the Origin of Species in 1859, led to the present understanding of the theory of evolution. It is not quantitative in the sense that it is readily subject to statistical analyses (or, at least, the original methodology did not assume it was necessary). Yet a more profound empirical work would be difficult to identify.

Empiricism is based on the existence of observable data. The nature of the data may take many different forms and is subject to manipulation depending on what information the empiricist is seeking. The organization of the data in a particular context or format constitutes a data set. The collection of archaeological artifacts in the British Museum constitutes a data set. Whether it is quantifiable or not, or subject to statistical analysis, is beside the point and says nothing about its legitimacy as a data set. It is no more or less legitimate than a data set that can be entered into a computer and interpreted through statistical analysis. It serves little apparent purpose to claim that one type of analyses is more empirical than another. Analyses are based on empirical evidence or they are not (e.g., logical evidence). One study is not more empirical than another because its analysis is based on data that is quantifiable and the other is not, and a data set is not defined by whether or not it can be analyzed using a given mathematical formula. Arguments to the contrary violate the language of science (semiotics) that is based, in part, on the need to find common understanding of language that has applicability to a broad range of individuals from a variety of disciplines. This is especially important with respect to experiential learning that draws scholars from so many different fields.

Understanding the method of accumulating empirical data, organizing them into data sets, and analyzing them is, of course, crucial to the evaluation of research. The comparative method is a methodology that has been used with effectiveness in the research on service-learning. Arend Lijphart wrote what many political scientists believe is one of the clearest and most succinct analyses of comparative methodology and its utility in the discipline. Much of his analysis applies to the use of comparative methodology in research on service-learning as well, and is worthy of some elaboration.

Lijphart compared and contrasted comparative methodology with experimental methodology, among others. The experimental method is a methodology favored by scientific researchers when it is appropriate to do so. "The experimental method, in its simplest form, uses two equivalent groups, one of which (the experimental group) is exposed to a stimulus while the other (the control group) is not. The two groups are then compared, and any difference can be attributed to the stimulus". But social norms limit the degree to which social scientific research that focuses on human behavior can place humans in a controlled setting for purposes of practicing the experimental method.

A much more frequently utilized methodology in research on servicelearning is the comparative method, which, while not the equivalent of the experimental method, nevertheless is regarded as a method of discovering empirical relationships among variables. This is done most effectively, if four rules are adopted whenever possible. One of these rules is to increase the number of cases as much as possible, echoing the call for increased research on service-learning that is voiced throughout the book. A second rule is to reduce the property-space of the analysis. For example, if one were doing a comparative study on patterns of service projects it would be more feasible to divide the service activities into a relatively few, broad categories rather than to try to identify every specific activity. This gives the researcher more cases for every cell of the matrix, which increases the confidence she/he may have in the interpretation of the results. A third, related rule is to focus the comparative analysis on the key variables. "Comparative [analysis] should avoid the trap into which the decision making approach to the study of international politics fell, of specifying and calling for the analysis of an exhaustive list of all variables that have any possible influence on the decision-making process". The second and third rules speak to the need for uniformity and continuity in research methodology.

A final rule is to focus the comparison on comparable cases. "In this context, 'comparison' means similar in a large number of important characteristics (variables) which one wants to treat as constants, but dissimilar as far as those variables are concerned which one wants to relate to each other". One means for accomplishing this is by engaging in longitudinal analysis. Longitudinal studies allow the researcher to observe a given data set at Time $_T$ and compare it with observations of the same data set after a given interval, Time $_{T+]}$. One of the advantages of longitudinal studies is the opportunity to control for variability in the population if the same data set is observed over time. However, the greater the interval or intervals between observations, the less confident the researcher can be that observed differences or similarities are attributable to a given dependent variable.

Scientific Method and Nature of Evidence

The scientific method is a methodology for practicing empiricism. It is not the only methodology, but it is certainly one that was dominant in the 19th and 20th centuries, and it appears unlikely that it will give way to another methodology early in the 21st century. It is a methodology that is very powerful, in part because its rules are relatively simple to understand. It is based on the premise that empirical knowledge is connected with experience in such a way that it can be tested. A theory or hypothesis is empirical to the extent that it allows the possibility of a counter-instance to stand against it. That is, there is the possibility that it can be refuted through empirical evidence. Rigorous application of the scientific method is the Falsifiability Principle as articulated by Popper:

In other words: I shall not require of a scientific system that it shall be capable of being singled out, once and for all, in a positive sense; but I shall require that its logical form shall be such that it can be singled out, by means of empirical tests, in a negative sense; it must be possible for an empirical scientific system to be refuted by experience.

We say that a theory is "corroborated" so long as it stands up to these tests. The appraisal, which asserts corroboration (the corroborative appraisal), establishes certain fundamental relations, viz.compatibility and incompatibility. We regard incompatibility as falsification of the theory. But compatibility alone must not make us attribute to the theory a positive degree of corroboration: the mere fact that a theory has not yet been falsified can obviously not be regarded as sufficient.

What the Falsifiability Principle avoids is the assumption that confirmation alone constitutes proof. Inductive proof would mean that one could predict the consequences or stasis of all forms of observable behavior. In most instances involving empirical knowledge, this is not possible. For example, if one observed x number of a given species of animal and that animal was always the same color, one might be led to conclude that all species of that animal are a particular color. Proof would require that one observe every species of the animal to verify the color. But the demands of such verification are unrealistic. One cannot be certain that there is not at least one member of the species that does not exhibit symptoms of albinism, for example, and has no color.

Appreciation of the Falsifiability Principle can be useful when encountering those unfamiliar with the scientific method who have made erroneous assumptions about what it can and cannot do. For example, this writer has had to dampen expectations by his research sponsors and other interested parties that one can either prove or disprove the validity of service-learning as a pedagogy through quantitative analysis. One means to address this expectation is to explain the Falsifiability Principle within the context of the scientific method. It is a concept relatively easy to both explain to and be understood by the lay public.

But the Falsifiability Principal can create its own set of problems for the social scientist if it is accepted as the standard by which all social scientific research, including that which pertains to service-learning, is measured. As noted earlier in this chapter, social scientific research does not take place in the controlled environment that is characteristic of chemistry, for example. This has led to much debate about the degree to which social science is really a science. Those who are the intellectual progeny of the logical positivists would generally argue that it is not. In the words of Goodwin and Klingemann: "The truths of political science, systematic though they may be, are and seem inevitably destined to remain essentially probabilistic in form. The 'always' and 'never' of the logical positivist's covering laws find no purchase in the political world, where things are only ever 'more or less likely' to happen" (p. 9). The same argument would seem to hold for almost all of the social sciences. Social scientists, including those who conduct research on service-learning, sometimes fail to understand this essential character of their work. It may be that this failed understanding is part of the reason why some social scientific research pertaining to service-learning lacks clarity and can leave the reader confused. The following examples serve to illustrate this point.

One of the commonly misspecified or, perhaps more accurately, unspecified concepts in the service-learning literature is anecdotal evidence which is often cast in a pejorative light. Exactly how one should define anecdotal evidence is unclear given its varied usage in the literature. Stripped to the core, it would seem to be evidence that is empirical but that is not subject to the rules of the scientific method. Although evidence that fails to meet these rules is of limited utility, it does not follow that anecdotal evidence is inherently useless as is sometimes implied in the literature. Indeed, the value of the evidence may be limited only by the absence of a research design capable of taking full advantage of what the evidence has to offer. Early observations contrary to the laws of classical or Newtonian mechanics could be described as anecdotal, but they were nevertheless taken seriously. Some of these observations helped lay the groundwork for quantum mechanics and the atomic era. Anecdotal evidence can offer rich insight into patterns of behavior that otherwise would not be perceived. Evidence that would be accurately defined as anecdotal has offered rich insight into this writer's understanding of patterns that emerged from quantitative analysis of survey data. A more egregious error in the literature is a tendency to identify any research that is not subject to quantitative analysis as anecdotal at which point it is dismissed out of hand. This is wrong for two reasons: (1) It demonstrates a misunderstanding of what anecdotal evidence is, and (2) it demonstrates a failure to appreciate what anecdotal evidence has to offer to the careful researcher.

Another area where the absence of clarity has caused confusion is the assumption that quantitative research that employs statistical models is ipso facto more objective than research that is defined as more qualitative. For example, one of the characteristics of the service-learning literature is the implicit (often explicit) assumption that the results of action research and other similar variants of ethnographic study are somehow less persuasive than survey data subjected to quantitative analysis. The use of terms such as rigorous methods and hard research are often associated with quantifiable data and analysis as if this made such research more objective. But all methodologies, those that employ quantifiable data or otherwise, are based on assumptions that are ultimately subjective. Models that employ sophisticated mathematical formulae are ultimately grounded in one's understanding of the world and how that understanding is grounded in the model. Evidence for this understanding is offered by formal theorists themselves.

Otomar Bartos wrote eloquently and simply about this matter in his analysis of the difference between Markov chain models and game-theoretical models of human behavior two types of models that can be represented by complex mathematical formulae. Bartos wrote that the "Markov chains models represent the approach which aims at describing how men actually behave, while the game-theoretical models exemplify how men should behave". Which model is more appropriate depends on what it is the researcher wishes to investigate. This leads to two points: (1) All models of human behavior and the modes of analyzing data within the framework of any given model are ultimately based on some subjective criteria about the researcher's understanding of the world, and (2) the misspecification or misapplication of formal mathematical models will surely lead to faulty analysis. The implications for action research (indeed, for all research methodologies) are straightforward: Understand and state clearly the strengths and weaknesses of the methodology employed, and the means for mitigating the weaknesses to the extent that is possible.

Theoretical Base of Service-Learning

One final point about the research on service-learning pertains to the theoretical underpinnings on which much of the literature rests. No one can doubt the significant and central importance of John Dewey's philosophy, particularly as it pertains to education. Service-learning advocates rely heavily on Dewey for theoretical justification of the pedagogy. But it behooves scholars interested in understanding the potential of service-learning and engaging in research about it to look at a broad range of theory, which has the potential to buttress and to suggest insights about how to approach research that a more narrowly defined body of theory might not.

If more researchers were able to bring to bear the theoretical arguments in their own disciplines and substantive areas of interest that are applicable to service-learning, the field would be the richer for it. This is one of the great strengths of interdisciplinary study and all researchers and theoreticians interested in service-learning ought to be taking better advantage of it. Although this is not the place for an exhaustive theoretical discussion, three examples of well-known contemporary theorists help illustrate this point. One of these is the work represented by Paulo Friere and his understanding of dialogical education. His belief that the educational process is dependent on the extent to which individuals commit to mutual co-inquiry and learning from one another on an equal footing offers much potential insight into the way one thinks about service-learning.

A second theoretical framework for thinking about service-learning that is worthy of more attention is the idea of emancipatory learning represented by the work of Jiirgen Habermas and Carroll Pateman, among others. Within this framework, taking ownership of one's education is not only conducive to maximizing the possibility of one's ability to develop the skills of lifelong learning, it may also be a necessary condition for developing and sustaining a democratic society.

A somewhat different theoretical framework looks specifically at the role of the humanities and their ability to connect citizens to a sense of community. The contributors to Standing with the Public:

The Humanities and Democratic Practice are representative of this framework. Such work is important because it attempts to integrate learning associated with what are often perceived as the more esoteric disciplines with the real world; something that experiential education strives to achieve. Each of these three frameworks offers complimentary insight into the student-teacher-community triad, which comprises the service-learning core. They may help focus the attention of researchers more broadly than simply on the impact service has had on students, which has been the primary focus of attention.

Summary

This chapter has identified several contexts and issues within those contexts that pertain to methodology and research in service-learning. These include methodological issues within the service-learning research community itself. Especially pertinent is a better understanding and clearer articulation of the meaning and interrelationships of empiricism, the scientific method and the nature and use of evidence. Always a challenge, the difficulty of this task is compounded by the political debate surrounding the merits of service-learning. Those who define both the advantages and limits of their research with care and integrity will conduct the most valuable research. This represents the best chance for researchers to provide a base of data that is not only independent of the prevailing political breezes but that may actually serve to affect them as good scholarship can. Properly conducted and reported, those committed to research in the field of service-learning may contribute to informed public dialogue on education that will constitute significant service to our civil society and democratic culture.

4

Researching the Production of Speech Acts in Research Methodology

Introduction

A speech act such as apologizing, requesting, complimenting, or complaining, the first concern of second-language acquisition (SLA) researchers has been to arrive at the set of realization patterns typically used by native speakers of the target language, any one of which would be recognized as the speech act in question when uttered in the appropriate context. We have referred to this set of strategies as the speech act set of the specific speech act.

In order to arrive at a speech act set, it is necessary to define the preconditions and interactional goals of the speech act in question and to identify performative and semantic prerequisites for the realization of these goals. If we take the act of apologizing, for example, we could stipulate that an apology is called for when there is some behavior that violates social norms. When an action or an utterance (or the absence of either) results in the fact that one or more persons perceive themselves as deserving an apology, the culpable person(s) is (are) expected to apologize. According to Searle, a person who apologizes for doing A expresses regret at having done A. Thus, the apology act takes place only if the speaker believes that some act A has been performed prior to the time of speaking and that this precondition has resulted in an infraction that affected another person who now deserves an apology. Furthermore, the apologizer believes that he or she was at least partly responsible for the offense, so that making amends is an interactional goal.In the case of the apology, it is necessary to separate the performatives (e.g., I'm sorry) from other semantic formulas by which an apology can be realized, such as an explanation and justification for the offense (e.g., The bus was late and so I couldn't possibly get here on time) or an offer of repair (e.g., I'll do it tomorrow). The speech act set of apologizing has been found to consist of at least the following main strategies or semantic formulas:

1. An expression of an apology, whereby the speaker uses a word, expression, or sentence that contains a relevant performative such as apologize, forgive, excuse, be sorry.
2. An explanation or account of the situation that indirectly caused the apologizer to commit the offense, used by the speaker in an indirect speech act of apologizing.
3. Acknowledgment of responsibility, whereby the offender recognizes his/her fault in causing the infraction.
4. An offer of repair, whereby the apologizer makes a bid to carry out an action or provide payment for some kind of damage that resulted from the infraction.
5. A promise of non-reoccurrence, whereby the apologizer commits him/herself to preventing a reoccurrence of the offense.

In order to investigate the speech act of requesting, it was necessary to validate empirically a scale of imposition from the most direct and imposing request to the most indirect and least imposing one. Perhaps the earliest empirical SLA research on requests involved having natives and nonnativies of English rank order the degree of politeness of a series of request strategies in the context of making a purchase. The request strategies themselves came from a theoretical claim that in making requests, imperatives are less polite than declaratives, which are in turn less polite than questions. For the natives, five levels of politeness were empirically validated, from the elliptical imperative and the imperative (give me steak and fries) on the lower or least polite end to the past tense interrogative model (could you give me steak and fries?) on the upper or most polite end. The nonnatives generally agreed with these rankings, although they reversed the order of two lower level requests. (The natives rank ordered the declarative with no modal, I want steak and fries, lower than the declarative using a present tense modal, I'll have steak and fries, whereas the nonnatives reversed this ordering.)

One of the most comprehensive empirical studies of speech act behavior, both for its breadth and depth, has been that of the Cross-Cultural Speech Act Research Project (CCSARP), which compared speech act behavior of native speakers of a number of different languages with the behavior of learners of those languages. The CCSARP has also produced useful instruments for data collection and a coding scheme that has been widely replicated in other speech act studies. In addition, several excellent surveys of the research literature have appeared, which help to define and shape the field of investigation with respect to speech act research.

Sociocultural and Sociolinguistic Abilities

Speakers and hearers are successful speech act users when they have mastery over the speech act sets for speech acts in the language in which they converse. Such mastery calls for the ability to provide both socioculturally and sociolinguistically appropriate behavior.

Sociocultural ability refers to the respondents' skill at selecting speech act strategies that are appropriate given (a) the culture involved, (b) the age and sex of the speakers, (c) their social class and occupations, and (d) their roles and status in the interaction. For example, in some cultures (such as U.S. culture) it may be appropriate for speakers, as a repair strategy, to suggest to the boss when to reschedule a meeting that they had missed through their own negligence. However, in other cultures (such as Israeli culture) this type of repair strategy might be considered out of place in that it would most likely be the boss who determines what happens next. Thus, the sociocultural ability is what determines whether a speech act set is used and which members of the set are selected for use.

Sociolinguistic ability refers to the respondents' skill at selecting appropriate linguistic forms to express the particular strategy used to realize the speech act (e.g., expression of regret in an apology, registration of a grievance in a complaint, specification of the objective of a request, or the refusal of an invitation). Sociolinguistic ability reflects the speakers' control over the actual language forms used to realize the speech act (e.g., sorry vs. excuse me, really sorry vs. very sorry), as well as their control over register or formality of the utterance, from most intimate to most formal language. For example, when students are asked to dinner by their professor and they cannot make it, the reply No way! would be a possible form to use with the semantic formula "refusal." The problem is that sociolinguistically, this phrase would constitute an inappropriate refusal, unless the students had an especially close relationship with their professor and the utterance were made in jest.

Selecting the Appropriate Speech act Strategy

The process of selecting the socioculturally appropriate strategy and the appropriate sociolinguistic forms for that strategy is complex, because the selection is conditioned by the social, cultural, situational, and personal factors already indicated. Strategy selection and selection of forms often depend on the social status of the speaker and the hearer, because in most societies deference toward a person of higher status, for instance, is realized via linguistic features (e.g., using vous rather than tu) or via modification of the main speech act strategies (e.g., adding intensity to the apology or purposely refraining from cursing). Thus, coming late to a meeting might evoke a more intensified and possibly invective-free apology when the apologizee is the boss, rather than a friend. Other factors such as age and social distance are part of the social set of factors that might play a significant role in strategy selection.

It has been found that situational factors also play an important role in strategy selection. Some situations generalize across cultures and hence will elicit similar strategies in different languages, whereas other situations are more culture-specific and are likely to cause cross-cultural problems. In one of the situations involving apology that was used in the CCSARP, a waiter brought the customer the wrong order. The waiters in all the languages under investigation avoided the expression of personal responsibility, perhaps because admitting such a mistake might cost them their job. On the other hand, the cross-cultural study of complaints showed that noise made by neighbors is perceived as a serious offense that warrants a complaint within some cultures whereas in other cultures it is viewed as a less significant offense. Furthermore, it has been found that situational circumstances are more likely to lead to personal variation than are social or pragmatic factors.

Focusing on Speech act Production

Research has demonstrated that in speech act behavior, as in other language areas, there is a discrepancy between a learner's perceptive and productive abilities. Thus, in a study done with immigrants in Israel it was found that although it might take 8 years to acquire nativelike perception of speech acts, a nonnative learner may never truly acquire nativelike production of such utterances. As Kasper and Dahl noted, most of the early studies of speech act behavior investigated the nonnatives' perception of speech acts carried out in the second language. Perhaps the very complexity involved in production then prompted a major focus on the production of speech acts.

Once again the research focus is shifting back toward perception of production, but this time with more sophisticated studies involving video taping. Most recently there have been two doctoral dissertations completed on this theme, one dealing with perceptions of Ll apologies and one dealing with perceptions of L2 apologies, requests, refusals, and complaints. Yet, although the focus on perception may be in the process of renewal, there are still areas concerning the production of speech acts, particularly the cognitive processing aspect, that are in need of further investigation. In the present chapter we discuss methodological issues in researching the cognitive processes involved in the production of speech acts in a second language.

Methods for Collecting Speech act Data

The complexity of speech act realization and of strategy selection requires very careful development of research methods for describing speech act production. In the field of language assessment, there is a current emphasis on the multimethod approach. The consensus is that no single method will thoroughly assess the behavior in question. In speech act investigations, the challenge is, likewise, to find some means of combining different approaches to describe a single speech act among natives and nonnatives of a language. The ideal cycle of data collection has been perceived as one that includes different collection techniques.

Investigators would start with the generation of initial hypotheses based on observational data from natural speech in Ll and L2, whether collected initially in Ll or simultaneously in both languages. Then we would elicit simulated speech such as that in role-plays, to test the initial hypotheses. From there we might go on to a paper-and-pencil task such as discourse completion in order to focus on specific realizations and manipulate the social and situational variables. If we are concerned with the perlocutionary aspect of speech acts, we might want to use acceptability checks in order to validate the range of acceptability within a speech community. Finally, we might be advised to validate the findings by means of further naturalistic, observational data.

Discussions of the relative strengths and weaknesses of each of these research methods have appeared elsewhere and so we will not discuss them here. Unfortunately, it is difficult to obtain extensive observational data on speech acts across languages because the speech act being studied may not often appear naturally. As for discourse completion, it is a projective measure of speaking and so the cognitive processes involved in producing utterances in response to this elicitation device may not truly reflect those used when having to speak relatively naturally.

Although we mention discourse completion data, we focus this chapter on the more direct method for studying how complex speech acts like apologies, complaints, and requests are produced, namely, the role-play interview. We enumerate certain pitfalls associated with this method. But by the same token, there are a number of benefits. For one thing, it is possible to simulate conversational turns and to have the interlocutor apply conversational pressures that are not present in discourse completion tasks, even if rejoinders are added around which respondents must write in what they would be likely to say.

Use of Verbal Report in Studying Speech act Production

In an effort to understand better the choices made by respondents when engaged in a speech act production task (naturalistic, role-play, or discourse completion) or a perception task (acceptability checks), we could make use of verbal report techniques. The cognitive processes that learners go through in order to produce or perceive speech acts are not available to outside observers and are usually not even attended to by the learners themselves. It would appear that only through verbal report are researchers able to tap some of these cognitive processes by calling the learners' attention to them. We could, thus to indicate that it could be used with any form of speech act production or with perception.

To our knowledge there have as yet been only four studies of speech act production behavior using verbal report. Two of these used discourse completion as the data elicitation format, and two of them involved role-plays. The first, by Motti, involved 10 intermediate EFL university students in Brazil who, after filling out a discourse completion task calling for apologies in English, were asked to retrospect individually in Portuguese regarding a series of variables, including their depth of analysis of the situation before response and the extent to which they thought in the foreign language, English, or in Portuguese Ll while preparing and writing their responses. Motti found that respondents thought slightly more in English than in Portuguese in the planning and execution of their utterances and were preoccupied with correctness. They also reported paying more attention to another's status than to age.

In the second study, Robinson had 12 native Japanese-speaking females respond to six written discourse completion items calling for refusals of requests and invitations in English. The respondents were asked to think aloud as they filled out the task, and their verbal reports were tape-recorded. Immediately after completing the task, the researcher interviewed the subjects individually for 20 to 30 minutes regarding the content of their utterances from the think-aloud session, playing back the tape-recording to remind the respondents of specific thoughts. Although they were given the option of responding in Japanese, all the respondents performed their verbal reports in English. The investigator interpreted this use of English for verbal reporting as a result of her inability to speak Japanese. The use of verbal report in this case helped to reveal a sociocultural problem, namely, that Japanese girls are brought up to say yes, or at least not to say no. Therefore, the task of refusing was difficult for them to perform.

Although it is unreasonable to ask speakers to provide such data while they are engaged in speaking-given the intrusive nature of verbal report techniques—it is possible to obtain retrospective verbal report either between tasks or immediately after the tasks. A recent study that called for role playing and then verbal report after all the tasks had been completed was that of Frescura. Role-play data on apologies were tape-recorded from native Italian speakers in Italy, native English speakers in Canada, Italians residing in Canada, and English-Canadian learners of Italian. After being tape-recorded in six role-play interactions, the respondents were asked to listen to all six recordings and to provide retrospective verbal report on: (a) how close to real life they felt their performance to be, (b) how dominant they felt their interlocutor was, (c) their sensitivity to the severity of the offense and to the tone of the complaint, and (d) (for Italians in Canada and learners of Italian) their possible linguistic difficulties. Frescura's use of verbal report helped her establish, among other things, that the learners of Italian tended to think in English first before responding to the role-plays.

The first study to combine verbal report with role-play is that of Cohen and Oishtain. The study sought to describe ways in which nonnative speakers plan and execute speech act utterances. The subjects, 15 advanced English foreign-language learners, were given six speech act situations in which they were to role-play along with a native speaker. The interactions were videotaped, and after each set of two situations of the same type, the tape was played back and the respondents were asked both fixed and probing questions regarding the factors contributing to the production of their response to that situation.

In the administration of the role-play interview, the interlocutor gave the respondents an opportunity to read the descriptions of two brief role-play situations at a time (two apologies, two complaints, and two requests in all). Then she slowly read each situation out loud, gave the respondent time to think of a response, and then gave her an opener and had the respondent role-play with her. The interaction was videotaped and audiotaped as well. In a previous study where the verbal interaction had been recorded only on audiotape the structure was fixed an opener was followed by a single response from the respondent. In this case, flexible structuring of the role-play was used. The native English-speaking interlocutor determined whether the interaction had reached its natural and logical end usually after four or five exchanges.

The probing interviews conducted after each set of two speech act situations were intended to employ retrospective self-observation in order to obtain verbal report data about the cognitive processes that went into the production of speech act realizations. The interviewer's probes were conducted in what was the native language for I I of the respondents, and a language of greater proficiency than English for the other 4 respondents. An effort was made to have the respondents be precise and to give examples where possible. The subjects were interviewed in three sessions after the apology, complaint and request situations instead of waiting until after all six speech act situations, in order to obtain a more accurate retrospective report of behavior. It was feared that the delaying of the verbal report would reduce the reliability of the protocols, even using the videotaped behavior as a memory aid. When the respondents were not sure as to what they did and why, the interviewers played the relevant portion of the videotaped session a second or even a third time. This usually helped to jog the respondent's memory.

Role-Play Interview as A Research Method

The use of the role-play interview in other words, an oral and/ or written prompt regarding a given situation and then role-play as a simulation of actual behavior needs to be examined closely in each research context. To what extent are any such research instruments really semiethnographic or reflective of natural behavior, as suggested by Oishtain and Blum-Kulka? The remainder of the chapter deals with issues that verbal report techniques have highlighted with regard to the use of role-plays in collecting speech act data.

Cultural and Personal Reactions to the Situations

Whereas an effort may be made to select situations that are cross-culturally appropriate (i.e., that have the same cultural weight in different cultures, such as a neighbor playing loud music late at night), it is possible that one or another of the situations could still be viewed by the given respondent as not constituting a sociocultural infraction. For example, being half an hour late to meet a friend to study for an exam may not be considered an offense in Latin America or in the Middle East. In fact, it may be considered rude or unusual behavior to appear right on time.

On the personal level, respondents may point out that a given role-play situation occurs all the time. They may, in fact, indicate that they had performed that speech act in that very same situation the previous day (e.g., requesting that a neighbor turn down loud music late at night). In other cases, respondents may make it clear that they have never had to perform that speech act in that situation. In instances where the respondent has never had to react in such a situation (e.g., apologizing for keeping a classmate's book two weeks beyond the agreed date), it could be argued that the instrument is forcing unnatural behavior and that if the respondent is not a good actor, the results might be problematic. In cases where the respondents are asked to play a role that is out of character for them, the challenge for the researcher is to distinguish the respondents' sociolinguistic proficiency from their situational adeptness.

One way to handle this would be to allow respondents to opt out of the speech act, as we do in real life. If they deflected the stimulus, the interlocutor would not pursue the issue. This is often the case in the real world, where a person may opt not to apologize, complain, or request something. Allowing for opting out, however, leaves holes in the data, and so researchers and evaluators tend to request that respondents produce an answer for each situation even in face-threatening situations.

The use of verbal report in the Cohen and Oishtain study revealed the degree of planning that certain situations may activate in the speaker. In other words, the situation itself may have properties that cause it to stimulate planning more than do other situations, regardless of the personal characteristics of the speaker. For example, students' asking their teacher for a lift home—where the inequality of status was found to play an important role in the mind of the respondent—was shown to prompt a conscious style shift, at least after the teacher pretended that she did not hear and replied, "What?" In addition, if they felt that they were in the right, as in a complaint situation, then some of the respondents reported planning less than when they felt the need to make amends, as in the apology situations.

Language for the Task Description and for the Prompts

If the role-play situations are written in the target language, this procedure usually provides sociolinguistically appropriate words and phrases that can be copied directly into the response if the respondents pick up on this. In the Cohen and Olshtain study, for instance, several respondents reported taking phrases directly from the text that described the situation phrases that were only partially in or absent from their productive knowledge. For example, in the "lift" situation, a respondent noted that she took "my bus has just left" directly from the text. Also, whereas she would ordinarily say "token," she requested a "phone token" in the "token" situation because that was written in the text. In that same situation, several respondents reported that they had used the word urgent only because "it was included in the situation." They noted that they would not have used it otherwise.

Sometimes the process was a bit more complex and involved the combining of the respondent's own material with that in the text. So, in the "lift" situation, a respondent described how he arrived at asking the teacher, Debbie, "Can I come by your car?":

First I thought "with your car, with you" and that I would not mention the car because I didn't know how to indicate hamixonit shelax 'your car' [in Hebrew]. I worried that she would think I wanted to go for a ride with her. "To get a ride with you" would be an expression I wouldn't know how to use. "Can I come" are words that I know how to use. After I heard Debbie read "by car," I said "by your car."

In addition, there were numerous cases where respondents did not make use of clues that were in the written descriptions of the situation. For example, in the situation calling for a request from the teacher for a "lift" home, there were respondents who reported that they disregarded this clue and had difficulties finding a word in English for this request. The Semi-direct Oral Proficiency Interview (SOPI), for example, gives the prompts in the native language of the respondent rather than in the target language being assessed. Consequently, no clues are given for the response.

The Validity of Verbal Report for Speech act Research

There is always the danger that if the interviewer makes leading suggestions in an effort to elicit verbal report, the respondents may fabricate inaccurate descriptions of what they did to produce utterances. Also, there is the possibility that the interviewer might make false assumptions based on intuitions regarding the verbal report and might put words in the respondent's mouth, as in the following case from Cohen and Oishtain: "I could see you were focusing on grammar." In this instance, the informant indicated that he was not doing so. On the plus side, verbal report interviews provide feedback from respondents regarding aspects of their behavior that would otherwise be left to the intuitions and speculations of the investigator.

Likewise, there is the concern that reported behavior may not truly reflect actual behavior. The use of immediate retrospection (immediate playback of the tape after two situations) may help to diminish the likelihood of the retrospections being fabricated, but there is still this possibility. In the Cohen and Olshtain study, no effort was made to investigate the relationship, for example, between the report of planning and actual evidence of planning (e.g., pauses in delivery). It has been suggested that looking for tangible signs of planning in the videotaped role-play interactions could serve as a means for corroborating verbal report data indicating that planning was going on.

Finally, in the Cohen and Olshtain study, the question arose as to when to stop the role-play in order to have the respondents retrospect. It was decided that if the retrospection had been delayed until the end of the session, then valuable verbal report data would have been lost, even with the replaying of the videotaped role-play interactions to help jog the memory. Yet by having the retrospection corpe at three intervals during the role-plays, there was a possibility that efforts taken to heighten awareness about a particular processing strategy could have inadvertently triggered that strategy, as respondents progressed from the first response session to the second and the third. Thus, asking respondents to indicate the language in which they were thinking may have stimulated the respondents especially the trilingual ones—to think in a language in which they had not been thinking previously.

Conclusions

The chapter began by noting that, although much work has been accomplished with respect to the empirical validation of speech act sets, much work still remains to be done. It was also noted that speech act behavior is so complex because the performance of any given respondent is dependent on a host of sociocultural and sociolinguistic abilities, each of which calls for a sensitive measurement effort. We pointed out that, although the field of speech act investigation began with studies of perception, moved to production, and now is swinging back to more sophisticated studies of perception, there are still numerous areas for investigation with regard to speech act production. This chapter focused on one of these.

The research cycle of observation, role-play, discourse completion, and acceptability checks was presented. We indicated that each of these data collection techniques has its own merits, but that it is the use of more than one technique that provides us with important triangulation. We suggested that in addition to considering the techniques that are useful for the description of speech act behavior within a group, the researcher of speech act behavior also needs to understand better the choices made by individuals. It is here that verbal reports can be most valuable in order to understand further the cognitive processing involved in producing speech act utterances. The last portion of the chapter raised some issues about the use of the role-play interview, which were brought to the fore through the use of verbal report. The concerns raised with regard to the use of verbal report, such as the relative benefits of immediate versus delayed retrospection, simply underscore the need to carry out more empirical research on the use of verbal report in investigating complex language tasks such as speech acts.

The field of speech act research is still fledgling compared to other fields of investigation, we have not reached the point of mandating one or another research method for one or another purpose. The safest way to proceed is to use multiple measures, in order to triangulate the measurement of the speech act phenomena in question. No doubt we need to continue to conduct studies utilizing the various measures and to continue to scrutinize each one in some detail. Hence, we had no intention of arriving at pronouncements about the preferred use of role-play measures. We simply assert that researchers need to use such measures with a keen awareness as to their potential strengths and weaknesses.

5

Local and Long-Distance Anaphora in Research Methodology

Introduction

The central problem to be addressed in this chapter is whether the grammars of interlanguages (IL) adhere to the constraints of UG, or whether in some cases they fall outside of these constraints. A related problem to be addressed involves the type of data and argumentation that bear on this problem. Much of the literature on the central problem, whether ILs obey UG, claims that L2 grammars do conform to the principles of UG, though there has been room for disagreement. The vast majority of studies addressing the related question, that of the type of data needed to support the claim, have reported aggregate data rather than data from individuals. In this chapter, it is argued that data from individuals, rather than group data, are necessary to test whether IL grammars adhere to the principles of UG.

The results of the present study suggest that, other research notwithstanding, some IL grammars apparently do fall outside the boundaries of UG. However, the existence of such violations is not, in itself, a threat to the position that ILs are governed by UG, because it may in fact be possible to predict these violations.

Thus, if it is shown that some IL grammars violate principles of UG, the task is to explain why the particular ILs in question violate UG principles, and why the violations happen in just the way that they do.The organization of this chapter is as follows. First, I briefly describe the Binding Principles, the associated parameters, and their relationship to some previous work in SLA. I then lay out the rationale and methodology for the present study and report the results. Finally, I discuss these results and their implications for SLA theory.

Background: Ug, Binding, and Sla

UG, as put forth in Chomsky and elsewhere, is a set of abstract and general principles assumed to be adequate for characterizing the core grammars of all natural languages. The central goal, under Chomsky's approach, is to account for the systematic variation found among the world's languages, and the relative speed and uniformity with which children acquire their native language. To this end, UG is postulated as basic to the innate human language faculty. UG consists of principles that form the basis for all languages. The observed systematic variability found among languages is accounted for by hypothesizing that some principles of UG permit variation along certain well-defined parameters. These parameters can be viewed as principles containing variables whose values must be filled in. Primary language acquisition takes place, according to this view, as the child-learner molds these principles of UG into the native-language grammar by determining the values of the various parameters.Two such parameters are the Governing Category Parameter and the Proper Antecedent Parameter, both of which are associated with the Binding Conditions, shown in (1):(1) Binding Conditions:

a. An anaphor is bound in its governing category.
b. A pronominal is free in its governing category.
c. R(eferring) expressions are free.

These principles determine when expressions in a sentence are properly bound (i.e., coreferential). For the purposes of this chapter, we will concern ourselves only with Principle A, involving the binding of reflexives, also known as anaphors. The Binding Conditions specify the structural configurations for coreference in terms of the notion governing category, which for English is, roughly speaking, a minimal category containing a subject.

Thus, for example, himself in (2a) must be bound by John because both of these expressions are contained in the same minimal category containing a subject, namely, the subordinate clause. On the other hand, herself in (2b) cannot be bound by Mary because these two expressions are not contained in the same minimal category containing a subject, namely, the subordinate clause. (2) a. Bill knew that Johni hit himself b. *Mary $_i$ knew that John hit herself.

Although sentence (2b) is not grammatical in English, this sentence type is grammatical in some languages. The Binding Conditions allow for this possibility through parametric variation. The relevant parameter, stated in (3), specifies the various domains in which binding can take place in any given language by specifying the structure that defines a governing category for that language. (3) Governing Category Par ameter (GCP): gamma is a governing category for alpha iff gamma is the minimal category that contains alpha, a governor for alpha, and has

a. a subject; or	English
b. an INFL; or	Italian
c. a TNS; or	Russian
d. an indicative TNS; or	Icelandic
e. a root TNS	Korean/Japanese

The GCP is essentially a hierarchy that divides languages into types according to how close two expressions in a sentence can or must be in order to be properly bound. English-type languages are the strictest in that they require local binding in which the reflexive and its antecedent must be in the same simple clause. Korean and Japanese, on the other hand, are less strict and allow nonlocal binding in which antecedents of reflexives can be indefinitely far away in the sentence; other languages fall between these extremes. The difference between languages of type (3a) and those of type (3e) with respect to the GCP can be illustrated using the sentence in (4), whose clausal structure is roughly that in (5a).

(4) Bill persuaded Charlie to consider Mick fond of himself.

(5) Binding possibilities in Japanese and English

a. $_{S1}$[NP $_i$ V $_{S2}$[NP $_j$ V $_{S3}$[NP $_k$ V refl] $_{S3}$] $_{S2}$] $_{S1}$]
b. i j k i/j/k/ (Japanese)
c. i j k *i/*j/k (English)

In an English sentence like (4), himself can refer only to Mick, the NP that is a clausemate of the reflexive, and not to Charlie or Bill. However, in the Japanese equivalent of a sentence like (4), the reflexive can refer to Mick, Charlie, or Bill. Thus, the governing category in a Japanese-type language is much wider than that in English.The other parameter in question, the Proper Antecedent Parameter, shown in (6), has two values that specify whether the reflexive must be bound by a subject NP or can be bound by any NP within the governing category.(6) Proper Antecedent Parameter (PAP):A proper antecedent for A is

a. a subject NP
b. any NP whatever

The English setting for this parameter is (6b), as is shown by sentence (7), in which either the subject or the indirect object NP may bind the reflexive, yielding two possible interpretations.

(7) John showed Bill a picture of himself.

In Japanese, which is set for value (6a) on the PAP, the counterpart of this sentence has only one interpretation, namely, the one in which the reflexive is bound by the subject NP.

Manzini and Wexler pointed out that there appears to be a correlation between the GCP and the PAP, such that languages that have the unmarked setting (3a) on the GCP have the marked setting (6b) on the PAP, and conversely, that languages that set the GCP for the marked value (3e) have the unmarked setting (6a) on the PAP. In other words, languages that allow nonlocal binding require the antecedent to be a subject NP, whereas languages that restrict binding to a local domain allow the antecedent to be any NP. What is apparently excluded by the two parameters are languages that are too liberal in that they permit binding to be both long-distance and local while allowing both subject and nonsubject orientation, and languages that are too restrictive in that they allow only local binding and only subject orientation. The allowed and disallowed possibilities are summarized in (8).

(8) Logically possible combinations of binding domains and antecedents:

	Local	Local & Nonlocal
Subject only	Type A (unattested)	Type B (Japanese, Korean)
Subjects & nonsubjects	Type C (English)	Type D (unattested)

As mentioned earlier, a number of recent articles have studied the role of these two parameters in the grammars of interlanguages. Because space does not permit an extensive review of this literature, I recapitulate some of the salient points of this body of work.

The first SLA study in this area was a pilot by Finer and Broselow, which used a picture identification task to elicit interpretations of coreference from six Korean subjects on English sentences containing the two types of complement clauses exemplified in (9).

(9) a. Mr. Fat believes that Mr. Thin will paint himself.

b. Mr. Fat asked Mr. Thin to paint himself.

The subjects had to determine which of two pictures corresponded to the sentence in question. Given a sentence such as (9a), for example, subjects had to choose between two pictures, one in which Mr. Thin was painting himself and one in which Mr. Thin was painting Mr. Fat.

Finer and Broselow reported that the subjects, as a group, assigned local coreference in sentences like (9a) and nonlocal coreference in sentences like (9b). They drew the following conclusions: (a) the subjects had not yet learned the more restrictive English setting for the GCP, (b) their subjects did not simply transfer the Korean setting of the GCP, and (c) the Korean subjects, as a group, used a setting of the GCP in between that of English and Korean, somewhere around the (3c) or (3d) value.

This pilot study by Finer and Broselow was followed up by a number of studies that expanded on it. These later studies, with the exception of Hirakawa, supported the finding of the Finer and Broselow pilot that L2 subjects tended to bind reflexives locally in tensed embedded clauses, and nonlocally in infinitival clauses. Hirakawa, in contrast, reported that her subjects made many more errors on sentences containing tensed complement clauses than did Finer and Broselow's subjects. Thus, Hirakawa argued that her subjects did not adopt an intermediate value for the GCP but instead set the GCP for their ILs at the widest possible value (that is, (3e)).

Studies that have considered the Proper Antecedent Parameter have shown consistently that L2 subjects generally bind the reflexive to a subject NP more often than to a nonsubject.

Thomas looked at nonnative binding with respect to two target languages. She considered Japanese and Spanish ESL learners, on the one hand, and English and Chinese L2 learners of Japanese on the other. She found that most English subjects bound the Japanese reflexive locally, although some nonlocal binding was allowed by subjects with higher proficiency. Interestingly, about half of the Chinese subjects bound the Japanese reflexive only nonlocally.

One of the goals of this research on binding in SLA has been to determine whether the IL grammars involved adhere to the principles of UG. In general, the findings of these studies have been the following: (a) the IL settings for each parameter are not merely transferred from the native language (NL) but are set at a value somewhere between that of the NL and the target language (TL) (though see Hirakawa, 1990 for a different result), and (b) the IL settings for each parameter are squarely within the limits prescribed by UG.

Some dissension on this second point has come from Thomas, who argued that the findings of Finer and Hirakawa run contrary to UG on two counts. First, both Finer and Hirakawa reported that in 20% of the L2 responses, a reflexive was bound by the object in a sentence such as (10).

(10) Mr. Fat gives Mr. Thin a picture of himself.

And second, both studies reported that English reflexives in complement clauses were bound only by the subject of the matrix clause in 2% to 38% of L2 responses. Thomas cited this as a problem, claiming that UG principles do not sanction either of these response types.

The problem I adduce here is not limited to the findings reported in the Finer and Hirakawa studies but is endemic in all of the research reported thus far on L2 binding and much of the research attempting to test UG principles in SLA. The problem is twofold: First, previous research in this area has reported aggregate results rather than results for individuals, and second, principles of UG have been interpreted directly with respect to data instead of with respect to IL grammars. I will take up each of these points in turn.

Consider first the question of group results. It has never been shown, or even argued, that IL grammars reflect the linguistic knowledge of groups of learners; rather, it has been assumed, perhaps tacitly, that IL grammars pertain to individual learners. Thus, in testing whether principles of UG hold for IL grammars, there is a problem with reporting results for groups rather than individuals, namely, that it thereby becomes impossible to determine whether the UG principles in question are being adhered to. What has to be determined from the reported data is whether the individual IL grammar of each of the subjects adheres to the constraints imposed by UG. To the extent that this is true, it can be successfully argued that UG governs ILs.

However, if a study reports that one of the L2 groups gave local responses on English reflexives in 80% of the cases, as does Thomas, this result does not tell us whether the principles of UG are being obeyed unless we know how those responses are distributed across the subjects. Clearly, the case for UG can be made if all of the subjects scored 80%. If, on the other hand, the 80% group result is a consequence of subjects' compiling many different scores, some of which indicate systematic adherence to UG principles and others that either are unsystematic or indicate nonadherence to UG, then the case for UG governing SLA is not at all clear.

This brings us to the second point. One cannot determine whether UG constraints have been violated simply by examining the errors. This is because the principles and parameters of UG do not directly constrain utterances but instead constrain grammars, in this case, IL grammars. What is crucial, therefore, is not the errors themselves but the analysis of those errors. Thus, Thomas' claim that the responses of Finer's and Hirakawa's subjects for sentences such as (10) are problematic for UG cannot be upheld unless it can be shown that the IL grammars that produced these responses are not in conformity with UG. And this, in turn, cannot be determined unless we know how the deviant responses were distributed across the subjects.

To sum up this section, previous research on binding has reported group rather than individual results, making it impossible to determine the extent to which UG constraints have been followed or violated. In the present study, therefore, the results will be presented for individuals.

Methodology

The present study builds in part on the methodology of two previous studies: that of Finer & Broselow, who used a picture identification task, and that of Thomas, who gathered data from two target languages, English and Japanese.

The subjects for this study were drawn from four groups. The L2 groups included 24 university-age native speakers of English learning Japanese as a foreign language and 25 ESL learners from four native-language backgrounds: Arabic, Japanese, Mandarin, and Spanish. The L2 Japanese group was drawn from students who were in their third and fourth year of studying Japanese. The L2 English group was drawn from students in the ESL Intensive Program at the University of Wisconsin at Milwaukee. The two L1 control groups consisted of 25 native speakers of English and 24 native speakers of Japanese.

Following Finer and Broselow, a picture identification task was used in which the subjects had to match a picture with a sentence containing a reflexive. The subjects worked their way through a booklet, each page of which contained a pair of drawings with the target sentence typed across the top of the page. The directions told the subjects that they were to choose the picture that the sentence best described, and that it was possible for the sentence to describe only one of the pictures, neither of the pictures, or both of the pictures. To avoid certain methodological problems that have been ascribed to Finer and Broselow's picture identification task, the instructions also reminded the subjects that, before choosing just one of the pictures as the answer, they should always check to see if both pictures corresponded to the sentence. To see whether the subjects understood the directions, they were given a short practice exercise. The test itself was not timed; the subjects were allowed to work at their own pace.The sentence types used in this study are displayed in (11) and (12) and fall into four different categories.(11) Type Example

a. Mr. Small hit himself.
b. Mr. Small said that Mr. Big looked at himself.
c. Mr. Big asked Mr. Small to hit himself.
d. Mr. Big gave Mr. Small a portrait of himself.

(12) Type Example

a. Big-san wa jibun wo mimashita.
b. Small-san wa Big-san ga jibun wo mita to iimashita.
c. Big-san wa Small-san ni jibun wo miruyo tanomimashita.
d. Big-san wa Small-san ni jubun no shozoga wo agemashita.

Type (a) includes simple sentences containing reflexives and object pronouns in which the reflexive must refer to the subject of the sentence. Type (b) includes sentences containing a complement clause where the clause boundary is clearly marked by the complementizer that. In sentences of type (b), the reflexive can refer only to the subordinate subject, and not to the superordinate subject or some entity outside the sentence. This is also true for type (c), except that in this case, the lower clause contains an infinitive instead of a tensed verb. Sentences of type (d) contain an object NP followed by a "picture" noun phrase containing a reflexive. (See Appendix for samples of the materials used.)

Results

As discussed in the previous section, the objective of the study was to determine whether an individual's IL grammar adheres to the constraints of UG. Thus, the performance of each subject on a given sentence type was assessed as to whether or not the performance was systematic. Because there were four tokens of each sentence type (with the exception of Japanese type (d), which had only three tokens) it was decided that the threshold for systematicity was three out of four (two out of three for Japanese type (d)). Thus, for example, a subject's IL was deemed to have local binding in tensed clauses if that subject chose the pictures that represented local binding in three out of the four cases involving a sentence like (11b). Conversely, the subject's IL was deemed to have nonlocal binding if the subject chose the nonlocal picture in three out of four cases. The same criterion was applied to sentences like (I I a) and (11c) for the determination of the binding domain and to sentence (11d) to determine whether the subject bound the reflexive only to subject

NPs or to nonsubjects as well. If a subject did not reach the criterial threshold of three, the IL was deemed to be unsystematic with respect to that aspect of coreference assignment.

Across the top of Table 5.1 are listed the possible binding domains: local only, nonlocal only, both local and nonlocal, and unsystematic. Within each domain, the orientation of the reflexive is listed, that is, whether the reflexive was bound only to a subject, whether it was bound to a subject or object, or whether the orientation was unsystematic. The first group listed is the native English control group, which uniformly bound the reflexive in a local domain. However, 15 of the 25 subjects bound this reflexive only to a subject NP, which accords with the findings of previous work.

TABLE 5.1 Number of Subjects in Each Combination of Binding Domain and Orientation

LocalOnly	NonlocalOnly	BothLoc+Nonloc	
	S	S+O	Unsys S
S+O	Unsys S	S+O Unsys Unsys	
L1E	15	6	4
L2E	6	3	2
Mn	2	1	3
Sp	1	J	4
L2J	6	1	2
2	5	5	4
L1J	2	1	13
1	4	1	1

Note. Loc. = Local, Nonloc = Nonlocal, Unsys = Unsystematic, S = Subject, O = Object, E = English, Ar = Arabic, Mn = Mandarin, J = Japanese, Sp = Spanish.

TABLE 5.2 Group Results for Comparison with Previous Studies TL = English

	Local Binding		Orientation	
Group	Tensed Clause	Infinitive Clause	Subj Only	Subj & Object
L1E	99%	98%	65%	35%
L2E	91%	82%	64%	34%

TL = Japanese		
Group	Nonlocal Binding	Subj Orientation
L1J	88%	70%
L2J	65%	44%

Note. E = English, J = Japanese.

Six subjects allowed the reflexive to be bound by a subject or object, and 4 subjects were not systematic in their orientation. The English L2 group was broken down according to NL background: There were 13 Arabic subjects, 5 Mandarin speakers, 4 Japanese speakers, and 3 native speakers of Spanish. The vast majority of these subjects bound the reflexive locally; one Arabic subject allowed both local and nonlocal binding and one Spanish subject performed unsystematically. It is interesting to note that the vast majority of L2 speakers whose performance was systematic permitted the reflexive to be bound only by a subject NP. Only four Arabic speakers allowed binding by either a subject or an object.

The native Japanese speakers also evinced some interesting patterns. Fourteen of the subjects bound the reflexive only to a nonlocal antecedent, 13 of these bound the reflexive to a subject, and one behaved unsystematically. Six subjects allowed both local and nonlocal binding and 2 allowed only local binding. The vast majority of the subjects whose IL showed systematicity bound the reflexive to a subject NP; only one allowed binding to a nonsubject also.

The group showing the most variability was that of English speakers learning Japanese. Seven speakers allowed only local binding and 2 evinced only nonlocal binding; 14 subjects bound the reflexive both locally and nonlocally. In the groups that bound the reflexive only locally or only nonlocally, the orientation, where systematic, was exclusively toward a subject antecedent. Where the binding was both local and nonlocal, the orientation was generally subject-only.

TABLE 5.3 Individuals Results for Native English Speaker Control Group

Locality Unsys Loc	Orientation Only Nonloc	Speaker Both Subj (Only Subj & Obj Unsys)
1	+	+
8	+	+

10	+	+
11	+	+
13	+	+
15	+	+
16	+	+
17	+	+
18	+	+
19	+	+
20	+	+
21	+	+
23	+	+
24	+	+
25	+	+
5	+	+
6	+	+
7	+	+
9	+	+
12	+	+
22	+	+
2	+	+
3	+	+
4	+	+
14	+	+

Note. Unsys = Unsystematic, Loc = Local, Nonloc = Nonlocal.

Discussion

In this section I consider whether the subjects' IL grammars are in conformity with the settings of the GCP and the PAP that are allowed by UG. In other words, we will be interested in how the ILs in question are distributed with respect to the typology of binding domains and reflexive orientation shown

TABLE 5.4 Individual Results for ESL Subjects

Locality Unsys Loc	Orientation Only Nonloc	Speaker Both Subj (Only Subj & Obj Unsys)
Ar 1	tns / inf	+
Ar 15	tns/inf	+

Ar 17	tns/inf	+
Ar 18	tns/inf	+
Ar 19	tns/inf	+
Ar 23	tns/inf	+
Ar 24	tns/inf	+
Ar 25	tns/inf	+
Ar 26	tns/inf	+
Ar 27	tns/inf	+
Ar 28	tns/inf	+
Ar 29	tns/inf	+
Ar 30	tns/inf	+
Mn 3	tns/inf	+
Mn 7	tns/inf	+
Mn 8	tns/inf	+
Mn 9	tns/inf	+
Mn 21	tns/inf	+
Sp 10	tns/ inf	+
Sp 12	tns/inf	+
Sp 14	tns/inf	+
J 16	tns/inf	+
J 20	tns/inf	+
J 31	tns/inf	+
J 32	tns/inf	+

Note. tns = tensed clauses, inf = infinitival clauses, Ar = Arabic, Mn = Mandarin, Sp = Spanish, J = Japanese.

Our concern, therefore, will be only with those IL grammars that are systematic and not with those categorized as unsystematic. The particular focus of this section is those ILs that appear not to adhere to the constraints of UG. The discussion of these grammars will approach this problem from two different points of view. When faced with ILs that appear not to conform to UG, we consider the implications for SLA theory, on the one hand, and for linguistic theory, on the other hand.

We first interpret the data from the SLA theory standpoint and consider the ESL group. Of the 25 subjects in this group, 17 performed systematically with respect to both binding domain and orientation of the reflexive.

TABLE 5.5 Individual Results for Native Japanese speaker Control Group

Locality Unsys Loc	Orientation Only Nonloc	Speaker Both Subj (Only Subj & Obj Unsys)
8	+	+
10	+	+
1	+	+
5	+	+
6	+	+
7	+	+
14	+	+
14	+	+
16	+	+
17	+	+
18	+	+
20	+	+
21	+	+
23	+	+
24	+	+
13	+	+
4	+	+
11	+	+
12	+	+
22	+	+
3	+	+
2	+	+
9	+	+
19	+	+

Note. Unsys = Unsystematic, Loc = Local, Nonloc = Nonlocal.

16 subjects bound the reflexive only locally, and one allowed both local and nonlocal binding. Now, of these 17 cases, only 3 fall into an attested category in (8), namely A, whereas 13 fall into type A and one falls into type D. Thus, only 3 of the 17 cases are Englishlike, whereas 13 would be classified as too restrictive and one would be considered too liberal. What is more interesting is that these cases

cannot be explained as a consequence of NL interference, because both Japanese and Mandarin have nonlocal binding, and because both Arabic and Spanish allow subject and nonsubject antecedents for reflexives.

If we look at the native speaker controls, we see that similar orientation was also exhibited by the majority of speakers in this group. The native speakers were completely robust with respect to binding being only local; however, of the 21 subjects showing systematic performance regarding orientation, 15 (71%) bound the reflexive only by subject NPs. These results are in accord with those reported for the native control groups in Hirakawa and Thomas and for children learning English as their L1 in Read and Chou Hare.

TABLE 5.6 Individual Results for Native English Speakers Japanese

Locality Unsys Loc	Orientation Only Nonloc	Speaker Both Subj (Only Subj & Obj Unsys)
7	+	+
15	+	+
19	+	+
20	+	+
[illegible]	+	+
24	+	+
21	+	+
4	+	+
10	+	+
9	+	+
5	+	+
13	+	+
14	+	+
17	+	+
2	+	+
3	+	+
8	+	+
12	+	+
23	+	+
11	+	+

6	+	+
16	+	+
1	+	+
18	+	+

Note. Unsys = Unsystematic, Loc = Local, Nonloc = Nonlocal.

One possible explanation for this preference is the fact that the combination of local binding and subject-only antecedent is the least marked configuration: All languages apparently allow a reflexive to be locally bound, and all languages allow subjects to bind reflexives. The apparent problem arises in that this constellation of binding and orientation is not allowed by UG and is presumably not attested. One way around this quandary is to claim that the grammar of the English controls does in fact evince local binding with both subject and nonsubject orientation, but that speakers may employ a strategy that uses an unmarked configuration of these principles.

This same explanation could then be extended to the IL grammars of L2 learners. The claim would be that these IL grammars are unmarked variants of the target grammars, and that the IL grammars arise from the same strategy, perhaps a learning strategy, that we saw represented in the data from the native speakers. Under this scenario, the L2 learners construct an IL that makes use of the unmarked configuration of principles, even though the grammars of both the NL and the TL contain the more marked instantiations of these same principles. In sum, the explanation for why these IL grammars are of the unattested type A is that the learners construct a less marked version of the TL. A similar explanation was proposed for both negation and relative clause formation by Hyltenstam.

We turn now to the L2 interpretations of Japanese reflexives by native speakers of English. Of the 24 subjects tested, 6 performed unsystematically: one with respect to the domain of binding and 5 with respect to orientation. Of the remaining 18, 6 interpreted coreference exclusively within a local domain and only with subject antecedents. This response pattern is the same as the one exhibited by many of the native speaker controls and has already been discussed. It is, grammatically speaking, similar to neither English nor Japanese.

There are two other Japanese L2 groups to be considered. In the first, two subjects bound the reflexive exclusively within a nonlocal domain, and only with subject antecedents. In the other, 10 subjects allowed both local and nonlocal binding; of these 10, 5 had subject orientation and 5 had both subject and object orientation. Only one of these configurations is allowed by UG, namely, type B in (8), which combines both local and nonlocal binding with subject orientation. The other two are apparently not allowed by UG and need to be explained.

The group that is easier to explain is the one allowing both types of binding and both subject and object orientation. This configuration characterizes the disallowed and apparently unattested type D language in (8). One plausible explanation for its occurrence is NL interference. The subjects have apparently learned that Japanese allows both local and nonlocal binding but have not yet learned that the antecedent in Japanese must be a subject. They consequently transfer the English principle, which allows binding by both a subject and an object. This hypothesis is supported by the findings in Thomas, who reports that Chinese L2 learners of Japanese bind the reflexive extensively to a long-distance antecedent that is exclusively a subject. Because Chinese has setting (6a) on the PAP and English has setting (6b), transfer would seem to explain the differences between these two groups with respect to Japanese binding.

The responses of the other L2 Japanese group, the one containing the two subjects who preferred only long-distance binding, are not as easy to explain. Notice, in particular, that this type of binding was actually preferred by a majority of the native speaker controls for Japanese and is also reported as a preference for the controls in Hirakawa and Thomas. It is, however, not allowed by the GCP, which claims that any language that allows reflexives to be bound over more than one clause, should also allow them to be bound within a single clause. Thomas proposes to explain these facts by showing that subjects underreport their intuitions. This is ultimately not an explanation because it begs the question why the subjects underreport in the way that they do and not in some other way.

One way to account for this behavior and still maintain the assumption that the Japanese subjects are employing an unmarked configuration of principles would be to speculate that the inclination to bind the reflexive only by a matrix antecedent in fact reflects a preference for the matrix subject as a binder over an embedded subject. Assuming that binding by only a subject NP is the unmarked case, then, in a language such as Japanese, which allows nonlocal antecedents, binding by the matrix subject, rather than one of the embedded subjects, could turn out to be the unmarked case. Under this view, which is admittedly speculation at this point, the anomaly of the exclusive nonlocal binding would reflect a preference for binding by the matrix subject.

Although this position is speculative at this point, it is nevertheless a testable position. If we hypothesize that the preference shown by some learners for binding by a nonlocal NP is in fact a preference for binding by a matrix subject, then we would predict that, in a three-clause sentence such as (4) (repeated for convenience as (13)), the NP Bill would be the preferred binder of the reflexive. Under the alternative hypothesis that only a nonlocal NP can be the binder, either Bill or Charlie should be a potential binder, but not Mick. Unfortunately, the evidence we have so far suggests that our hypothesis cannot be maintained. Hirakawa tested three-clause sentences and did not find a preference for binding by the matrix NP.

(13) Bill persuaded Charlie to consider Mick fond of himself.

Perhaps a better explanation is the one outlined by Lakshmanan and Teranishi, namely, that the verbs used in the test sentences introduce a semantic bias toward binding by the matrix NP. If this position can be maintained Lakshmanan and Teranishi do give evidence in its support then the results in question do not have to be explained on acquisition grounds, because the findings are apparently the consequence of a flaw in the test instrument.

Having discussed how the L2 binding patterns that do not conform to the configurations allowed by UG impinge on SLA theory, we turn our attention to the implications of these patterns for linguistic theory. The point to be made is the following. If interlanguages are in fact natural languages, as has been argued, then they should fall under the purview of linguistic theory. This being the case, the fact that our data reflect binding patterns not yet attested in L1s could indicate that such primary language types do in fact exist but have not yet been discovered or documented by linguists. In other words, under this view, interlanguages would serve as an indicator of the types of primary languages that one should expect to find. Along these lines, U. Lakshmanan reports that Tamil has a reflexive that requires nonlocal binding, which is theoretically disallowed by the current formulation of the GCP.

The position that ILs may reflect the types of primary languages that linguists should expect to find is not unreasonable when one considers that only a handful of languages have been tested against the parameters in question, and only a few languages have been found for some values of the GCP. For example, Manzini and Wexler cite only Italian for value (3b), and only Icelandic sig and hann for values (3c) and (3d), respectively. To be sure, other languages have been adduced elsewhere; however, the point remains that, to date, there has been no published attempt that systematically characterizes a sizable number of languages with respect to the typology in (8). Thus, the fact that there exist some ILs that fall into unattested categories in (8) can be argued to be at least as much a problem for linguistic theory as it is for SLA theory.

Conclusion

In conclusion, we have presented data on L2 binding of reflexives with a view toward testing the hypothesis that UG principles hold for IL grammars. With respect to this position, we have argued that (a) this hypothesis can be tested most clearly by reporting data for individuals rather than for groups, and (b) at least two cases where the IL grammars conflicted with UG could be explained on other grounds, namely, in terms of markedness or in terms of the language-contact situation and NL transfer. We have considered some of the implications of these findings for both SLA theory and linguistic theory.

The word research is derived from the Latin word meaning to know. It is a systematic and a replicable process which identifies and defines problems, within specified boundaries. It employs well designed method to collect the data and analyses the results. It disseminates the findings to contribute to generalizeable knowledge.

The five characteristics of research presented below will be examined in greater detail later are:

1. systematic problem solving which identifies variables and tests relationships between them
2. logical, so procedures can be duplicated or understood by others
3. empirical, so decisions are based on data collected
4. reductive, so it investigates a small sample which can be generalized to a larger population
5. replicable, so others may test the findings by repeating it

6

Reliability of Second-Language in Research Methodology

Introduction

There is a theoretical distinction to be made between grammaticality judgments and acceptability judgments, despite the fact that the terms are often used interchangeably. The former, in strict linguistic terms, involve those sentences that are generated by the grammar, whereas the latter involve those sentences about which speakers have a feel of well-formedness.

It is now commonplace for scholars to think about language not only in terms of language use in everyday communicative situations, but also "as an object of analysis and observation in its own right". Grammaticality judgments are one (but certainly not the only) form of metalinguistic performance, or language objectification. One way of objectifying

language is to state whether a given sentence is acceptable or not. Responses to questions of acceptability are used to determine grammatical properties of language. That is, they are used to determine which sentences are possible and which are not in the grammar of a particular language.

Second-language researchers examining linguistic characteristics of learnergrammars have often used grammaticality judgments as data. However, the use of grammaticality judgments in second-language research has not been without difficulty or without controversy, as Birdsong and others have pointed out. As is evidenced by other chapters in this section, issues relating to reliability and validity are still debated.

More than two decades ago, Selinker argued that researchers should "focus analytical attention upon the only observable data to which we can relate theoretical predictions: the utterances which are produced when the learner attempts to say sentences of a TL". The exclusive focus on production data and the uncertainty regarding what is involved in providing judgments have led to a mistrust of this research instrument among some researchers in the field of second-language acquisition. But, as Chaudron pointed out in his literature review, grammaticality judgments are complex behavioral activities that must be used with caution and with full understanding of their limitations. Nonetheless, despite such controversy, grammaticality judgments have been and continue to be used in second-language research. Interestingly, however, we often find that researchers who do use such data include a paragraph or a section in which they provide justification for their use.

If grammaticality judgments do not measure what they are purported to measure (validity), their use should be called into question. If one cannot access consistent judgments (reliability), this would also be reason to call their use into question. Given the centrality of grammaticality judgments to second-language acquisition research, both validity and reliability must be investigated.

The main question this chapter addresses is: How reliable are grammaticality judgments as measures of a learner's grammatical knowledge? With regard to the task itself, there is clearly a difference between primary-language judgment data and second-language judgment data. In the former, one is asking native speakers to judge sentences of their own language system in order to gain information about that same system. That is to say, the two systems are isomorphic. In the case of second-language judgments, one is asking learners to make judgments about the language being learned at a stage in which their knowledge of that system is incomplete. Here, however, inferences are being made not about the system they are being asked about, but about some internalized system. In other words, there may be a mismatch between the two systems in question.

Indeterminacy

The question of indeterminacy, which refers to the learner's incomplete knowledge or absence of knowledge of parts of the second-language grammar, is of central importance in any discussion of research methodology in second-language acquisition. Adjemian claimed that indeterminacy is a fundamental property of learner-languages: The salient characteristic of ILs is that they are linguistic systems which by nature are somehow incomplete and in a state of flux".

As Schachter, Tyson and Diffley pointed out, there are many sentences about which second-language learners have indeterminate knowledge. This is not to say that native speakers of a language, either individually or collectively, do not have indeterminate knowledge, for surely they do. In fact, linguists recognize this on the printed page by placing question marks or question marks plus asterisks before certain sentences. For L2 learners, it is clear that indeterminacy exists, and it is conceivable that it embraces an even greater range of data than for native speakers of a language. Because there is a wide range of data that are potentially indeterminate, it is particularly important that we have a principled basis for determining what is truly representative of a learner's knowledge and what is not. How can we know which data are good data and which represent spurious exemplars of grammatical structures? This distinction is reminiscent of Corder distinction between errors and mistakes. Clearly, we want grammatical descriptions to be based on actual knowledge rather than on guesswork or extraneous factors.

Tapping determinate knowledge is less problematic when using production data because, barring some sort of slip, the language produced is presumably generated by the learner's grammar. However, it is well accepted that unconstrained production data (free speech data) are inadequate for specific grammatical studies because the examples of a given grammatical structure are often lacking. As Corder aptly noted: "Elicitation procedures are used to find out something specific about the learner's language. To do this, constraints must be placed on the learner so that he is forced to make choices within a severely restricted area of his phonological, lexical or syntactic competence".

But with grammaticality judgments what we are asking learners to do is evaluate sentences of a language that they do not have total control over; many of the sentences being asked about are beyond the domain of their current knowledge. Thus, responses to these represent little more than guesses. What we want to know is which sentences actually represent those sentences that are part of a learner's grammatical knowledge and which ones do not. Through the use of grammaticality judgments, we can establish whether learners' grammatical knowledge includes information about the impossibility of particular forms. This, of course, is of utmost importance when working within a theoretical framework such as Universal Grammar or within a typological universal framework, because in both instances one would want to know whether learners are able to violate universal principles. Thus, grammaticality judgment data provide a means to determine not only the possible utterances but also the impossible ones.

Relationship to Competence

As Birdsong noted, there is a danger of attributing to metalinguistic performance a "straightforward deterministic relationship to linguistic competence". There are numerous misconceptions in the literature of what grammaticality judgments represent. They are not a direct reflection of competence, for competence is an abstraction. There is no question that they provide performance data, but these performance data (because they provide information on allowable and disallowable sentences) do give us insight into competence.

White, in her discussion of the misconceptions that abound regarding the nature of competence, provided quotations from the literature in illustration. I repeat them here because they reveal how misinterpretations have occurred and continue to occur.

I am unable to accept that the preferred data of many UG-oriented researchers, grammaticality judgments, afford some kind of direct window on competence. A grammaticality judgment is just as much a performance as any other kind of language use.

Researchers working in the UG paradigm assume that such results are a direct reflection of the learner's underlying competence and therefore evidence in support of UG.

Researchers in the UG/SL framework still face a fundamental question of what 'counts' as appropriate data. Cook champions the use of grammaticality judgments as evidence for competence.

As White indicated, those working with grammaticality judgments as a research tool have not claimed a direct line to abstract representations. She cited the following as evidence:

In practice, we tend to operate on the assumption, or pretense, that these informant judgments give us 'direct evidence' as to the structure of the I-language, but, of course, this is only a tentative and inexact working hypothesis. In general, informant judgments do not reflect the structure of the language directly.

A grammaticality judgment is no more central to UG than is any other experimental technique. It is tarred with the same brush of performance.

Linguistic competence is, of course, an abstraction. There is no direct way to tap competence, but various aspects of linguistic performance can give insights into competence. Some aspects of performance are more revealing than others.

More recently, G. Martohardjono stated, "Although based on competence, grammaticality judgments are not uniquely comprised of competence."

Thus, in any discussion of grammaticality judgments (or other elicitation techniques, for that matter), it is essential to keep in mind what they do and do not reflect. Grammaticality judgments do not give us direct access to learners' competence; they do, however, provide us with information about what are possible and impossible sentences in the learner-language.

Issues of Reliability

If we return to Corder's distinction between errors and mistakes, where the former refers to repeated use of a form and the latter to something more akin to a slip of the tongue, something easily correctable, and if we agree that we want our linguistic generalizations to be based on other than spurious data, we need a basis for eliminating just those data that are not representative of a learner's linguistic knowledge. One such means is through measures of reliability. Sentences about which there is no clear judgment are not sentences that should be included in our descriptions of second-language grammars.

With regard to reliability, questions abound and research presents conflicting results. I describe three representative studies that suggest the unreliability of grammaticality judgments.

Birdsong reported on a judgment task in a study of learners of French as an L2 in which 4 sentences were repeated within a task of 60 sentences. He found that for each of his 12 subjects, there was at least one pair of identical sentences for which judgments differed between the first and second appearance of the sentence.

Ellis presented the most recent attack on the reliability of grammaticality judgments. He attempted to discredit the reliability of a set of data in second-language acquisition research, pointing out that there had never been a test-retest reliability study carried out on the same group of learners. He studied the consistency in judgments of Japanese and Chinese speakers on English dative alternation, to rectify this shortcoming. He gave learners the same grammaticality judgment task twice, with a two-week interval between tests. On the basis of his results, he concluded that the variation in judgments from Time 1 to Time 2 suggested the lack of reliability of this instrument. However, a closer look at his instrument and the interpretation of results reveals problems. First, it is not clear how we can interpret his results, inasmuch as he did not cite a reliability coefficient despite the fact that the purpose of his study was an assessment of reliability. Second, there were slight differences in the methodology from Time 1 to Time 2. For example, in the Time 2 test for one of the groups, only a subset of the Time 1 sentences was presented.

Finally, to illustrate the uncontroversial nature of the controversy, consider a study by Christie and Lantolf. They focused their research on aspects of UG, in particular on properties of the Pro-drop Parameter. Their subjects were English speakers learning Italian. There were two tasks, a grammaticality judgment task and an oral narrative task (depicting the events of a film).

Fifteen months after the original data collection, the same grammaticality judgment task was administered to a subset of the original group. At this point, the subjects were more advanced in their Italian language studies (one of the subjects had spent time in Italy in the intervening period). In addition, oral protocols were administered at Time 2 to two of the subjects. We are not told whether or not it was the same elicitation measure as that used at Time 1. The results for the grammaticality judgment test for these two learners were quite similar from Time 1 to Time 2. Although no statistical comparisons were made, let's assume that in statistical terms there was no difference.

As far as the oral data are concerned, Christie and Lantolf focused on the use of grammatical subjects, in particular on whether there were full NP subjects, null subjects, or pronouns. Again, there were no statistical data presented, but it does appear that for one of the subjects there was a substantial difference from Time 1 to Time 2. That is, there was an increased use of null subjects (0 at Time 1 and 10 at Time 2) and a decrease in the use of full NPs (8 at Time 1 and 5 at Time 2). Thus, she appeared to move toward the standard target-language forms. To summarize, there was one subject with no difference on the grammaticality judgment task and a large difference on an oral task (possibly the same oral task). Christie and Lantolf conclusion was the following:

This finding is particularly interesting if one takes into account the results on the grammaticality judgment task, where neither of these two subjects made substantially different judgments from Time 1 to Time 2. It seems, then, that judgment data may not necessarily inform us of a learner's changing interlanguage grammar, since the results of the latter basically remained unchanged after 15 months, even though the oral narrative showed a major change for one subject but not the other.

However, we could just as easily discredit the oral data and say the following:

This finding is particularly interesting if one takes into account the results on the oral data task, where one of these subjects made substantially different judgments from Time 1 to Time 2. It seems, then, that oral data may not necessarily inform us of a learner's stable interlanguage grammar, because the results of the latter changed after 15 months, even though the judgment data showed no change for either subject.

In other words, it is commonplace to discredit grammaticality judgment data unquestionably, and in this case with a paucity of evidence. I argue that all data elicitation measures must be examined to determine what they can and cannot inform us of. The present study attempts to provide evidence regarding one aspect of one elicitation measure: the reliability of grammaticality judgment data.

Judgment Data are Gathered and Used

Before reporting the results of the present study, I briefly review some recent work that reflects a variety of ways in which grammaticality judgments have been used. In looking at the literature, we find that there are three main dimensions in which grammaticality judgments vary. First, researchers differ in whether or not they ask learners to correct those sentences that are judged ungrammatical. Second, differences occur in what is being asked: In some cases learners are asked for judgments on single sentences; in others they are asked for preference judgments. In other words, given two sentences, which is preferred? Within grammaticality judgment tasks, another difference arises: Some sentences are contextualized; some are not. A third dimension has to do with the number of possible responses that one can give. In some cases, responses are dichotomous; a sentence can be either grammatical or ungrammatical. In others, there is a range of possibilities that include the degree of confidence a learner has in making responses. Additionally, researchers vary widely in the number of sentences subjects are asked to give judgments about, ranging from 30 or 40 to more than 200.

Analyzing Results

To illustrate the range of data we deal with in second-language acquisition research and the range in interpretation of results, it is useful to take a look at a few recent studies. Bley-Vroman, Felix and Ioup, in their investigation of Subjaceny and the Empty Category Principle, asked subjects to judge 32 sentences in one of three ways: the sentence is a possible English sentence, the sentence is an impossible English sentence, Not Sure. When analyzing the results, however, what to do with the Not Sure responses became problematic. Their solution was to count the Not Sure responses as if they were incorrect responses (i.e., marked as possible for ungrammatical sentences and impossible for grammatical sentences), a solution that they felt was justifiable, in large part, because there were so few responses in the Not Sure category (3.6% for the nonnative speakers). This post hoc arrangement was not principled because it is unclear what would have happened had there been a much larger percentage of Not Sure responses.

A second study is that of Coppetiers, in which he counted the responses to the Not Sure option as if they were correct responses.

A third study is that of Schachter and Yip. In their study, Schachter and Yip looked at the relationship between processing constraints and grammaticality judgments. They included 54 sentences, to be judged on a 4-point scale as clearly grammatical, probably grammatical, probably ungrammatical, or clearly ungrammatical. In this study they did not allow for a Not Sure option. Their display of the data and their descriptive statistics maintained the separateness of these categories. The question remains: How do we interpret the middle two categories (the "probably" ones)? Does this type of judgment reflect a learner's linguistic knowledge?

In a fourth study, Gass and Ard were looking at the acquisition of the progressive. As in the Schachter and Yip study, they used a four-way distinction, ranging from definitely correct to definitely incorrect. Their statistics incorporated these four distinctions, as they were looking at patterns of responses across language groups. However, the same question is raised as was raised with regard to the Schachter and Yip study: What does one do with the "possibly" answers?

Finally, we turn to another variation on the use of grammaticality judgments, a study by Schachter on Subjacency. Four possible responses were allowed in this study, as in the Schachter and Yip study, but here the responses were collapsed so that judgments of clearly correct and possibly correct were counted as correct responses. As with other studies, questions arise: Do we use a confidence scale, without some justification for that scale in our analysis of the results?

The Study

The present study takes a slightly different perspective on ways in which grammaticality judgments are used, considering reliability as a function of syntactic constraints.

Subjects

The data base comprises judgments on relative clauses by 23 Chinese, Korean, and Japanese ESL learners at the English Language Center of Michigan State University. The subjects were all attending ESL classes to satisfy the language requirement specified by university policy for students wishing to pursue studies in substantive disciplines.

Materials

Test sentences reflected relative clause positions on the accessibility hierarchy, a hierarchy that makes predictions about the frequency and occurrence of relative clause types in languages of the world. The accessibility hierarchy is given in (1):

(1) SU > DO > 10 > OPREP > GEN > OCOMP

The accessibility hierarchy is to be interpreted in such a way that if a language has, for example, OPREP relatives, it also has all relative clause types higher on the hierarchy (to the left), in this case SU, DO, and 10. Languages differ as to the lowest relative clause type they allow, and there is no way of predicting a priori the lowest position for any given language. In attempting to understand the extent to which learner-languages obey primary-language constraints, researchers have attempted to consider the accessibility hierarchy in the context of second-language learning. In general, it appears that the same constraints that govern primary languages do indeed hold for second languages.

Because this study deals with differences between determinate and indeterminate knowledge and because the accessibility hierarchy appears to represent some reality in terms of knowledge strength, it is hypothesized that the effects of reliability will be reflected in hierarchical orderings. That is, it is predicted that reliability will be greatest on SU relatives and least on OCOMP relatives.

Method

Subjects were given 30 sentences about which they were asked to make judgments: 6 distractor sentences and 4 sentences (2 grammatical and 2 ungrammatical) of each of the 6 relative clause types (see Appendix). Subjects were first asked to judge categorically whether the sentence was grammatical or not by indicating Correct or (I)ncorrect on their answer sheet; they were then asked to assess the degree of confidence they had in their judgment. The response sheet included a scale from +3 to -3, given in (2):

(2) -3	-2	-1	0	+1	+2	+3
definitely incorrect			unsure		definitely correct	

A value of -3 meant that subjects were 100% certain that the sentence was incorrect and +3 meant that they were 100% certain that the sentence was correct. Other values indicated different degrees of certainty, with zero signifying Not Sure. Subjects were told that there was no time limit, but that they were not to go back and change responses to earlier items. Two sample sentences were provided.

There were two administrations of this test with a one-week interval between the two. For each student the order of sentences was randomized in both the first and second version. Thus, 46 versions of the test were generated. After the first administration students were not told that there would be a second administration. In the intervening week, moreover, there was no instruction on relative clauses. Of course, despite the fact that there was no specific instruction in the intervening period, there remains the possibility that the first administration affected the subjects' knowledge base.

After the second administration, 4 subjects were interviewed to see if they could provide us with information on why they made changes.

Results And Discussion

In displaying the results, two aspects of the data are considered: reliability and hierarchical orderings. For ease of comparison with other secondlanguage studies, the 10 and OPREP positions are combined.

The results from a Pearson Product-Moment Correlation. There are two correlations presented, one for dichotomous judgments and one for the judgments on the 7-point rating scale. As can be seen, correlations were significant in both instances (.5979, $p < .01$, in the case of dichotomous judgments, and .6443, $p < .01$, in the case of judgments on a 7-point scale).

TABLE 6.1 All Sentences Combined (552 Sentences)

Dichotomous Judgments		Seven-Point Scale	
r	p	r	p
.5979	<.01	.6443	<.01

TABLE 6.2 Changes in Judgments from Time 1 to Time 2

Number of Points Changed in 7-Point Scale	Number of Instances
0	317
1	105
2	22
3	20
4	22
5	30
6	36

In Table 6.2 are given the changes made on the 7-point scale. We see that in the majority of the sentences there was no change from Time I to Time 2 (317) and also that when there were changes, they were minimal.

In the production measure, subjects were asked to combine two sentences to form a relative clause. The similarity of the patterns is clear. In the case of accuracy on a production task and reliability from Time 1 to Time 2, the pattern of the results is the same, including the oddity of the GEN position.

TABLE 6.3 Changes by Subject

Subject Number	Changes on Dichotomous Scale (n = 24)
1	5
2	5

(Contd)

3	1
4	5
5	5
6	6
7	4
8	1
9	5
10	7
11	4
12	6
13	8
14	2
15	3
16	1
17	3
18	1
19	11
20	1
21	10
22	3
23	10

TABLE 6.4 Reliability by Sentence Type (552 Sentences)

Sentence Type	Dichotomous Judgments		Seven-Point Scale	
	r	p	r	p
SU	.7620	.001	.8302	.001
DO	.5990	.01	.5861	.01
IO/OPREP	.6348	.01	.5832	.01
GEN	.6517	.01	.6806	.001
OCOMP	.4789	.05	.5442	.01

It has been suggested that individual variation may be a major factor in inconsistent responses. Consistency may vary between subjects and, if so, this would mean that person-factors that contribute to inconsistency would have to be identified, and that sampling in future studies would have to take this into account.

However, for the most part we see that there is not a wide range of variation from Time 1 to Time 2. Only three subjects (19, 21, and 23) seem to show considerable variability in their responses. If we further examine where those changes were made, we see that the greatest consistency is in those sentences that are high on the hierarchy and the least consistency is in those that are low. Thus, even when there is inconsistency, it is predictable on the basis of syntactic information.

What has been established thus far is that reliability is a function of syntactic factors. But what is of additional interest is the establishment of a means of extracting from the data those sentences that are determinate. It will be recalled that one of the major issues of this chapter is that of indeterminacy and the concern that some of the grammaticality judgments of learners represent little more than guesswork. What was of interest in this study was a methodology for eliminating just those sentences. Put differently, if we are to understand the nature of second-language acquisition, we must have some means of determining which sentences reflect a subject's knowledge base. To consider this question, those sentences on which there were major jumps from Time 1 to Time 2 were eliminated.

In Tables 6.5 and 6.6, we see what would happen if we eliminated from consideration just those sentences for which specific learners had demonstrated erratic responses. Specifically, all sentences in which there was a change of 6 points, that is, from +3 to -3 or vice versa, or 5 and 6 points, were eliminated. It was hypothesized that these indicated pure guesses and/or that factors other than linguistic knowledge were contributing to the results.

TABLE 6.5 Reliability by Sentence Type with the Extremes of 6 Points Removed (516 Sentences)

Sentence Type	Dichotomous Judgments		Seven-Point Scale	
	r	p	r	p.
SU	.8206	.001	.9025	.001
DO	.8034	.001	.8425	.001
IO/OPREP	.6348	.01	.7300	.001
GEN	.7385	.001	.7916	.001
OCOMP	.5933	.01	.7055	.001

TABLE 6.6 Reliability by Sentence Type with the Extremes of 5 and 6 Points Removed (486 Sentences)

Sentence Type	Dichotomous Judgments		Seven-Point Scale	
	r	p	r	p
SU	.8616	.001	.9374	.001
DO	.8154	.001	.9249	.001
10/OPREP	.8676	.001	.8892	.001
GEN	.8244	.001	.8851	.001
OCOMP	.7306	.001	.8411	.001

There is justification for such a move. After the second administration, a small group of subjects was interviewed, in the hopes of obtaining information as to why they changed responses from Time 1 to Time 2. In most cases there was little if any change. That is, the results of Time 1 and Time 2 were identical. For one of the subjects, however, there were a large number of changes. He was unable to provide any reason for such changes until at one point he offered the following statement (R = Researcher; S = Subject):

(3) R: Do you know why you're not so sure here?
S: I think it's definitely correct.
R: O.K. Um.
S: I think that happens because I have three tests tomorrow and the next day so . . .
R: So you have a lot on your mind.
S: Yea.
R: Yea.
S: So I'm so tired . . .
R: That it's hard to concentrate . . .
S: Yea.

In general, we see that without much loss in data, reliability coefficients are extremely high. This, of course, is not unlike what is done in scientific experiments when high and low scores are removed from the data pool. Thus, by removing what appear to be spurious data, most of the original data set remains, and we can feel more confident that these data represent a learner's linguistic knowledge.

Conclusion

It is clear from the results of this study that the issue of reliability cannot be separated from issues of indeterminacy. That is, from previous research it has become clear that the orderings of the Accessibility Hierarchy are reflected in acquisition orders and in acquisition difficulties. Interpreting these findings in terms of indeterminacy, the positions lowest on the hierarchy are those that are indeterminate. They are also the ones where, given our definitions of indeterminacy, we would expect less reliability.

The reliability coefficients, in general, indicate that although there is some variation from Time 1 to Time 2, the overall picture is one of consistency. The use of a 7-point scale permits sifting of the data to examine further the differences in judgments on two occasions by the same subjects.

The data do not provide evidence for the view that judgment data are unreliable. Nor do they provide support for the view that individuals behave in an inconsistent manner. On the other hand, there is evidence to suggest that low reliability occurs in just those areas where greater indeterminacy is predicted. Goss, Zhang and Lantolf claim that "we need to be certain that these judgments are predicated on linguistic principles rather than on some other factors." By comparing judgment data with data based more directly on linguistic principles, it has been shown that judgment data can, when used properly and appropriately, be useful in secondlanguage acquisition research. In sum, we find that grammaticality judgments are indeed reflective of patterns of second-language use.

7

Proactive Talk of Research Methodology

Introduction

Non-critical understandings of radio as a talk site perhaps indicate the extent to which radio is a victim of its own success at naturalising itself within multiple layers of social and cultural activity. In its heyday-the 1930s and 1940s radio's developing production techniques rapidly became buried beneath the exigencies of wartime censorship. The subsequent emergent dominance of television saw to it that radio in Australia, as elsewhere, became the poor relation in media studies. Its dramatic transformation into an interactive talk site, through the developing prevalence of interview over commentary genres, remained largely unnoticed in media studies, as did the development of new formats with the arrival of talkback technologies. Radio's latter-day flexibility, its use of modern outside broadcast techniques and cellular phone links, and the pluralism of vocalities produced by the enduring success of the community broadcasting movement, have each been under-recognised and rarely discussed within media scholarship.

One result of this inattention to contemporary developments has been the inadequate critique of the persistent construction around radio of a myth of spontaneity and free participatory access, in turn giving rise to the sense that radio talk is initially identical with unmediated everyday social conversation. This perception has proven at once a strength and a peril. While at one level it has opened radio as a source of powerful and very often disputational social 'talk' texts to research, it has too often failed to deal with that talk as text', specifically situated within complex layers of radio production and listener reception, as well as socially and culturally embedded within established discourses. Analysis of radio talk too often fails to take into account those other conversations with which it is always intertwined. Those studies which have been undertaken, for instance Higgins and Moss and Scannell, either submerge the medium of delivery in the analysis of ensuing social relations and power differentials or, conversely, limit the social analysis, in detailing the talk of specific format genres.

Since radio is the only mass communication medium limited to a single sensory output, perhaps it is the seeming purity of its exclusive basis in talk which has led to its being critically conceived as particularly close to the broader discourse practices of its social setting. But, while radio talk is undeniably a powerful agent of discursive social formation, it is not and can never be an entirely 'natural' site. At a point when its powers are demonstrably accelerating in a period of re-emergence, its new formats are showing its capacity once again to 'vanish' perceptually into an intensified hyper-naturalising whose progress we can trace as it occurs around us. The re-technologisation of new layers of ubiquitous siting, such as radio rediffusion in shopping malls, elevators and workplaces, or during telephone call-waiting, demonstrates how contemporary radio as a medium should call for more, rather than less, critical attention. And, as part of this rendering aware of the existence of an increasingly omnipresent radio voice within everyday existence, there needs to be a technique which can estrange that radio voice, to divide it from the talk of everyday conversation, and reveal the complex layers of its own particular selectivity. My work seeks out and stresses what the production practices of 'talk radio' bring to what is increasingly under scrutiny as 'radio talk'.

Radio as a Discourse

While my own study shares Fairclough view that radio talk, like all media text, has much to reveal about the transformations currently occurring inside and alongside dominant discourses, my contribution to this field is a focus on how radio as a set of institutional practices, in regard to both its station-based production and its listener reception, continues to elaborate distinctive discursive forms and power relations. While these are continuous with, and even overtly promote, those broader social discursive patterns which Fairclough identifies as contributing to the establishment and maintenance of specific orders of discourse, their effectivity is not only intensified by the processes of mediation which the broadcast spoken word still carries, but is formed into peculiarly multilayered structures by the processes of broadcasting 'production'.

Radio is more than simply a technology of delivery or a representational text. It has developed strategies which can simultaneously familiarise and defamiliarise talk in ways immediately perceptible to any individual who is interviewed or who phones in to a talkback program and subsequently hears themself on-air. Radio has its own distinctive techniques for selection, regulation, and transformation of talk, all the time constructing myths about itself representing itself as immediate, spontaneous, low-tech, accessible, democratising and 'real'. So successfully has it developed and deployed these techniques for the production of particular forms of radio talk, and the simultaneous suppression of its own formative and regulatory practices, that it has become a site where a powerful, top-rating station such as Sydney's talkback specialist, 2UE, can insist on your right as a listener-caller to their programs to 'have your say', without arousing any consciousness of the ironies of the invitation.

Analysis of radio talk, and especially of that which, like the discourses within and around talkback, represents itself as openly 'interactive' with (misnamed) 'listeners', must take into account those elements of radio practice occurring during the professional production of that talk, as well as in the highly active 'reception' of listener 'talkback'. Here I accept Fairclough's schematisation, admitting into the analysis the complex meshing of what he calls his 'threedimensional conception of discourse'. This positions the 'discursive practice' of production, distribution and consumption of texts as always and everywhere carried out within, and on behalf of, broader social practices—at the same time admitting, as in Hall's formulation, the existence of negotiative and resistive responses as well as consensual reception. Where my analysis differs from Fairclough's (other than in its focus on radio, a rare sectoral choice in Fairclough's work) is in its consideration of those parts of the resultant radio 'text' not produced by interactive talk with the community of listener-callers. I accentuate instead those aspects of the talk which result from the in-studio broadcast practices of program presenters, acting as 'talk hosts.' The talk as it goes to air with its invitations to respond is already simultaneously caught up in other dialogues: those covert or even disruptive exchanges with in-studio production team colleagues, which manage the flows of broadcast talk. In other words, my analysis recognises that a part of the elaboration of the 'relational' aspects of radio discourse practice is initiated before what Hall would see as distribution of this mediated talk-text. It is this processing which then models discursive relations for those other talk relations which ensue, first as listener-callers 'talk back' to the program hosts on air and, subsequently, as they talk through 'reception' within their own social networks. Perhaps most significantly, I problematise this extended relational processing in the conversations which ensue with listener-callers, not by accounting for the differences between officially 'on-air' texts and in-studio talk, but by uncovering marked continuities.

Talkback radio claims that it centres around the potential for participant callers freely to 'air their point of view', yet it simultaneously constrains that participation within a range of control techniques. The in-studio communication behaviours shown in the off-air talk of production teams have much to reveal about the processing of this particular illusion of free access. Those audio channels which do not usually go to air, on which frenetic instructions, interpersonal banter, time-control cues and even frustration-release comments constantly occur, have a powerful influence on the structuring of on-air talk. The 'at home' situatedness of the listener-caller is equally formative. The interventions of partners, mates, party guests, kids and even pets 'get into' what is said, not as irrelevancies or interruptions but as significant elements in the formation of the talk. The now classic insistence of talk hosts to callers that they 'turn down their radio' to prevent distorting feedback through the telephone, acts as an important element of the transformation from listener to listener-caller: a re-channelling of the voice and an implicit assent to the many regulatory processes which going on-air entails. Each process involves elements contributing to the social positioning of radio talk within the broader contexts of power-within-discourse. Talk radio is never the intensely focused two-way interaction it represents itself to be. Instead it is 'opened' at each end simultaneously into the broader social, with all that that entails.

It is these dimensions of radio as a consistent and coherent 'practice' which this chapter attempts to reintroduce. I do not, however, undertake this through observational study of the in-studio behaviours of production staff or those of listener reception—although each might profitably be undertaken, and full observation study of radio reception in particular is markedly overdue. I work instead to foreground the ways in which what can be called the radio texts, the conversations which result from the interaction of talk show hosts and their callers, can themselves reveal in-studio, regulatory practices at work. I seek out the textual moments in a given broadcast where the smooth linearity of production to reception is disrupted; where there are what Fairclough calls 'cruces and crises' in the discourse and especially in the relational work of that discourse. Nor are disruptions difficult to detect. Indeed, so prevalent are the breaches in the techniques and behaviours that radio discourse seeks to establish, that they dominate transactions between hosts and callers. They can be seen to have a major influence on the production of a dominant relation of (conversational) exchange. If, as many commentators have observed, talk radio discourses do go on to modify broader social discourses in their turn, I contend that it is at the moment of active co-production between broadcast team, on-air host, and 'caller-on-behalf-of-all-listeners', that meaning is most forcefully made, and power relations forged.

Radio Talk's Unique Discursive Space

In the first instance, the discourses established within radio talk are a product of their connection at one end of the continuum that is broadcast talk, to the 'in-studio' locatedness of the talk show host and his production team (in Australia, most hosts are male; most production teams are female). It is at this point that they engage with the institutional discourses of a professional media organisation: language policies, advertising or sponsorship roles, and so on, and beyond the organisation's ideological positioning within the public service, commercial or community. Whether A, B or C-licensed, a given Australian radio station maintains watchful limits on the talk which constitutes its program delivery. It directly controls on-air talk through the broad generic restraints of program formatting to the narrower constraints involved in the regular feedback on presentation behaviours from program managers to onair staff and production teams. Indirectly, a radio station's controls are extended through its response to ratings, licensing and other policy regulation, and the flow of advertising or sponsorship revenues.

Operating even more implicitly are specific sets of what Bourdieu would recognise as 'dispositions', manifested in the attitudes and practices of broadcasters. Particular forms of vocality, acquired registers, expertise within formats and favoured speech genres, together comprise a broadcast performance which listeners are encouraged to regard as indicating the existence of a distinctive individual 'personality', but which the radio industry's hiring-and-firing procedures and selection of personnel to work particular shifts demonstrate are acquired skills.

These preferred behaviours, rendered and read back as 'personality', do not operate only in constructing that flow of conversation with interviewees and callers. In commercial talkback in particular they are also demonstrated on a daily basis in the negotiations and contestations occurring in-studio, enmeshed in the talk of production teams. Intersecting the broadcast comments of the presenter are the unheard organising conversations of technical and program producers; researchers and news journalists; and receptionists and call-screeners, who prearrange and pace the flow of talk. The increased seepage of such in-house talk into what is actually broadcast says much of the powers of contemporary radio talk's myths of its own spontaneity and 'interpersonal' immediacy. Conventionally suppressed on the advice of training procedures and station manuals as 'unprofessional', such halfjoking collusion with breaches of good conduct and 'correct' public discourse practices, shows how far institutional radio talk's familiarity and friendliness is building a private into a public voice.

The tendency is conterminous with Tolson isolation of 'populism' as a major transformation in the order of public media discourse: a blending of earlier and more formal 'public service' informational styles with a drive towards entertainment. At the same time, it engages a long-established tradition inside radio's own programming practices which Hilmes describes as a simultaneous marking out of the 'sacratised', or not-to-be-mentioned-on-air, and its selective violation. The success of many of America's early radio shows she attributes to this tendency: 'it may be the very balancing acts performed by these programs that made them so popular'. In talkback radio it is the rehearsal of combative semi-insult and apparent professional ineptitude which licenses participation from listeners; a kind of highly-skilled and carefully produced amateurism which works as an anti-glossiness in the on-air presentation, and so invites 'the everyday' voice of the caller onto the air. The process is most consistently modelled in those violations of formality and consensual, seamless, professional radio flow allowed to go to air on commercial talkback.

Such comment and banter should, however, not be seen as a disruption to the flow of broadcast talk. On the contrary, it is continuous with its broader ideological positionings. It both speeds up the pace of exchanges by adding to their mass, and adds to the characterisation of the talk as combative, argumentative and competitive. As Fairclough would have it, this is a moment where the 'communicative event' in this case, spontaneous criticism, personal or social, directly voiced intersects with and endorses the 'order of discourse'. Talkback radio conversation, a genre whose greatest successes occur within the free-market 'enterprise discourse' of commercial stations, thrives on competitive argument.

The programming presentation 'talk' behaviours most consistently engaged in in a night-time talkback program: 'The Stan Zemanek Show'. Here the host's persona is built around an untrammelled and aggressive masculinity, developed over familiar patriarchal notions of unassailable authority and a perverse yet concomitant larrikin disruptiveness and resistance to regulation-all played out as argument. Broadcasting on top-rating Sydney talkback station 2UE, home to John Laws and Alan Jones (nationally topranking talk hosts), host Stan Zemanek, with over twenty years experience in radio and a staggering weekly programming output of between fifteen and twenty-five hours of talkback, regularly breaches the flow of listener-directed talk to give priority to those in-studio staff and broadcasting procedures usually unheard. He becomes, in Goffman terms, both 'author' and 'animator' of the discourses at play in his programming. He is attending to talk which produces and gives priority to his own power as it places him at the centre of a production team, and at the same time allowing it to be 'overheard' by what is effectively, at that moment, a secondary audience of at-home listeners. Zemanek's behaviour within the conventionally unheard exchanges of in-studio talk demonstrates the continuity, and thus doubled power, of his position.

At one level many of his spontaneous comments on his own broadcasting practice appear as very much the sort of errors that Goffman analysed in his 1981 study. Zemanek reveals, however, a far more cavalier attitude towards the preservation of an aura of expertise than was the case for the 'announcers' of the earlier, more formal radio formats that Goffman analysed, or even for the strongly performative stylings used in DJ programs on music radio from the 1950s on. Zemanek actively reveals the often chaotic technical processes at work around him as he broadcasts.

The following texts are extracts from 'The Stan Zemanek Show', Radio 2UE, recorded 1-4 April 1996.

Extract 1

The extract breaches the immediacy of the broadcast relation between host and listener in two ways: first, by indicating the presence of the technology and, second, by the recognition of a multiple presence within the studio, where 'we', and not 'I', turn on microphones. The immediate swing into listener address, 'good evening and welcome', does nothing to mitigate the heavy criticism of the 'aside', in which the host addresses in-studio staff. Both breaches show openly the split focus of talk-program address.

Extract 2

[The host comes out of a pre-recorded segment without engaging the seven-second delay required for phone-in security.]

Z: It was 14 after the hour: this i-i-is, Stan Zemanek; and what am I gonna do now? I suppose . . . go into . . . delay.

While the host now accepts it is his own responsibility to correct the microphone delay, again he has no hesitation in talking the problem through on air, actually displaying those elements of broadcast practice designed to protect hosts from abusive callers, and so supposed to remain concealed. In a later exchange with a young caller who has Internet expertise, the host works to rebuild exactly this illusion of a non-technically-mediated immediacy of relation to his listener-callers yet, at the same time, cannot resist the technology's efficacy in 'magically' endorsing his own powers. The following exchange with caller 'Michael' reveals the centrality of the host's technical control over listener-caller voices and so enhances the importance of the destabilisation allowed in moments of banter or criticism with staffers especially those which involve technical matters. They are, as Hilmes has suggested, instabilities set up and rehearsed to reassert rather than to release control.

Extract 3

[The caller, 'Michael', tells the host about the existence of a Stan Zemanek 'hate' page on the Internet. The caller has altered the 'hate' page to a 'like' page, and hopes to impress the host.]

M: Hi how are ya Stan?
Z: Yes Michael.
M: (uhh, uhh) Yeah uum (uhh) you know how that person rang up said he was gonna do a hate page on the Internet?
Z: (:::) Yeeess?
M: A long time ago?
Z: Yes . . .
M: Well um he actually, did it,
Z: Did he really?
M: Yep
Z: He did a whole hate page on me!
M: Yeah! (uhh) but, um, I did a favour for you Stan:
Z: Yes . . .
M: I changed it. I wrote: 'The best things about Stan'.
Z: Oh this'll be good!
M: An' um, I've had some, ah, someone sent me five letters? And they said, um, he doesn't like, how you cut off people?
Z: Yes—
M: But he likes um the show.

M: Can you like on the show tell them about the, show? I mean about the Internet? Um, the hate, er, like page?
Z: Well I mean, I don't know anything about it—how about you send me in all the information?
M: Send you all the information?
Z: Yeah, send me all the, er send me all the information by mail.
M: By mail but I'm—
Z: See we don't have the Internet here at 2UE we're not that up to date.
M: Eh? What about your house, do you have the Internet?
Z: No we don't.
M: You don't! (haha)
Z: No we don't. I can't even work a computer.
M: Oh ha ha ha!
Z: I have about a dozen computers but I don't know how to work either one of them.
M: Oh Stan I was wondering
Z: Yes—
M: —how do you cut off people?
Z: Very easily:

The extract is particularly interesting given the arrival at 2UE in the following month of their own Internet website, preparations for which must have been well under way when Zemanek received this call. The final rejection of this caller is of course specifically motivated by a question (lines 51 and 53) about concealed radio practice: the host's capacity to cut off a call with the flick of a switch. This question has the potential to unearth some of the host's own professional abuses of a still powerful, if outdated, technology but at the same time the host's reticence in approaching new technologies (and especially somebody else's 'new') is there throughout the discussion. It is at one level an extraordinary position from a commercial talkback host so strongly directed towards the constant renewal of consumer desires for the new. Yet the position is consistent with his awareness of the conservatism of his mostly ageing audience, and of the degree to which the intensified access to opinion formation represented by Internet use threatens his own dominance via radio. His slip in grammatical control over the number of computers he has ('I have about a dozen computers but I can't work either one of them', line 49) and his apparent openness in admitting a lack of expertise in the new technology, are immediately compensated by his refusal to explain his control over the old, and by his demonstration of the power he thus retains, cutting off the caller who has dared to question him. Nor is this preservation of power to himself, and attribution of weakness or error to others, an isolated moment.

Extract 4

[The host comes out of a cart-taped promo-sting, and has trouble with his headphone sound levels.]

Z: Why are my headphones sooo . . . (::) so, ah, top? (::) Why are they . . . I don't know why (uhhh). This studio just seems to change, from day to day to day (hh) (:::) One of these days, somebody's going to wake up and say (uhh) (::) 'Let's get it fixed . . .' (Public voice resumes) 13 13 32, aand, what have we got here: Terry hello!

Extract 5

[Coming out of a live-cross sports report, the host has failed to consult with the call-screener over an incoming VIP call: he goes off-air to do so. When he returns, his microphone is still engaged to the call-screener's—so he picks up and transmits the next call in both 'real time' and 'delay time'.]

Z: [music sting] YEes! 13 13 32 is-our-tele-phone-nu-mber. And, um just excuse me folks I've just gotta tell Natasha something. [5 seconds of dead air] OK. Thank you very much for that; sorry, folks, I just have to (er-er) take those little breaks—every now and then: Hello! Hello—Wayne! (::) [2 second delay-sound feeding back through the host's microphone, off broadcast output: thank you much for that: sorry fo -'] Way-ne! [delay sound: 'take those little breaks every now and then') I see-ee (ahem) [mic. lead noise] Are you there Wayne? [mic. lead noise, phone beep] Hello! [phone hangs up: engaged beeps] See! [engaged beeps as host speaks] Fantastic, isn't it. [beeps] Absolutely wonderful. [beeps] The apprentice Labor people [beeps] they haven't yet quite worked out [beeps] how to work a phone [beeps] They don't have the brains [beeps] to be able to sort of converse on the telephone and [beeps] to er communicate with their fellow human beings

The host is already working here to recover the breaches in those barricades of powerful speech behaviours and technical devices behind which he constructs his unassailable position of authority. It is arguable, given the range of such moments across shows, extending even to examples which capture staffers' voices on the host's microphone as they respond to his off-air demands, that such comment from the host operates less as a revelatory breach in control than as yet another opportunistic incursion into a new area of social space: the usually unheard form of in-studio communication. This, in effect, adds to the pervasiveness, and so the power, of the Zemanek position. After all, inside this newly revealed social space, the host is still dominant, making open demands on a group of very much subordinate, and universally female, production staff, who thus come to occupy, in technology analyst Sadie Plant terms, the inside of the machine':

In a sense, women have always been the machine parts for a very much male culture. Women have been the means of reproducing the species, reproducing communications—secretaries etc. which is obviously similar to the role of machines and tools.

Ultimately then, this interior world, in which every aspect of the host's demands for the authoritative information and technical enhancement that sustain his power must be met and where lapses are just as instantly exposed and criticised, is also reproductive of male power. Certainly, whenever there is error or inadequacy in the technologically-armoured carapace of the host's voice as powerful persona, the host's self-representation of inviolable authority, it is attributed at once to women staff.

Extract 6

[Music: Johnny-be-good—host begins to speak before the end of the track.]

Z: Yes [music] Oh! [music] oh! [Music] Yes—that is Johnnybe-good and that is Doug Parkinson and let me tell you they're gonna be all over the joint: ah, so you, better get along, to see the Doug Parkinson Buddy Holly Show, ah, because it is fantastic (uhh) Apparently they're, aaahh, they're still travelling around: they're gonna be at the Parra Riverside Theatre at Parramatta on the 20th of April, and ah, Yalla Wool Shed, ah that's down near Wollongong, on the 26th and 27th of April, ah, and ah Belmont Sailing Club up here in ah Port Macquarie on on as they head off on their northern New South Wales tour, (::) What is it I say? (:::) Did I say La—(::) I said

PORT Macquarie did I? OK it's LAKE Macquarie, thank you Shirley—well you are from that way aren't you. You're just a Newcastle girl at heart aren't you. (:::) Hunter Valley. (::) Muswellbrook. I see. OK. (Uhh) well now that we've found out where Shirley ah comes from, ah anyway, ah up there at uh Lake Macquarie on ah Belmont there Belmont Sailing Club on the 4th of May.

Extract 7

[Caller 'Rocky' in a reasonably friendly, bantering tone, accuses the host of behaving badly to an earlier female caller.]

R: . . . but I agree with that last lady mate (ha) you are a pig, there's no question about that.

Z: I am a pig! Shirley: this man just called me a pig! can you believe that?

Z: Now, listen, my producer's here, and, um, she's the reason why this show's the way it is

R: (indecipherable)—my heart's bleeding for you

Z: Well I mean she's the one that tells me what to do, I ju—I don't—I just sit here and I'm just a mouth piece for Shirley.

R: . . . well that's true.

Z: Shirley do you think I'm a pig?

S: [voice off] No . . .

Z: I'm—there's—there was (hahaha) a little bit of hesitation in that (hahaha) Shirley! Hahahaha! There was a bit of hesitation in that! Ohohohohoho! Oooh, Shirley! (:) Can I have another cuppa tea please?

Extract 8

[Host moves into a new call sequence: uncertain of the next technical change; he is presumably taking off-air instruction from producer Shirley through his headphones.]

Z: Yeees, OK, what have I got here, what do I have to do now? I'm just taking directions from the lovely Shirley, an' I think I'll press this button:

In each of these examples women staffers, attempting to remedy the host's technical incompetence or factual error, are submitted to a kind of direct or indirect teasing mockery which is not far removed from manipulative violence. Producer Shirley, in Extract 6, making an important correction to the locale of an advertised performance-a sponsor's product, and so an element central to the show is first of all bunted hard with reference to her obscure country origins, then manoeuvred into appearing to be wasting program time with trivia, and finally slapped firmly into place as 'tea maker' to the star. She is rendered first as local, rather than having the globalising powers to rove at will across sectors which the host preserves for himself; then she is demoted to the merely domestic. When, in the subsequent call, Extract 7, 'Rocky' rebukes the host over just such a contemptuous and violent treatment of an earlier female caller, the host retaliates by claiming, in a surprising mock-anti-heroic ploy, to be 'Shirley's mouthpiece' at her beck and call so effectively shifting all blame for program misdemeanours onto her. It is however a timely reminder of the one element of accuracy in his portrayal of the power relations in play in-studio: the producer's capacity to be speaking off-air to the presenter throughout his on-air conversations, and so to be, in effect, inside his head.

What is centred here by the hurt the host's persona has sustained, once outside an arena of his own control is the degree to which his vocal presentation, his radio style, constitute a powerful masculinity, built against any hint of female authority or autonomy. This is beyond the representations of patriarchal authority detailed in earlier studies of radio talkback in which paternalistic male authority directly asserts itself and seeks to control female opinion and behaviour. While 'The Stan Zemanek Show' overtly revisits this aspect of patriarchal authority, what is under scrutiny here is the role that radio can play in the constitution of masculinity, rather than simply its rehearsal in relational talk with women callers. The spread of that constitutive masculinity across all layers of social space, the private as much as the public; its equation with dominant social values; and the apparent fixing of those values in the construction of a coherent, stable and powerful 'King Stanley' as the ultimate embodiment of a dynamic 1990s entrepreneurial masculinity, work together in a continuous line from in-studio spats to every other form of on-air interaction.

Radio's Discursive Gendering of Social Space

The beliefs expounded in 'The Stan Zemanek Show' are thus founded on the daily elaboration of a myth of outwardly-directed male agency over the reality of in-studio female control. The myth is then extended outwards from its base in bullying control of female staffers, to a rehearsal of its powers in combative exchanges with aggressive male callers. Setting up a relation of dispute and argumentation through his construction of an unassailable masculine authority, extended to his male callers as a challenge to try out their power against his own, Zemanek produces a rarely-countered gender divide in his callers. Female callers respond with collusive strategies which operate as a form of fan adulation and even as direct financial gain for the host, as regular women callers set up social groups to track his cabaret performances across metropolitan Sydney's Rugby League Club venues and to sell tickets to their friends. The collusive nature of these calls is displayed in their endorsement of every opinion the host voices, and in their personal response to criticism of the host from other callers. The collusive relation is capped by an extensive program of gift exchanges (most often sponsors' promotional give-aways in return for home-baked treats) which epitomises the classically patriarchal role played out with women callers.

Male callers are positioned in a more complex relation. In accepting the invitation to verbal combat, which the technological inequality of their bandwidth-suppressed voices and the host's powers to override their opinions never allow them to win, aggressive male callers still reproduce the host's authority. He is consistently the 'winner' in each debate, however, and the ratings victor in the red-hot and no-holds-barred verbal sparring which results.

There is on-air undeniably what Hutchby has identified as an 'asymmetry' in Zemanek's social relations. It runs all the way from the host's power to represent even his own errors in studio as the mistakes of his colleagues, through his persistent use of a range of other abuses of conversational power relations. When he disrupts conventions of conversational and disputational turntaking by overriding responses with the 'ducker' device (an automatic control on the microphone which runs the host's voice over the caller's), by cutting callers off to ensure that the host has the last word, or even by summarising a call after it has been cut off, the technically-enhanced powers to control conversational exchanges help to produce what is subsequently read as a powerful masculinity within the talk of this form of contentious talkback. As with the commercial exchanges which such talk shows promote, and the intensely competitive marketing ethics they both espouse and deploy, all the talk texts admitted to air and especially those selected for replay as promotional clips or for marketing as CD compilations demonstrate submission to the powerful talk strategies of the host. The more aggressive the contention and argumentation, the more dramatic the conflict the greater the power exercised by the host, and the higher the ratings.

Turntaking, Fairclough reminds us, 'depends on (and is a part of) power relationships between participants'. Hutchby analyses its regulatory systems to isolate asymmetrical power relations in argumentation, demonstrating in great detail the strategies used both to prolong and control debate and to end it at moments of peak advantage. His analysis does much to identify techniques that Zemanek can be shown to use to assert his own persona as one of unassailable authority. But beyond the systems of interaction, both Zemanek and his callers explicitly equate this combative structuring of talk with the sorts of physical and aggressive masculinity once identified with Australian larrikinism. Caller 'Henry', angry with Zemanek for both his racism and his scorn for the older forms of physical power displayed, for instance, in the heroic manual labour of wharfies, reads the host's talk performance as the explicit invitation to combat that such talk actually enacts. Henry's response to the host's aggressive banter presumes an already articulated masculine discourse of insult and challenge to combat and, in so doing, creates a new context for their actual articulation, by challenging the host to abandon the unlocatability of his mediated, virtual radio self, safely within its studio and protective technologies, in favour of a and rights.

By showing the pervasiveness and tenacity of the largely unnoticed and taken-for-granted work that all members do with membership categories, I have implied that a first step in challenging discourses and practices is to recognise the force of categorisation practices in social and institutional life. This chapter has sketched some initial procedures for doing the recognition work in the analysis of a text or transcript. First, identify the categories in use, especially those that are otherwise taken for granted as points in a matrix of some social institution or encounter. Second, show how various attributes, activities, qualities are attached to categories and, if relevant, how they are contested or disattached. Monologic texts and dialogic texts may well differ in the arrays of candidate activities proposed for different categories. Show how categories are related, and how they are related through descriptions of activities. Look especially for tenacious category-bound activities such as babies cry or need help, mothers help. These are the categories that lock the discourse into place, and possibly the practices that flow from them.

The specification of how discourses are secured through membership categorisation work assists the identification of how discourses are called on and how they are invoked in the mundane activities of talking, hearing, reading and writing. The use of membership categorisation analysis is always local, and always occasioned: done on an occasion of talk or writing, reading or hearing. Culture is internal to action, and can be found in the course of membership categorisation work as well as in an array of other social practices.

Membership categorisation device analysis offers a socially critical perspective on text and culture by showing a different order of phenomena in texts and in talk than is retrievable through other critical discourse analysis approaches, and by locating 'culture' in social practices. The social practices to which membership categorisation work is central include describing, accounting, and reasoning. Recall in the first example the teacher's attempts to have students find a reason for mothers to be helping at school that day in the story. For the teacher at least, there seems to have been one real reason why the mothers were there that day. That mothers were there, and that they were there to help, was treated as obvious. The students were encouraged to think about the surface of the story (the plot, the events) and not the category-predicate connections that underpin the 'reality' of the story.

While I have proposed that membership categorisation work can be studied as a means of locking texts, talk and discourses into place, and therefore 'excavating' their foundations, it needs to be recognised that this does not provide directly for the characterisation of texts, talk and discourses as conservative or not. The judgement about that matter comes from observations of how they work in situ or in general to arrange relations of power, privilege and advantage.

That is, the political valency of a categorisation analysis is found in its material, social, symbolic applications and consequences, rather than in its contents or form per se.

8

Linguistics and Discourse Analysis in Research Methodology

Introduction

At the beginning of the twentieth century, Saussure came to the view that the proper focus for the new kind of study of language he envisaged was langue (the abstract system of language that underlies actual language use) and not parole (language in actual use). Such a view involved a profoundly idealist conception of language study, one in which the decontextualised study of grammar (or syntax) came to be seen as the apex of scholarly achievement in the emerging discipline of linguistics. This was a world where the emergence of discourse analysis (concerned as it is with parole) would have to wait another fifty years, though the necessity of studying conversation was indicated well before this by the British linguist, J. R. Firth in a paper originally published in 1935:

Neither linguists nor psychologists have begun the study of conversation; but it is here we shall find the key to a better understanding of what language really is and how it works.

Even those linguists directly indebted to Firth were slow to take up this challenge and, through much of the twentieth century, it was not heard at all. For Noam Chomsky, that most widely-known contemporary linguist, linguistic theory could comfortably be conceived of, fifty years after the publication of Saussure's major work, as 'concerned primarily with an ideal speaker-listener, in a completely homogeneous speech community'.

However, it was almost inevitable that analytic tools developed under this idealist regime would be turned to social/political use in the 1960s and 1970s, given the general politicisation of that period and the emergence of socially-oriented concerns with language the beginnings of what was to become sociolinguistics. In the United States and the United Kingdom, concerns about schooling focused linguistic attention on questions of race and class; in Germany, a concern with the situation of non-German 'guest-workers', involving a complex of questions from schooling to political rights, led to parallel investigations of the everyday language use of actual people. The political flavour of this period emerges very clearly from the introduction to Dittmar's book:

In the last decade sociolinguistics has become a powerful factor in promoting emancipation. Attempts have been and are being made to attenuate conflicts in schools and to remove the obvious inequality of opportunity of broad sections of the working classes and peripheral social groups by systematically exposing the connection between speech forms and class structure, and by application of the insights gained to specified social contexts.

The emergence of sociolinguistics produced a new kind of linguist who moved between the academy and the classroom, shopfloor, street or therapist's office, armed with a metaphorical toolbox filled with linguistic tools in one hand and, in the other, that increasingly ubiquitous material box—the tape-recorder. Sociolinguistics was the vanguard of a new kind of parole-oriented linguistic work. It, and the new 'discourse analysis' which was soon to follow, were characterised by: a substantial focus on spoken language; a recognition of the need for new technical vocabularies concerning both language and the social in dealing with such material; a willingness to go outside linguistics for such vocabularies; and a failure to interrogate adequately many of the terms of those vocabularies.

Legacy of Saussure

The eighteenth-century appearance of increasingly formalised knowledges concerning 'labour, life, language' in the emerging disciplines of economics, biology and linguistics marked a significant moment in the transformation of Europe from earlier forms of knowledge and social organisation to those characteristic of modernity. Labour, life and language have all been significant sites for the forms of control of populations which characterise modern systems of governance. In the case of language, control of which (that is, whose) language was to 'count' was critical to the disappearance of old regional or local identities and the building of new, national identities. The emergence of the nation-state in nineteenth-century Europe was preceded by the relentless movement of rural populations to the city, a process accelerated in the developing countries where such population movement became more and more transnational. The inevitable consequence of such movement has been the large-scale disappearance of linguistic diversity as a function of geographical location and its replacement with the contemporary diversity of urban language variation, understood in terms of hierarchies of social differentiation involving particularly class, race and ethnicity.

Closely associated with the nineteenth-century emergence of the European nation-state have been language standardisation and the provision of universal education, the latter (particularly in the form of literacy education) usually functioning as a vehicle for the spread of standard language. Speaking 'the' national language constituted a claim to a national identity and, hence, a new kind of self—an emergent, even if never completely seamless, process in the complex balancing of the imaginaries of nation against region and locality.

The twentieth-century emergence of the multilingual state, together with the spread of English as an international language, have made the relations between language, nation and identity even more ambiguous. The nation-state outside Europe, in the former colonies of Asia, Africa and the Americas (including those, such as Australia and Canada, which are dominated by Europeans and are substantially English-speaking) is typically multi-ethnic and multilingual and, if not officially English-speaking, is likely to make considerable use of English in education, government and business. The implications of such usage for identity and nation are enormous.

This is the contemporary scene within which the texts and meanings that speakers/listeners and readers/writers need to negotiate are increasingly produced and contested. Yet the models of language that are the currency of contemporary linguistics, including discourse analysis, are in certain key respects based in the late nineteenth and not the late twentieth century. Central to this perspective is the figure of Saussure, grounded in the nineteenth century but casting a shadow across all twentieth-century work on language and, ultimately, discourse.

The nineteenth century was a time of major intellectual work on language. This work included feats of historical reconstruction, most spectacularly of the Indo-European language, the original speakers of which inhabited what is now central and eastern Europe several millennia BC. This ancient language was the precursor of what is now known as the Indo-European language family which includes not only most of the contemporary languages of Europe but also languages extending from Europe through parts of the Middle East into northern India. Ferdinand de Saussure, trained in this 'comparative' tradition and an elite performer within it, subsequently reacted against both its historicism and the minutiae of its habitual data (typically, speech sounds and lexical items). He had a grander sweep in mind for his new science of 'semiology', encompassing both language and other semiotic systems.

Mainstream twentieth-century linguistics has been substantially shaped by two ideas taken from Saussure. The first idea is the conviction that language should not be studied with a focus on change over time, that is, historically, but from a more synoptic perspective-what it looks like at a particular point in time (in Saussure's terms, synchronically rather than diachronically). The second idea is that what should be studied is the abstract system of language (langue) that underlies language use and not instances of actual use (parole). In particular, the view of the emerging discipline of linguistics, substantially until the 1970s, that langue and not parole was the proper concern of scholarship about language, ensured that linguistics in the first half of the twentieth century had problems even beginning to address any aspect of language above the level of the sentence. Compounding the effects of the discipline's preferred focus on grammar and phonology was the 'capture' of much Anglo-American linguistics by the psychological behaviourism of the 1940s and 1950s. This led to eschewing the possibility of any kind of 'scientific' focus on meaning, that is, what actual people are actively constructing through their language practices. Since meaning, in any conventional scientific' sense, could not be 'observed', it came largely to be ignored. The combined effect of these two influences, (linguistic) Saussureanism and behaviourism, produced a strong 'technicist' bias which marks linguistics to this day.

The successful linguistic challenge to behaviourism came, very early in his career, from Chomsky in a blistering review of behaviourist B.E Skinner 1957 book, Verbal Behaviour. Chomsky's own subsequent work in linguistics, however, produced side-by-side with his influential work of social and political critique, did not take a social direction but rather was informed by philosophy and related disciplines, including cognitive psychology. This led him to a formal rather than a functional model of language, a model in which language was understood to be in some sense 'hard-wired' into the individual and only marginally 'acquired' socially: thus, speaking to young children merely gave them data to work on. Though Chomsky himself did not develop forms of social analysis within linguistics, others did, and Chomsky's fame, as a radical intellectual, no doubt contributed to linguistics coming to be seen as both intellectually challenging and an avant-garde site for bright young radicals of the 1960s and 1970s.

The conjunction of the radicalism and intellectual challenge of linguistics with the increasing availability of the tape-recorder, providing a means of 'fixing' the flux of talk, brought about a major change in the discipline, which now routinely includes discourse analysis in most programs in linguistics. The kind of non-intrusive investigation of urban language variation that began to develop in the late 1960s, however, required easily portable machines that could be batterypowered. Armed with such machines by the 1970s, graduate and even undergraduate students, and their teachers, fanned out through the urban areas of the United States, Britain, Australia and elsewhere to map how people talked.

It is hardly surprising, then, that, under these conditions, discourse analysis within linguistics became substantially synonymous with the analysis of spoken language. This bias can be read as yet another manifestation of the 'phonocentrism' that characterises Western society, that is, its privileging of the spoken word and hence speakers in terms of such notions as 'truth', the real' and 'authenticity'.

The field of discourse analysis now includes an increasing body of work dealing with written language. Much of this work has been carried out within the critical discourse analysis and social semiotic traditions (see below, for further detail), which tend to work across the speech/writing divide, drawing on descriptive/analytic technologies able to handle both. Areas of substantial work include news/media/ advertising, literary stylistic work drawing on linguistics and student writing, especially the Australian work by Joan Rothery, J.R. Martin, Frances Christie and others.

The opposition between spoken and written discourse, or 'talk' and 'text', can be read as an assertion of the validity as research object of instances of (spoken) parole alongside the more overtly structured and organised forms of written discourse. The status of an actual piece of writing as just as much parole as an instance of speech is not necessarily always transparent. This is particularly so when the stringent demands for 'correctness' in writing are couched in terms of rules directly invoking the presumed regularities of langue. Further, the fact that the term 'text' has come increasingly to be used for both spoken and written instances of language in use suggests that the dynamism and multidimensionality of much interactive talk has been assimilated to the more synoptic and static understanding of writing as (completed) product, the norms for which provide the measure against which any 'text' is to be judged.

From this perspective, 'text', applied to spoken language, can be read as a structuralist claim on parole. This claim not only suggests an illusory completeness and finality to much speech (and, hence, to its 'analysis') but also, since the 'texts' of speech are commonly equated with their transcriptions, establishing an idealist control over parole, rendering it that much more langue-like, and hence fit for linguists.

What has been lost in this process is the materiality of speech its rhythms, its tunes, its vocality, its timbres, its voice qualities features long regarded by many linguists, conveniently, as merely 'expressive'. And with that materiality, a sense of the particularity of who is speaking is lost—a grievous loss of focus not on individuality, as such, but on positionality. For speech is necessarily embodied, not just in 'the grain of the voice' but in the gestures, postures and movements of speakers, all of which articulate deeply cultural and social selves through their learned corporeality. The investments of speakers in what they and others say, a key aspect of positioning, is commonly much more legible from the corporeality of the speaking body than from words and sentences alone.

Discourse Analysis as Technology: Tools Description

This section turns to a closer look at some key aspects of work both within and outside disciplinary linguistics constituting the emerging field of discourse analysis in particular ways. It indicates disciplines outside linguistics, as well as aspects of linguistics itself, that have made significant contributions to discourse analysis as 'sociolinguistic analysis' but excludes the various borrowings from cognitive psychology, such as schemata and scripts in discourse processing. The aim is to provide a 'map' of the sociolinguistic terrain that gives salience to both its 'socio' and 'linguistic' dimensions, as constructed by the descriptive and interpretive tools mobilised by discourse analysis.

The tools of discourse analysis differ, depending on the discipline they are drawn from. What the various approaches to discourse analysis have in common is that they are highly technical and proliferate 'analytic' tools. This technical approach makes a kind of sense when the analytic task is understood as a semiotic object. It deals better with discourse as object rather than as semiotic (meaning-making) phenomenon, however.

Conversation Analysis is an interdisciplinary concern: major contributions have been made by philosophers, sociologists and linguists. Yet the rules and units framework which, we claim, informs them all, is perhaps especially typical of linguistic models. Its preoccupations are with segmentation, classification and combination. Types and tokens, syntagms and paradigms these are the classic concerns of descriptive and structural grammar, and they are present to a high degree in most currently influential approaches to conversation.

It is not entirely surprising, then, that those scholars demonstrably engaged with questions of language and discourse outside linguistics are somewhat dismissive of the empiricism and 'hardening of the categories' they see as characterising much linguistic work; including discourse analysis.

Such problems are exacerbated when 'interpretive' terms, including class, gender, race, face, power and solidarity, are 'borrowed' from various kinds of social theory in order to address relations between language and culture/society. The approach to other fields of knowledge for working vocabularies was initially an exciting development, suggesting a new openness to interdisciplinarity, particularly with respect to socially oriented fields. A degree of such openness remains an attractive feature of contemporary discourse analysis, suggesting possibilities for further productive developments. However, much of the interpretive terminology has tended to be used in reified and realist ways analogous to the ways in which structuralist 'units' are identified and used within linguistics itself as simply 'facts' about the world. Such usage makes sense of the disconcerting practice of linguists referencing key social terms largely within the linguistic literature itself. There may be a citation of some originary figure in sociology or social psychology, such as Goffman, Roger Brown or Bernstein, but there is no sustained engagement with social theory.

The sociological categories which continue to be used within sociolinguistics, for example, have been trenchantly critiqued by Glyn Williams. Williams identifies the sociology of sociolinguistics as derived from a particular kind of theory (Parsonian functionalism) of the 1950s and 1960s, never updated much less critiqued within linguistics. A similar critique can be mounted in the field of language and gender, cutting across both sociolinguistics and discourse analysis. Linguistic work on gender is still largely informed by understandings based in the liberal and radical feminisms of the early 1970s and not in the more complex theorisations of gender and the social available through recent feminist work such as that of Elizabeth Grosz, Teresa de Lauretis, bell hooks and Judith Butler, whose work on performativity, might reasonably be assumed to be of particular interest to linguists.

If there are problems with sociocultural interpretive vocabularies, borrowed from outside linguistics, what has been the situation with technical vocabularies borrowed for more descriptive purposes? At first glance, the contribution of two bodies of work of major significance has been extremely positive. Speech act theory (from philosophy) and Conversation Analysis (from ethnomethodology) have made possible new kinds of attention to the interactional and social work done by utterances, and have contributed to a new respect for spoken language. The technical uptake, by linguists, however, has not always been so positive.

The critical move of speech act theory, as it was developed in the work of Austin and Searle, was that utterances did not just refer a central tenet of much theoretical work on language in both philosophy and linguistics over a long time but could do several different kinds of 'work'. This included very literal kinds of work in the case of 'performatives' such as 'I name this ship The Golden Fleece' and 'I sentence you to be hanged by the neck until you are dead'. Such speech acts (naming, sentencing) actually produce effects: they do not simply refer, in the way that the clause 'the cat sat on the mat' is presumed to do. Paying attention to how an utterance is taken up (its illocutionary force) also makes clear that the relationship between the structure of an utterance and its meaning may not be simple and straightforward. Even though speech act theory did not work with empirically-derived data, from people speaking in 'real-life' situations, its principle of attending to the work done by utterances, not just to their structure, has been of considerable importance in a variety of forms of conversation analysis.

The take-up of speech act theory within linguistics has been various, and variously problematic. Wierzbicka , opens up the diversity of meanings of speech acts but operates with reductive conceptions of culture and the social while Martin's work on conversation closes down much of the open-ended possibility of speech act theory by developing a highly grammaticalised version of the exchange structure approach that Taylor and Cameron criticise:

In considering the problem of sequential ordering as it arises in models using speech act theory, we touched on the subject of quasi-grammatical rules and their role in conversation analysis. The issues and problems which rules of this kind raise assume a central importance in the 'exchange structure' model. Though in some ways it resembles the speech act approach, the exchange structure model of conversation analysis is one of the most unreconstructedly 'grammatical', and therefore exemplifies a number of pitfalls in the rules and units framework with especial clarity.

The second area outside linguistics that has been a source of techniques for the analysis of interactive talk is ethnomethodology, that branch of sociology concerned with the means by which the activities of everyday social life, including interactive talk, are achieved, originating with the work of Harold Garfinkel and continued by Harvey Sacks and others. The detailed attention of what became known as Conversation Analysis (CA) to the achievement of interactive talk included attention to how such talk was begun and ended and how turn-taking was managed. Conversation Analysis work is notable for the meticulous detail of its transcriptions with respect to pausing, overlaps, hesitations, repetitions and repairs, paying the utmost respect to parole by taking so much of its detail seriously.

Aspects of the technicality of CA, particularly its meticulous transcriptions, have had obvious descriptive appeal for linguists. Much less attention, and hence weight, has been given, however, to the stance of CA with respect to 'interpretive' categories. For CA practitioners, interpretive categories are not given but rather should emerge from the data itself and not be 'imposed' from the outside. The basic principle is that analysis should be 'emic' or participantoriented rather than 'etic' or analyst-oriented. Linguists, however, are not trained to take any perspective other than that of the analyst (that is, themself) into account. This is an ongoing problem with all linguistically-informed work, an inevitable consequence of the idealised status of 'text' in even the most contextualised approach.

Discourse analysis as it has developed so far, then, can be characterised by fluidities and rigidities in both its descriptive resources and protocols and in its links with disciplines beyond linguistics. It was, after all, within linguistics itself that spaces for discourse analysis opened up, in part because of other developments within the discipline. One such development was the comparative work, arising from Chomsky's cognitive orientation, investigating possible 'language universals'. Some of this work identified phenomena such as work on topic/focuswhich could just as readily be characterised in terms of 'discourse' as grammar. Work on textual cohesion also began to appear. Increasingly connections were made with the work of the Prague School by European linguists and by linguists working with Halliday. Such connections proved productive not only for literary stylistics but also for other kinds of textual work.

The growing legitimacy within linguistics of work on discourse also made it possible to attend to various phenomena which would not previously have been regarded as proper objects of linguistic enquiry, for example, conversational 'discourse markers' such as English well, yeah, now, right. The gradual relaxation of disciplinary 'policing' within linguistics was affected (and partially effected) by the increasing links discourse analysts were forging with practitioners doing related work in other disciplines. There were, however, limits to the legitimacy of such relationships: there was (and still is) more prestige to be found in links with philosophy and psychology than with literary stylistics and other forms of textual studies. Perhaps not a great deal has changed since Randolph Quirk, in his foreword to Cohesion in English, specifically noted the relevance of the previous literary work of both authors and the rarity of such engagement by linguists. The literary constitutes a double problem for discourse analysis, of course. It is written, while the privileged mode is spoken; and the literary belongs to the realm of the 'aesthetic' rather than to the 'scientific' fetishised by linguistics. The attachment of linguistics to a particular positivist conception of the scientific, however, not only limits the fluidity of the emerging field of discourse analysis in its links with other disciplinary enterprises concerned with language and text but legitimates ongoing rigidities in technical description. Logic and mathematics might have their fuzzy edges but linguistics prefers sharp edges and clean lines.

Text as Social Semiotic

One of the most interesting cases of ongoing tensions between fluidities and rigidities is that of systemic-functional, or Hallidayan, linguistics and its ongoing engagement with text, context and their interrelations. This work is of particular importance because it informs, in various ways and to varying degrees, much discourse analytic work within and beyond linguistics, particularly the various forms of critical discourse analysis. The rigidities are predictable, for a linguistic model, and concern the technical apparatus of systemic linguistics, particularly in some of its more recent elaborations. The fluidities of systemically-based approaches to discourse analysis are much less predictable and concern the various kinds of interconnections with social theory that have been made in the past and that are currently being elaborated.

The emergence of systemic-functional linguistics in the 1960s as an explicitly functionally oriented form of linguistics immediately put it outside mainstream formal (that is, Chomskyan) linguistics. Its particular heresies were its view of text (not word or clause) as the basic semantic unit and its understanding of text and context as profoundly, and constitutively, interrelated. Such a move away from linguistic idealisation pushes 'text' in the direction of mode of social action rather than purely semiotic object. That is, while verbal 'text', spoken or written, is certainly a semiotic object requiring 'analysis', it is also a form of action in and on the world. This kind of view led to Michael Halliday, key systemic theorist, being viewed by conservative linguists as a kind of sociologist and not a linguist at all.

The radical nature of Halliday's proposal required two interrelated moves. The first was to see the clause (the fundamental grammatical unit) as made up not of one but of three kinds of structure, mapped onto one another, each strand realising a different kind of meaning. The three kinds of meaning (or 'metafunctions') are: ideational (with its subcomponents experiential and logical), interpersonal and textual. These are concerned respectively (leaving aside the logical metafunction) with the representation of events (experiential meaning), negotiating social relations (interpersonal meaning) and creating texture—the weaving together of the experiential and the interpersonal strands of meaning (textual meaning). The second move was to see each metafunction, and hence the particular kind of grammatical structure through which it is realised, as related in a bidirectional way with aspects of context. In other words, language constitutes context as well as simultaneously being constituted by it. The conventional systemic term for the context-to-language relation has been 'realisation', distinguishing this approach sharply from models which use 'expression' and therefore assume that what is 'outside' language exists independently of it. Martin uses the term 'redundancy' and speaks of aspects of language and context 'redounding' with one another. The 'redundancies' hypothesised are between experiential meaning and field (what is 'going on' in a situation), interpersonal meaning and tenor (the relations between interactants) and textual meaning and mode (the role language is playing in the situation).

It is this kind of linguistics which has been taken up by three groups of scholars, with overlapping membership, who have seen its potential for 'critical' analysis, that is, for political critique. In the United Kingdom in the late 1970s, Gunther Kress, Bob Hodge and others spoke explicitly of 'critical linguistics' and addressed questions of ideology with a particular interest in media representation. Hodge and Kress subsequently became associated with a second group of scholars engaged in critical work in Australia through the 1980s and into the 1990s under the name 'social semiotics'. During the same period, the third group of scholars, Norman Fairclough and his colleagues at Lancaster University in the United Kingdom, were developing 'critical discourse analysis'. With the relocation of Kress and later van Leeuwen to the United Kingdom, and their closer working relation with Fairclough as well as European discourse analysts, the 'critical discourse analysis' label is now coming to be generalised. Thus, the subtitle of Caldas-Coulthard and Coulthard, containing chapters by Fairclough and some of his former students, and by Kress, van Leeuwen, van Dijk, and various Birmingham scholars, is 'readings in critical discourse analysis'.

What is particularly important about this body of work is its ability to move between the minutiae of a multistranded descriptive technology and some of the most productive frameworks for understanding social life as developed in broadly poststructuratist theories. Foucault has been particularly attractive his conception of persons constituted through discourse is most congenial to linguists familiar with a model of language as social semiotic, involving the necessary bidirectionality of the constitutive relation between text and context. Bakhtin is a regular reference point, particularly his work on the multi-voicedness of text, suggesting ways of exploring the operation of discourses in text that go well beyond purely grammatical accounts. Of growing importance is a range of work in feminist and, more recently, queer theory, especially on the body / corporeality. And, returning to text, narrative theory is increasingly being drawn on. Threadgold draws on a range of work in all these areas, for example.

From one point of view, this openness to contemporary theorisations of text, discourse and their relation to the social is quite characteristic of discourse analysis as a field. Discourse analysis, in its search for ways of understanding the cultural work carried out by (spoken) discourse, has been eclectic and much more adventurous than sociolinguistics. Discourse analysis has looked well beyond the 1960s sociology of sociolinguistics, borrowing from a range of social theory including social psychology, anthropology and various forms of sociology. Most of this work has, however, been concerned particularly with the social relations being negotiated. And once certain categories became established, there has not always been much questioning or further exploration. Thus, the categories of power and solidarity, first introduced into sociolinguistics from social psychology through the work of Roger Brown and his colleagues on terms of address, moved from there straight into discourse analysis with no further interrogation. And the feminist work on language and gender has done no active work to theorise power, despite its centrality to the ongoing argument about whether 'dominance', of women by men, or (cultural) 'difference' between women and men provides the better explanation of what happens linguistically. The lack of theoretical attention to power is even more surprising considering that work on language and gender has been carried out at a time when Foucault's theorisation of power has been immensely influential in the human sciences as well as subject to extensive feminist critique and rewriting. Likewise, Brown and Levinson's now canonical work on politeness uses Erving Goffman's notion of 'face', as well as power and solidarity, but includes no critical interrogation of them.

While discourse analysis as a field takes it as axiomatic that language plays a role in articulating identities and social relations, even if that role is understood to be expressive rather than constitutive, the engagement with the 'content' of texts has been more sporadic, more restricted and often quite reductive. Pragmatic work on presuppositions, for example, focuses very narrowly on what needs to be 'known' or assumed by listeners in order to understand utterances, assuming essentially a now outmoded sender-message-receiver model of communication. In contrast, CA, through its work on membership categorisation, offers one productive model for understanding how speakers constitute themselves as members of a particular culture through the categories they invoke and the ways in which they use them.

Critical discourse analysis, through its use of the Hallidayan technology for dealing with the clause-level constitution of representations (transitivity analysis), goes some way to attempting a more Foucauldian task exploring the nexus of power and knowledge—as it investigates how persons engage with various ways of knowing as they participate in the social relations appropriate to specific institutions. This exploration understands persons and their relations with one another as both constituted in language, not pre-given or outside language, and understands those persons and relations as necessarily constituted in relation to knowledge. It is in their relation to the knowledges of institutions that the representations deployed by language users are of significance.

The systemic-functional linguistic account of representation is anything but unproblematic—most critically, its technologies for exploring 'knowledge' in text are crude in comparison with the sophistication of transitivity analysis in the clause. In particular, its technologies are not sensitive to momentary eruptions of non-dominant discourses, so critical to understanding the complex positionings of subjects as always multiple, never singular. Further, the continuing structuralist imperative governing all kinds of linguistics to keep categories separate produces serious problems in attempting to interrelate the interpersonal and the experiential. It is these aspects of the systemic-functional model which are most closely aligned with the power/knowledge nexus. Critical discourse analysis practitioners, familiar with European traditions of critical theory and discourse analysis concerned with power/ knowledge, and the interrelations between representation and the positionality of speakers/writers, do seem in a strong position to offer a more integrated account of linguistic and other approaches to discourse.

It remains to be seen how far such integration might go. Pennycook, for example, explores the question of whether Foucauldian and linguistic approaches to discourse are ultimately 'incommensurable'. And Threadgold (personal communication) ultimately abandoned attempts to 'map' Foucault and Halliday onto one another, despite still teaching and writing using both the conceptual apparatuses simply would not translate. Apart from the possibly irreconcilable difference between a Foucauldian and a structuralist 'rules and units' approach to discourse analysis, perhaps the most intractable problem for linguists is that Foucault's notion of discourse is not restricted to language but concerns the whole gamut of cultural practices which 'speak' to persons but which they also 'speak', so bringing themselves into being as particular kinds of persons or subjects. Discourse analysts trained in linguistics, not surprisingly, have great difficulty with such a conception of discourse. The analytic practices of even those with great familiarity with European theory, and hence with a sophisticated conception of 'context', remain stubbornly 'linguocentric', despite their best efforts. This is true, for example, of Kress and most notably of Fairclough Discourse and Social Change. Here, perhaps, lies the real value of the multimodal work currently developing within the social semiotic tradition, spearheaded by the work of Gunther Kress and Theo van Leeuwen on visual images. In such work language takes its place as merely one of the multitudinous signifying practices that (in)form social life and is understood in relation to those other practices.

Discourse Analysis, Context and The Social

The inevitability of the text/context relation has been acknowledged from the beginning of discourse analysis as a field of study. 'Context' has been a key term in recognising the need to look beyond language to understand the work performed by discourse. Understanding that work includes understanding that who speaks—particularly if they are a child, a woman or non-white is commonly of greater importance in determining whether they are heard or not than is any question of content or presentation. It also involves understanding that that 'who-ness' is iteratively marked, on the body of the speaker including the grain of their voice, foregrounding the salient identity and backgrounding the inevitable multiplicity of actual persons. It is very clear that linguistics as such has nothing to say about such issues; they will have to be approached from elsewhere, from other disciplinary frameworks.

An explicit 'multidisciplinarity' has come to characterise the field of discourse analysis. There are several problems with the way this has been done, however. This chapter has already referred to problematic aspects of the ways in which various social categories have been 'borrowed' without being subject to further interrogation. The narrowness of the range of disciplines actively drawn upon has also been mentioned, along with some of the inevitable exclusions (particularly literary work). Beyond the particularity of such discipline-based work, there has been a growing body of European-based work on discourse and/or social theory which is barely attended to in the discourse analysis literature. Contributors to van Dijk two-volume overview of the field cite major European theorists including Barthes, Bakhtin/ Volosinov, Bourdieu, Derrida, Foucault, Habermas, Kristeva, Ricoeur-commonly involving only one citation, of the same one or two works; while another recent text cites only Macdonell introductory text on discourse. Even more rarely cited is the variety of 'textual' work done within rhetoric, composition studies and literary studies. In the face of the manifest incapacity of linguistics to offer any kind of adequate theorisation of context, despite various attempts, the failure to explore contemporary social/ critical theory, particularly the work of Foucault, seems inexplicable.

Returning to the question of discourse analysis and those disciplines/knowledges that it does engage with, what of the relation between discourse analysis and other disciplines? Has that relationship been one where the different contributors meld into some new kind of entity or, rather, has the relation been one of coloniser to colonised: other disciplines constituted simply as 'booty' to be systematically stripped down and plundered for whatever can be appropriated that might be of use to a fundamentally technicist project?

If the multidisciplinarity of discourse analysis fails to guarantee the adequacy of the understandings of context and the social that underpin it, what of the conjunction of critical discourse analysis/ social, semiotics/critical linguistics? Can it be differentiated from other forms of discourse analysis as a more credible interdisciplinary, or even transdisciplinary, enterprise, that is, a more integrated way of knowing? Several characteristics of that nexus lend it credibility. The first is the model of technical linguistic analysis that all share. The features that distinguish this model are its functional (as distinct from formal, as exemplified by Chomsky) emphasis and its interconnection of language and context. That is, the model allows attention to what language 'does' in the world and to how particular aspects of language relate to aspects of contexts, or situations, precisely because of the 'work' they do. Of all linguistic models, the systemic view of the two-way determination of the relation between language and context comes closest to current (poststructuralist) understandings, outside linguistics, of the work done by 'language' in constituting (and not just 'expressing') knowledges and persons.

Critical discourse analysis practitioners, unlike most other linguists, demonstrate familiarity with frameworks in the 'human sciences'. Not surprisingly, many such practitioners are not located within linguistics at all but rather in English, Communications, Media and Education. This is clearly relevant to the comfortable multidisciplinarity of their work but it is also relevant to the third characteristic of this work: the balance of the 'technicist' agenda compared with other dimensions of the work done, that is, the balance of linguistic to other forms of 'analysis'. Given the extensive elaboration of the technical apparatus of systemic-functional linguistics, this is an issue of considerable import. Becoming thoroughly familiar with Hallidayan functional grammar (let alone systemic work 'above', 'below' and 'beside' the clause) is a formidable task in itself. Training in Hallidayan linguistics continues to be even more relentlessly technicist than many other forms of linguistics (but see Terry Threadgold's interview with Barbara Kamler for the possibility of an alternative pedagogy which might somewhat redress this situation).

The most effective discourse analysis, however, involves being able to stand back sufficiently from that monolithic technical apparatus to make strategic selections of analytic focus, informed by other kinds of understandings of text, context and their possible relations. The best critical discourse analysis work is characterised precisely by an economy, even parsimony, of analytical technology informing (and informed by) wide familiarity with contemporary critical theory.

Conclusion

This chapter has addressed both the successes and some of the more problematic aspects of the increasingly complex terrain of linguisticallybased discourse studies. The successes lie, first, in the attention it is now possible to give to spoken language within linguistics and, second, in the progressive elaboration of text-analytic tools, drawing on vocabularies both from within linguistics and from other fields. The multidisciplinarity claimed for discourse analysis as a field, however, has in many respects promised more than it has been able to deliver. This is particularly the case when 'borrowed' vocabularies have (as they have all too often) become part of a technical apparatus used in ways which vindicate views of linguistics as a discipline utterly caught up within an empiricist scientific agenda.

The conjunction of critical discourse analysis, social semiotics and critical linguistics has been a somewhat more convincing, though not unproblematic, version of a linguistically-informed interdisciplinary discourse analysis, attempting to address the imbrication of language and the social. It is this work that is the most overtly political form of discourse analysis, offering not only critique of existing arrangements, but espousing an agenda of social transformation and change. It is difficult to see, however, how an exclusively linguistic agenda might be used proactively to imagine effectively, much less bring about, radical social change. This is in spite of the sophistication of the understandings of discourse practices and discursive formations that it has become possible to bring to bear retrospectively on the present.

The agenda of critique central to the critical discourse analysis project certainly makes available the kind of externalising 'outsider's' position from which it is possible to identify the positionings and interests of those with speaking roles in the ongoing choreography of social life. Those who actually take up such externalising positions are few, however, in comparison with the increasing number of people engaged in aspects of what Fairclough calls the 'technologisation' of discourse. By this he means the increasing use of linguistic (and other, particularly psychological) knowledge about language in the service of training in language or, more usually, 'communication' skills for workers and managers (in the workplace) and for children (in schools). The increasing availability of discourse analytic tools constitutes a critical condition of possibility for such technologisation, in those cultures where economic rationalist discourses have steadily increased the range of 'objects' of commodification, including the knowledges and skills of academics. Discourse technologisation certainty offers increasing opportunities for 'useful work' for practitioners of various kinds of discourse analysis. It may offer opportunities to better understand language use in contexts, particularly the workplace, that are crucially involved in the production of new forms of social relations. It certainly involves significant political and ethical problems.

It remains to be seen whether all that discourse technologisation can offer to discourse analysis practitioners is the choice between cooption or some restricted kind of oppositional stance. At the end of the twentieth century, the increasing imbrication of persons and institutions within relations of power makes imagining a viable position outside such relations increasingly difficult. Possibilities for an oppositional stance for any kind of resistance to the operations of new forms of power—are giving way to very different kinds of engagement with issues of power, government and their legitimation. Discourse remains at the heart of these issues, however, rendering critical forms of discourse analysis current and future of ongoing importance.

9 Membership Categorisation in Research Methodology

Introduction

Ethnomethodology provides a number of directions for analysing texts and talk as part of the ongoing assembling of social and moral order, and for analysing 'culture in action'. This chapter introduces one powerful analytic approach, membership categorisation, and shows its use by writers, readers, speakers and hearers in educational settings. Membership categorisation work is pervasive in the doing of descriptions, the making of claims, the organisation of social relations, and other aspects of the micropolitics of everyday and institutional life. This chapter contributes an approach to analysis that puts culture inside action, rather than action inside culture, already preconstituted.

By showing how membership categorisation is done in talk and texts, this chapter points to a 'critical edge' that can be provided by ethnomethodological and conversation-analytic work on texts and transcripts of talk in institutions and elsewhere. While Button provides detailed papers on how ethnomethodology offers a 'foundational respecification of the human sciences', this chapter's scope is limited to briefly describing some main concepts in membership categorisation analysis and applying them to some sections of text and transcribed talk. A second purpose, then, is to substantiate the view that categorisation work, in addition to its descriptive and explicative character already well documented in the literature, is powerful in the organisation of discourses. Specifically, I work with the idea that categories and categorisation work lock discourses into place, and are therefore ready for opening to critical examination.

Membership Categorisation Analysis

Membership categorisation analysis, as a subfield of ethnomethodology, arose in the early lectures of Sacks. Sacks explored how actual instances of talk-in-interaction constituted, in their own right, materials for sociological analysis. In his lectures on conversation, he showed how some classical problems of sociology-social order and social structure could be addressed by studying the organisation of talk-in-interaction. In addition, his studies have contributed very different takes on how 'culture' can be understood and studied.

The notion of membership categorisation addresses how people 'do' descriptions and how they recognise descriptions: matters of cultural knowledge and relevance. This interest is exemplified in his analysis of a story told by a child: 'The baby cried. The mommy picked it up'. Sacks made the point that we all 'hear' the mommy who did the picking up as the mommy of the baby who cried, not some other mommy. People accomplish this hearing routinely and economically by using the resources of what Sacks called the 'membership categorisation device': . . . any collection of membership categories, containing at least a category, which may be applied to some population containing at least a member, so as to provide, by the use of some rules of application, for the pairing of at least a population member and a categorisation device member. A device is then a collection plus rules of application.

Applied to the baby-mommy example above (elaborated in much more detail by Sacks), we connect the two persons by calling on the membership categorisation device 'family' which collects them both. This hearing is both adequate and economical. On other occasions the term 'baby' can be found to be part of other devices such as 'stage of life' (baby-child-adult).

Following the early work of Sacks, literature studying the membership categorisation activities that occur in a variety of settings has been published, including work on reading newspaper headlines, classroom interaction and police-suspect interrogations, among other topics. Such studies have been concerned with the descriptive and explicative work that is done in the course of talk-in-interaction, and have refined a number of the original notions proposed by Sacks.

Categorisation and Culture

Within ethnomethodology, a membership categorisation device is understood, not as a pre-existing structure of category-organised knowledge (a decontextualised notion, a reified entity like a schema, or a machinery, such as might be found in cognitive anthropology or linguistics), but as an always locally assembled corpus: a corpus that is occasioned and produced in a given moment of use. An implication of such local embeddedness and practical accomplishment of membership categorisation devices (for this occasion, this time) is: . . . not just that members use culture to do things, but that culture is constituted in, and only exists in, action. For membership categorization analysis, this means that the orderliness of cultural resources (categories, devices and the rest) is constituted in their use rather than pre-existing. Our central point is that it is in the use of categories that culture is constituted this time through.

What such a view offers is a radically different take on 'culture'. It has situated culture in action (which is a reversal of normative theories of culture) and suggests that we look at membership categorisation activities as 'culture-in-action'; or, put another way, that 'culture is internal to action'. So, to find culture, we look differently, and in different places, from those ways and places that more conventional theoretical approaches would direct us to look (and listen).

This approach to culture is a release and a relief from conventional formulations of culture as the way of life of a group, including norms, values, artefacts etc. that are prevalent at least in the field of education. It is a relief from the weight of a notion of culture where people 'share' and things connect and ideas relate, and a release from a unitary notion of culture as a single thing that a group has (a notion that is not undone by theorising subcultures within cultures and so on). Situating culture inside action opens the possibility of seeing the different, competing ways in which culture might be done. Studying membership categorisation work—looking at how people occasion and hear descriptions, connections, claims and other activities—is one way of addressing matters of text, discourse and power. That is the direction in which I take this chapter.

Membership Categorisation: Outline of Terms

Membership categories are categories of person, place or activity. The ubiquitous matter of reference to persons is a place to begin to appreciate how consequential categorisation is, socially, politically and morally. Any one person can be referred to through a range of possible descriptors: frequent flier, mother, stranger, daughter, Catholic, wife, taxpayer, teacher, Australian, witness, client, and so on. For any given person, all could be correct some for some of the time, some for all of the time. But, when is one made a 'daughter'? When is one relevantly a 'taxpayer'? The selection of descriptor is occasioned by the circumstance in which the description is done, but is not predicted by it. People can be surprised by who they are (made to be) this time, just now, right here.

A number of the categories above imply a second term to a standard relational pair, such as wife-husband or daughter-mother. Others have second terms which are strongly suggested, such as client-professional (a client is always somebody's client). Some categories in particular contexts will routinely, relevantly invoke a second term (Catholic-Protestant, but not necessarily, or everywhere), while other categories used in particular contexts can hint at silent but still relevant second terms (single-married-divorced). The hearing of the second term implied or suggested by the first is the joint activity of the speaker and a listener both using the resources of membership categorisation.

Membership categorisation devices are collections of categories plus 'rules' of application. Rules of application are not external rules or mandates, but summations of how members will ordinarily hear second and even third and fourth pair parts. Some examples follow of commonly used membership categorisation devices which can 'collect' (imply, invoke) a number of individual categories within them:

'family' (mother, father, children . . .)
'stage of life' (infants, children, adolescents, adults . . .)
'school' (principal, teacher, children, students . . .)

These membership categorisation devices show that the category 'children' might belong to any of a number of membership categorisation devices and it is a local matter for members to determine which device is in play this time, often by hearing a next item and locating the relevant list that way. Similarly, a description of a person as, say, a 'taxpayer', does not settle which categorisation device might be pertinent until some other terms are produced (taxpayer-government, taxpayer-politician, taxpayer-unions, or other locally occasioned contrasts).

There may be various degrees of association made in interaction

14 S: ((inaudible))
15 T: Good for you.

As the transcript shows, the category of 'mothers' receives considerable attention regarding its place in the membership categorisation device (the school class in that story that day, comprised teacherchildren-three mothers). The teacher's questioning arose from one student's observation that three mothers had come, and her questioning seems to pursue a reason for the mothers being there. The activity of 'helping' is bound to the category 'mothers' in the text, and also in the reading of the text. It is accepted by the teacher that the mothers had come to help, but that does not seem to be her puzzle for the students, 'why were the mothers there though? where were the children going?'. It seems that the solution resides in something about that particular trip on a bus to the woods—what the children were going to do—rather than in the qualities of (these three) mothers. There is no questioning of why mothers are there at all (rather than fathers, say), no questioning of the category selection or of its predicate, that mothers help. Later in the story 'Miss Brown and the mothers got into the bus too' and that is the last that is heard of the mothers in the story.

We can connect this text and its classroom reading with Smith commentary on the dependence of classroom work on mothering work, and the professional and institutional discourses and practices that secure mothers' work within extended organisational relations. While the students in the class, and probably the teacher as well, have not read Smith, they have read and reflected back the ideological order that the text both presupposes and, in this naturalised reading, itself achieves. Such complicity with the presence and later disappearance of mothers in the story line, and the representation of mothers' work as 'helping' the class in the text—though no specific things done are mentioned is one brief course of contact with the mothers-as-general-helpers discourse. Other points of contact would presumably be encountered repeatedly. For these reasons, 'critical' reading practices need to address the categories and predicates that underpin the natural logic of texts. These categories and predicates are the quiet centres of power and persuasion that naturalise texts.

Example 2: A Parent-Teacher Interview

The next example of membership categorisation analysis comes from a study of parent-teacher talk. In this example, a teacher and two parents of a secondary school student meet to discuss the student's progress in the year so far. There are clear indications here of proposals about the relation between the work of the home and the work of the school.

The analysis shows how the teacher and parents' category memberships are central to the organisation of the talk, how they attach particular 'activities' to the categories they speak from, or as, or to, and how they disattach others being assigned to them. The analysis also shows that the work of category-elaboration is synonymous with the assembling of institutional relations and that the categorisation work involves the production of sometimes competing (moral) descriptions of persons. The talk in this interview can be examined for the speakers' competing claims to competence and the pragmatics of their describing activities. I will focus here primarily on categories and activities.

The interview took place as one in a series that the teacher conducted at a parents' evening in a secondary school in

Queensland. The analysis will proceed in stages through the opening part of the interview, showing how the categorisation work proceeds sequentially.

Teacher	:	Ellen
Student	:	Donna
Parent(s)	:	Mother and Father

1 T: Ok all right we'll just forget it I should cover it up or something I hate tape recorders! (hh) Right um Donna um I just took over Mister Jay's class um four weeks ago so, I don't really know a lot about Donna's work I've had a quick look at her work in her folder, and from her marks she um, you seem to have, passed in the first part of the year and then really gone down in last two um, pieces of work which was a poetry oral? and a um a novel (2.0) a novel in another form that was putting part of the novel into another style of writing. Now um (2.0) in class (1.0) Donna's a little bit distracted? often? down the back there, with um the girls that she sits with, though she does give in class when she's asked to, she does do all her work, um I'm (1.0) would you like to—do you work with Donna at home with her schoolwork at all? do you see it at all or?

This opening statement by the teacher is replete with categorisation work. It can be treated as an initial sketch, a proposal, for who the participants relevantly are in this interactional event (their categorical incumbencies), what they do and should do (activities that attach to these categories), and how these categories and activities (should) connect. It is an initial map of the social and moral terrain in which representative of the school meets representatives of the home as idealised courses of action. Through re-categorisation work, some features of this map will be open to redrawing as the talk and its implications unfold.

The teacher first identifies Donna as the incumbent of the category 'students whose parents I am meeting tonight': 'Right um Donna um I just took over Mister Jay's class'. But her comment does more than this: it lines up herself as 'the teacher of Donna', and as 'a successor to Mister Jay', presumably the teacher she has replaced. This double categorisation is central in the teacher's characterisation of her own work. Simultaneously these words line up the parents as 'Donna's parents' and as people who might not know that she is now acting in Mister Jay's place. The further comment, 'so, I don't really know a lot about Donna's work I've had a quick look', additionally characterises the parents as 'interested in Donna's work' and wanting information from this teacher about it. 'I've had a quick look' also self-attributes the quality of being busy, perhaps, but certainly warns that she will not be completely informed about what she has attributed them with wanting to know.

There is then a sketch of her observations of Donna both from the markbook and from her first-hand knowledge ('seemed to have passed and then really gone down', 'often a little bit distracted . . . down the back with the girls that she sits with', though she does give in class . . . does do all her work'). These are produced, and hearable as, relevancies for parents as well as teachers. After a short pause the teacher issues questions to the parents which are themselves descriptions of activities which are attachable to the category of parents:

1 T: would you like to—do you work with Donna at home with her schoolwork at all? do you see it at all or?

This attribution of activities by a teacher to parents is a clear move in the description of home-school relationships, and particularly the work of the home, but equally the preceding desorption of 'Donna in class' casts these parents as needing or wanting to know all this about Donna, and it is for this reason they have come to the school this evening. With this handful of categories, and interactional work with them, the teacher has sketched a complex set of relations, knowledges and motivations. The parents are handed the floor at this point.

2 F: Not really no=
3 M: =(We very rarely) see her schoolwork
4 F: they generally disappear off to their edroomswiththeir
homework and um=
5 T: =Ye:es (2.0) Well um
6 F: We don't see much of (it)

The parents, led by father, have responded to the final questions, not to the preceding descriptions. 'Not really no' is a mitigated response, acknowledging that parents could be held accountable for doing these kinds of things: working with Donna, or even seeing her homework. The parents have accepted their accountability for not seeing (much) of Donna's homework but have done other than and more than confess: they have furnished a reason that could re-characterise Donna as a student who is keen to get on with her homework. This possible Donna could be one of the unspecified 'they' who 'disappear off to their bedrooms' so fast that their parents have not got a chance to see the homework. These same parents might well wish to see the homework but cannot. At this point, the parents have disattached from themselves any irresponsibility for not working with Donna at home.

The teacher proceeds with more apologies about not knowing enough about Donna, and the parents begin to ask some questions themselves. These questions return the accountability to the teacher and the school. The teacher turns the talk back to what she does know first-hand about Donna.

7 T: Let me see yes I didn't mark this this was all Mister Jay's (1.0) This is a summary, they had to summarise um this (1.0) um let's see where her, mistakes seem to lie. (3.0) Oh it seems all right. (3.0) Why did she only get four and a half for that Hmmm. It's awful when you're when you're talking about, something another teacher's (hh) done! (5.0) Only seems to have limited English grammatical mistakes, um (4.0) oh it seems fine it's not covered all in red,

8 F: mm no

9 M: ( )what's the problem with it then ( )?

10 T: I don't know. Obviously maybe it's the the standard or the urn (4.0) the ideas I'll see what Mr Jay's written here let's have a look. (2.0 Good more impact in conclusion is possible. That doesn't really say a lot does it.

11 M: Not really, no ( )

12 T: No. (3.0) Uh this is, I'm sorry about this because I haven't, been with Donna's class so I'm not sure, I've only just come back from leave. I know, the piece of work that I've done with the class was a, radio play which we've just done. And (2.0) we spent a couple of weeks in class learning about it and then we did um had some time to prepare it, and the girls the group of girls really didn't do a lot of work on it I wasn't really happy with the work that was done, and the work that did come out was um, read from Dolly magazine or Cleo just onto the tape? So I found that urn, that wasn't not just Donna the three of them together working together really didn't put a lot of work into it an' [I

The teacher turns to what she does know about: the radio play, and generates through this description a Donna who didn't do much work. Previously the teacher had said 'She does do all her work'. The classification of Donna as a particular kind of student is not a straightforward matter. Any of the descriptive detail produced earlier in the talk can be reworked in further pursuit of the apparent problem. The mother asks a question that could be heard as informational (who was she working with) or as accountable (if Donna is distracted, maybe she should sit with someone else).

13 M: [Who was she working with?

14 T: Umm (2.0) Joanne someone and Vicki(3.0), Joanne Williams

15 M: ( )

16 T: an' Vicki (2.0) Hawkins

17 M: ( )?

The parents appear to have gained some ground through getting these names. The teacher attempts a topic switch back to her own limits of knowledge about Donna. The parents then present another Donna, who hates oral. The force of this is to make oral hateable. Perhaps it is not Donna who is at fault but the character of the work she is asked to do. The teacher issues only some agreement tokens before changing the topic once again.

18 T: No. So on on the whole, um that's the only work I have real experience from, from (2.0) Donna. Um,

19 F: She said she wasn't keen on this oral

20 M: No she hates oral, she hates getting up an' [(standing up in front)

21 T: [Speaking, right

22 M: ['N if she ever has to stand up in front of the class, or anything like that she's not that

23 T: Yeah, [well

24 M: [( ) you know I suppose that a lot of kids are the same

25 T: Well this is um (1.0) this is where she's got a very low mark here. Wonder if her oral, oral paper's here. Oh it hasn't been put into her folder. [turn continues]

In what we can take to be carefully designed talk, teacher and parents are producing category-descriptions: of themselves as teacher or parent, of the other as parent or teacher, and of Donna in the classroom and at home. Donna is silent in all this talk about her. However, the talk is not only about Donna: it can be heard as self-description of competent category-incumbency as teacher or parent. The talk is about what activities could, should and do attach to a (competent) teacher or parent and to a (good) student. In this sense the talk is about possible ways of describing extended institutional relations as much as it is about Donna's academic work. In this instance, the categories themselves are quiet (and uncontested) but the predicates are not.

Conclusion

We can ask of all varieties of critical discourse analysis: Just what is it that is the target of the critique? How are you critical of it? Where does this criticism lead in terms of social practice? I have proposed that by studying membership categorisation work as done in the course of speaking, hearing, reading and writing, we are able to observe uniquely how categories and associated categorisation practices permeate and organise texts and talk. The more natural, taken-for-granted and therefore invisible the categorisation work, the more powerful it is. Like the foundations of a building, categorisation practices go deep underneath the surface of words, ideas, and images that are produced in conversations, texts, and dialogues. They provide for the shape and contours of the surface configurations. They are powerful also because they are double-sided resources for speaking and hearing, writing and reading: there is collusion in their deployment.

By extension, I have argued, we can identify the categories and the categorisation work that lock cross-situational discourses and practices into place. Rearranging categories and associated activities is difficult excavation work because one encounters a history of sedimentation of usage and, therefore, of commonsense and 'logic'. This has been encountered in feminist work which has attempted to dislodge persistent and pervasive connections between gender categories and associated activities such as forms of work and rights.

By showing the pervasiveness and tenacity of the largely unnoticed and taken-for-granted work that all members do with membership categories, I have implied that a first step in challenging discourses and practices is to recognise the force of categorisation practices in social and institutional life. This chapter has sketched some initial procedures for doing the recognition work in the analysis of a text or transcript. First, identify the categories in use, especially those that are otherwise taken for granted as points in a matrix of some social institution or encounter. Second, show how various attributes, activities, qualities are attached to categories and, if relevant, how they are contested or disattached. Monologic texts and dialogic texts may well differ in the arrays of candidate activities proposed for different categories. Show how categories are related, and how they are related through descriptions of activities. Look especially for tenacious category-bound activities such as babies cry or need help, mothers help. These are the categories that lock the discourse into place, and possibly the practices that flow from them.

The specification of how discourses are secured through membership categorisation work assists the identification of how discourses are called on and how they are invoked in the mundane activities of talking, hearing, reading and writing. The use of membership categorisation analysis is always local, and always occasioned: done on an occasion of talk or writing, reading or hearing. Culture is internal to action, and can be found in the course of membership categorisation work as well as in an array of other social practices.

Membership categorisation device analysis offers a socially critical perspective on text and culture by showing a different order of phenomena in texts and in talk than is retrievable through other critical discourse analysis approaches, and by locating 'culture' in social practices. The social practices to which membership categorisation work is central include describing, accounting, and reasoning. Recall in the first example the teacher's attempts to have students find a reason for mothers to be helping at school that day in the story. For the teacher at least, there seems to have been one real reason why the mothers were there that day. That mothers were there, and that they were there to help, was treated as obvious. The students were encouraged to think about the surface of the story (the plot, the events) and not the category-predicate connections that underpin the 'reality' of the story.

While I have proposed that membership categorisation work can be studied as a means of locking texts, talk and discourses into place, and therefore 'excavating' their foundations, it needs to be recognised that this does not provide directly for the characterisation of texts, talk and discourses as conservative or not. The judgement about that matter comes from observations of how they work in situ or in general to arrange relations of power, privilege and advantage. That is, the political valency of a categorisation analysis is found in its material, social, symbolic applications and consequences, rather than in its contents or form per se.

10

Power, knowledge and subjectivity in Research Methodology

Introduction

Important to current social theory is an understanding of the body not as separate from the mind the mind/body dichotomy of Western thought but as integral to 'the self'. In poststructuralist terms, this is understood through the concept of 'embodied subjectivity', where those social practices which form selves work through language and material practices to locate individual subjects in relation to institutional and cultural discourses. The body is thus produced by and exists in discourse, the term referring to 'sets of deep linguistic principles incorporating specific 'grids of meaning' which generate what can be spoken, seen and thought'. While discourse in this sense is differentiated from language, choices in language (as social practices) provide indicators as to how those discourses are being drawn upon by writers and speakers and to the ways in which 'users' position themselves and others. Questions can therefore be asked about how language works to position speakers in relation to what discourses, and with what effects.

Foucault further understands discourse as 'practices that systematically form the objects of which they speak. Discourses are not about objects; they constitute them and in the practice of doing so conceal their own intervention'. It is through discourse that meanings, subjects and subjectivities are formed. Much current semiotic work focuses primarily on reading bodies as they are inscribed with meaning in performance, the electronic media, photographs, art, dance forms and written texts, both literary and non-literary. What this chapter offers is a different set of insights which overlap but also extend this work. Drawing on poststructuralist and linguistic theory and methodologies, it first provides a set of tools to examine how the body is represented in texts derived from spoken language. Second, the chapter examines the effects of that talk as it acts on bodies, to promote certain kinds of bodily behaviour and social relations. The chosen site is a physical education lesson but the analysis could be extended to many similar sites where talk is central to the constitution of the body and promotes 'bodywork' in different ways for instance, coaching sessions, aerobics, tai chi, bellydancing and yoga classes.

Schooling, as a set of practices specifically intended to shape and train bodies, becomes a fruitful site to examine this process of subjectification. As Shilling points out, 'the moving, managed and disciplined body, and not just the speaking and listening body, is central to the daily business of schooling'. Focusing on how bodies are managed through disciplinary practices such as expecting children to sit still and quiet, to control their toileting behaviour-does not take into account how teachers' talk, together with the practices it expects, constitutes particular notions of the body.

In physical education, a site within schooling specifically focused on the body, teacher talk works both to manage/discipline bodies and to inscribe the body with particular meanings, that is, to (re)produce particular discourses which determine how bodies can be thought about and, consequently, how they can act in space and in relation to other bodies. For instance, teacher talk constitutes notions of the skilled/unskilled body, as well as the way the body learns (through the acquisition of skills broken down into their component parts). 'Bodywork' can thus be used to describe teacher talk both as it constitutes knowledge about the body and as it affects the way bodies work.

While this chapter does go beyond the language of the lesson to other material practices, it will focus on the spoken language of the teacher. It is important to acknowledge that there are problems with a singular focus on language. Bodies are certainly not only, or indeed mostly, produced in and through language. Rather, material practices such as dress, the organisation of space, the work done by bodies through exercise and by paid labour are all implicated in the construction of bodies as cultural products. Language, however, in both written and spoken forms, influences how we can think about/ conceive of bodies. It categorises and associates value with certain kinds of bodies rather than others and it can be employed to evoke bodily movement. For instance, through medical, legal, psychoanalytic and educational discourses, bodies are described and positioned in relations of value. School physical education is a site which, because of its focus on the body, brings a number of discourses and material practices to bear on the bodies of teachers and students. The questions, then, which motivate this analysis are as follows:

- What kinds of bodies are being constituted in physical education lessons?
- What discourses and material practices are drawn on to constitute bodies and in what relations of power?
- What are the consequences of such bodywork for individual subjectivities and social relations?

A Methodology

To make a closer study of how language use is implicated in the construction of knowledge and subjectivities, a finegrained tool of analysis is required, one which is able to provide a systematic analysis of spoken language going beyond mere 'insightful interpretation'. It might be argued that the analysis described below could result from a close non-technicalised reading of the texts. While this may be true for some texts, a systematic analysis of the grammatical and lexical patterns leaves such a reading less to chance and can provide insights into patterns of use which would otherwise have been unavailable. The analytic tools I use are derived from systemic functional linguistics, a system of grammar which recognises the ongoing social constructedness of meaning.

Language does not make meaning, nor can it be interpreted in isolation. Any poststructuralist analysis of language must take account of the social and cultural contexts in which texts are constructed. It must also consider the ways in which language use is constituted in the context of particular discursive relations which predict certain power relations. While Michel Foucault eschewed a close analysis of language, his work provides a means of understanding and interpreting the ways in which language and other social practices work to constitute specific relations of power. Such relations are not monolithic but are pervasive and negotiated and, through their subtle operations, work to form subjectivities. Foucault puts it thus:

But in thinking of the mechanism of power, I am thinking rather of its capillary form of existence, the point where power reaches into the very grain of individuals, touches their bodies and inserts itself into their actions and attitudes, their discourses, learning processes and everyday lives.

In a somewhat controversial move, Jennifer Gore has sought to construct an empirical technology which provides a means to examine the practices of power in pedagogy. While not using a linguistic approach, she has developed the following eight coding categories derived from a careful reading of Foucault Discipline and Punish with which to analyse her data. These are: surveillance, normalisation, exclusion, distribution, classification, individualisation, totalisation, regulation. What I have attempted to do in this paper is to go beyond Gore's examples, mostly recorded through fieldnotes, to focus on linguistic realisations of the categories identified through close analysis in a spoken context. The intention here is to be neither exhaustive nor prescriptive. Rather, through an examination of the way Gore's coding categories function in a specific text in a particular situational and cultural context, I will demonstrate the link between those categories and specific language choices. As Gore points out, no one category is exclusive of the others. Many of the examples provided below could and should be coded in terms of several other categories. All categories cover the exercise of power in relation to knowledge, interpersonal relations and subjectivities. The examples cited below specifically relate to the physical education text and are clearly not exhaustive for this text or any other. Non-verbal examples are taken up in the analysis of the lesson as a whole.

Normalisation

Normalisation is defined as 'invoking, requiring, setting or conforming to a standard defining the normal'. Normalisation suggests the correct and proper way, often in comparison to another way of being or acting. Grammatically this may be signalled by words such as 'normally', usually', or 'the best/better' or 'right' way of being or performing an action. For instance, in the lesson the teacher says 'normally we do co-ed'. This suggests that co-education physical education is the/a normal practice in contrast to single sex physical education. Most of the descriptions of how skills should be done are also examples of a normalising practice: they suggest that there is only one, correct way to perform the skill. Conditional clauses such as 'If you keep your knees into your chest, then you will roll over' arguably also have a normalising function.

Exclusion

Gore describes this category as 'the reverse side of normalization the defining of the pathological'. In this physical education lesson the female and male students have been separated. The separation is presented as a consequence of effects produced by the short skirts the girls wear as part of their physical education uniform. These effects include the girls seen as preoccupied with being looked at. Though the girls have no control over the choice of such a uniform, much less the gaze of the boys, they are the ones whose behaviour is effectively pathologised.

Classification

This category is defined by Gore as 'differentiating groups or individuals from one another, classifying, classifying oneself the classification of knowledge, the classification of individuals or groups'. The most obvious examples in language are those attributes which work in binaries such as physical/mental, hard/ easy, strong/ weak and attributive relational clauses such as 'girls are' But any language choice which divides the world into groups functions as a form of classification. Examples include differentiating boys from girls and linking particularly ways of acting and being with one group in comparison with the other; differentiating gymnastics and dance by their specific attributes from other forms of physical activity.

Distribution

This category deals with the distribution of bodies in space. Most of the organisational directives in the lessons fall under this category, for instance, the separation of girls from boys and commands which organise the class such as 'we'll have a line down here giving lots of room for girls to bring the mats out', 'we're separating you and 'one at a time please'.

Individualisation

This category is defined as 'giving individual character to oneself or another'. This is recognisable when individuals are named or addressed using the singular 'you' (maybe ellipsed (deleted) in commands) and their behaviour or appearance singled out for comment, for instance, 'Allison, if you face me you'll know what is going on'. It also covers situations where individuals are requested to answer questions or perform actions and where the individual speaking uses the first person pronoun singular (see Wright 1990 for a more detailed discussion of the functions of person pronouns in spoken texts). While the following example is not included in the texts below, it does come from the same lesson. It provides an example of how individualisation can often have a totalising effect as well: 'I'm a woman and women are allowed to change their minds.

Totalisation

Totalisation is defined as 'the specification of collectivities, giving collective character', often achieved through the use of 'we'. The collective 'we', where the teacher includes him or herself as a member of the class, is a very common feature of teacher talk generally. It is rarely a strategy that students have at their disposal. In the texts below it is employed frequently, for instance, 'we're not going to start with forward rolls today' and 'we'll have our usual partners please'. Totalisation also occurs when a particular group is linked to a set of attributes, for instance in the statement: 'we're particularly aiming at you people being more conscious of what you are doing instead of who's looking at you doing it'.

Regulation

As Gore points out, while all the categories could be seen to have regulating effects, this category was used where regulation was most explicit so that regulation was defined as 'controlling by rule, subject to restrictions, invoking a rule, including sanction, reward and punishment'. Linguistic examples of this include particularly statements which include 'must', 'need to', 'have to', 'should', as in 'have to get the blood circulating' and 'You should turn your feet out so little toes go to the floor'.

Physical Education and The Body

As teachers in the texts below make linguistic choices that constitute meaning and social relations, they draw on existing cultural and institutional discourses or sets of meanings already circulating and contribute to the (re)production of those discourses as they speak. To interpret any text it is necessary to be able to identify the intertexts from which it may be constituted, the cultural resources which are available (and, at times, not available) to the participants—both listeners and speakers—to be able to make meaning. The physical education lessons are constituted intertextually by drawing on a complex range of institutional discourses from education, sport, the academic disciplines associated with the study of human movement and, most recently, discourses linking exercise and fitness with health. These intersect with broader cultural discourses around gender, sexuality, ethnicity and bodies widely circulating through day-to-day interactions and particularly through the media.

Physical education, in comparison with other curriculum areas of contemporary schooling, provides the optimum opportunity for a detailed attention to the disciplining of the body and the production of embodied subjectivities. Physical education is centrally concerned with 'work' on the body, with the regulation and control of the body through the ritualised practices of both sport and physical education lessons and through the scientific and medical rationales that underlie these practices. In Australia the physical education curriculum is profoundly implicated in constructing gender differences and patriarchal/dominant versions of heterosexual femininity and masculinity. This happens primarily through the dominance of the curriculum by activities traditionally associated with men and boys and with the construction of hegemonic masculinity, namely sports and team games, and the consequent marginalisation of gymnastics and dance.

As well as discourses which constitute the body as gendered, there are many other systems of values and meanings which affect the body and are embedded in the practices of physical education. Richard Tinning, for instance, has identified the influence of the sets of values and beliefs associated with technocratic rationality, individualism, compulsory heterosexuality and mesomorphism. The two most prominent beliefs which need to be mentioned here are those which equate health with fitness and those which define physical activity in terms of performance and achievement. In Western society the commodification of the body, through the fashion and fitness industries and through the popular media, together with a prevailing anxiety about death through heart disease, has led to the equation of health with fitness. This healthy/fit body is a slim toned body, the apparent product of hard work through exercise and diet. The pursuit of fitness and a 'healthy lifestyle' has also been promoted by the state (for instance, the New South Wales 'Life be in it' campaign) as the practice of the responsible individual. The rationale for physical education as a legitimate subject in the school curriculum has often been argued on the basis of its presumed contribution to children's fitness through their participation in physical activity. Most physical education teachers would argue that one of their main aims is the promotion in their students of a commitment to a healthy lifestyle and regular exercise.

A further set of relevant discourses are those which promote the acquisition of skills and the improvement of performance as the primary purpose of school physical education. These outcomes are achieved through teaching practices based on the principles and understandings of the body derived from research in the human movement sciences, for instance, exercise physiology, biomechanics and motor learning. Learning is then taken as requiring the teaching of specific skills by experts who can demonstrate them, break them into their component parts for easier acquisition, organise activities which provide for repetitive practice, analyse skill performance and offer corrective guidance. This skill acquisition and training approach stands in opposition to other approaches which promote learning through movement. These emphasise the process of learning rather than the end product (performance). Movement education, a form of physical education developed by women in Britain and popular in girls' schools in the late nineteenth and early twentieth century, is an example of one such approach where the emphasis is on problemsolving through movement and body awareness.

The metaphor of the body as machine is prominent in both the healthy lifestyles and performance discourses. In one, the body is to be exercised and cared for, to be worked on to accrue health benefits; in the other, the body is to be trained to perform effectively and to achieve in competitive situations. Neither stands alone, both have many elements of compatibility with each other and with dominant discourses informing physical education. All are evident to some degree in the text which will be discussed below.

A Text Analysis

The text to be analysed comes from a Year 9 (fourteen years old) girls' gymnastics lesson taught by a female teacher. In many ways this is not a typical physical education lesson since physical education classes are increasingly co-educational. Classes including boys have differences which can be linked to the differences in the positioning of boys and their male teachers in relation to the discourses and practices associated with sport. However, the structure and more general features of this lesson still serve to demonstrate how language use produces particular notions of the body, including the gendered body, in the context of specific pedagogical technologies of power.

The transcript of the gymnastics lesson was made as part of a larger study in which teachers agreed to wear a microphone and were recorded using a professional Sony Walkman. Lessons were also videotaped and observational notes made. It is usual in physical education lessons for the teacher to do most of the task-related talking and there is usually little verbal interaction between teachers and students; consequently, most of the linguistic material that is available is from the teacher.

Physical education lessons, as a result of their organisation and use of space, lend themselves to the constant exercise of power through the techniques of surveillance and distribution. Students are frequently organised into differing configurations—singles, pairs, groups, teams n the space available according to directions from the teacher. Similarly, the open space of the gym or field provides the teacher with the opportunity to constantly monitor the students' behaviour. The very teacher-directed approach of most physical education lessons, marked by the dominance of commands, also indicates the regulatory potential of physical education: teachers determine where students will move, what they will do and how they will do it. While not all students concur, and many find subtle ways of resisting and engaging in their own forms of regulation and normalisation, the structure, organisation and typical interaction patterns of traditional physical education lessons lend themselves to the constant enactment of these techniques of power on the part of the teacher.

Classification, Surveillance and Normalisation

The lesson begins with a roll-call. The students are seated on the floor in front of the teacher while the teacher calls each name in turn and waits for the student's response. Students are allocated marks according to the completeness of their uniform. By Year 8 (thirteen years old), many of the girls can supply their own mark. In other words, they have by now internalised the effects of surveillance and can regulate their own behaviour (technologies of the self). Like most schools, the appropriate dress in this class means a specific uniform which goes beyond the necessity of safety—in this case, a short brown skirt or brown tracksuit pants with a pale blue t-shirt. These are clothes that the girls would not by choice wear on any other occasion and serve as an indication of compliance with school and class rules.

The roll-call provides an opportunity for surveillance and for remarking on the students' uniforms as an indication of their attitude to the lesson, of defining the standard and of establishing rules (normalisation). It serves to divide students into those who comply —those whose bodily inscriptions fit with the range of expectations- and those who do not (classification). Like most of a physical education lesson, the monitoring goes beyond uniform to an obseravation of body types—those who are slim and/or appropriately muscular, and can be taken to have an appropriate attitude to physical activity, and those who do not, and are presumed not to have.

Following the roll marking, the teacher (T) makes a number of statements which establish that the arrangement for this lesson has been changed (distribution). The change has taken place because the teacher was concerned that the girls may have been inhibited by the boys' scrutiny of their bodies (exclusion). In articulating her concern, she constructs the girls as objects of the boys' gaze under male surveillance. She also clearly differentiates 'boys' as a category with different attributes from 'girls' (classification) and characterises all the boys and all the girls as possessing the attributes described (totatisation).

T: With the 9B 2 girls you weren't with us last week, but what we've decided very briefly is with Year 9s we're separating you for gymnastics as I explained, from the boys in your class, whereas you normally do co-ed physical education. Doing that particularly in gym because of skirts, and you'll see that the girls who were here last week have been told that they're able to wear light pants, um tights, something suitable they consider to gymnastics, (someone talking in class) Listen please, (pause). Something that you consider to be suitable for gymnastics.

What will happen, Mr P and Mr S are taking all the boys in the three classes. At the moment they're going outside, but at times, we're doing gymnastics from now until the end of the term, they will be using half of the hall in here. So what we're particularly aiming at is you people being more conscious of what you're doing instead of who's looking at you doing it.

In this quote the teacher establishes the normality of relations where girls' bodies are subject to the scrutiny of the male students and where the girls are so preoccupied with this scrutiny that they cannot concentrate. It is also taken-for-granted (as normal) that female teachers will teach female students and male teachers will teach male students.

In the next section of the lesson the teacher, through a series of commands, organises the arrangement of the warm-up. The teacher has some linguistic choices about the way she does this: her commands can take a variety of linguistic forms including imperatives, declaratives or interrogatives.

This particular teacher tends to use declaratives when giving general instructions to the whole class. For example, rather than saying 'Find a partner and the two of you bring the mats out and place them in this half of the hall', she uses what could be understood as the less powerful 'we'll have our usual partners please'. In this quote, she also uses the communal 'we' and 'our' instead of 'you' and 'your' when she is clearly referring to activities in which only the girls will be involved (choosing partners). These grammatical strategies paradoxically provide examples of regulation and totalisation, as the teacher uses language which can be construed as an attempt to construct a teacher-student relationship which is more inclusive and less marked for unequal power relations. At the same time, she is involved in the technique of classification-joining herself with the group a strategy which is less likely to be available to the students. Its success as a strategy depends on how the students make sense of what she says in the context of the lesson, their experiences of teachers, and of this teacher, and what else the teacher does and says in this lesson.

The following excerpts from the gymnastic lesson are typical of the more general linguistic features usually identifiable in a physical education warm-up but they also provide some further illustrations of how gendered bodies are constructed in physical education. The basic unit of analysis in systemic functional linguistics is the clause, so the text has been 'claused' for easier analysis.

Teacher, Student

T: What's the purpose of doing a warm-up?.

S: Stretching our calves.

T. Stretching and,

S: (Unclear)

T. No, what else do we have to do other than stretching?

(Pause)

Have to get the blood circulating.

All right.

So that all those fibres, muscle fibres are being fed with oxygen, so that we're prepared to do physical work.

Right standing up very quickly. (Pause)
Right, just on the spot, just jogging.
(Pause)
[sound of girls jogging]
Right keeping those ankles right up off the floor. (Pause)
Don't have to come very high.

Right rolling wrists, make a wave with your forearms and your wrists, (Pause) [Giggling and talking in background]

and pressing against each, hands against one another.

And point those little toes to the floor. When you do gymnastics or dance, Allison if you face me you'll know what's going on.

You should turn your feet out so little toes go to the floor. Not big toes, but little toes. (Pause)

As is the case in most physical education lessons, the teacher does most if not all the talking, generally as a series of ellipsed commands realised by material processes ('press', 'stretch') and circumstances of place or manner. In many cases, commands are ellipsed to the point that only circumstances remain ('up', 'there', 'quickly'). The students are positioned as the recipients of a constant flow of talk to which they must respond by moving their bodies in specific ways. The students ('you') are the main subjects and actors in the clauses, with the body or parts of the body positioned as the object/goal to be moved in specified ways and in specified directions. The warm-up is based on the principles of movement derived from exercise physiology and from pedagogical imperatives about safety students must go through a warm-up, that is, move parts of their bodies in specified ways, so that they can participate in a skill practice without injury. The activities thus draw on particular knowledge regimes which are translated into specific practices by the teachers and the students.

Of all the segments of the lesson, the warm-up would have to provide the most potential for the expression of the regulatory practices and technologies of training that Foucault describes in relation to the disciplining of bodies in army training. Bodies are divided into component parts (calves, ankles, wrists, feet, elbows, toes) which must move or be placed in specific ways and within specific time frames. The physical organisation and the predominance of commands in the warm-up provides an optimum environment for creating relations of authority and control. Divergences from the appropriate execution of the activity provide the means for the assertion of the teacher's authority and her right in this lesson to regulate all behaviour pertaining to the body. Students are physically organised to facilitate surveillance by the teacher. They face the teacher and the pace of the instructions means that all students have to be paying attention so that they are performing the activities at the same time as the rest of the class.

In this text, what is of particular interest is the close attention to the positioning of parts of the body, to the placement of the feet and toes. The request to place the feet is explained in terms of the standards appropriate to gymnastics and dance, realised by the use of the obligatory form of the verbal auxiliary, for example: 'When you do gymnastics or dance . . . you should turn your feet out so little toes go to the floor. Not big toes, but little toes'. The 'you' both carries the meanings of you the specific students in the class and is a statement of rule 'one should', this is 'how things are done', drawing on a set of values and behaviours appropriate or 'normal' to a specific field of movement (normalisation, classification). This attention to the aesthetics and proper comportment of the body is taken up again in other parts of the lesson, for example when the teacher says:

Form, how we do things in gymnastics is important. Let's now start to get legs together if they're supposed to be together; straight if they're supposed to be straight. Think about your feet, and instead of having this big blob on the end of your leg, right, your foot becomes the same line as your leg. Start to look at how you're doing things.

Practice, classification and standardisation

Having completed the stretches, the practice stage is introduced by statements about the skills that will be practised in the lesson that day:

T: Rolls, we're not going to start with forward rolls today, we're going to start with backward rolls. (Pause: a few groans from girls) Backward rolls don't necessarily have to go over your head. What are the things to remember in a backward roll?

S: Keep your head tucked in.

T: Keep your head tucked in, yes, in any roll you have to keep your head tucked in 'cause basically you're trying to become like a ball aren't you. Something else, Yola? (Pause) What about your knees, where do your knees have to go in a backward roll if you're going to,

S: under (rest unclear)

T: Well under your chin or up to your chest.

You've got to keep your back rounded and your knees into your chest.

If you keep your knees into your chest then you will roll over.

If you're going to do a shoulder roll, keep your knees tucked and they go over your shoulder to one side, and then you don't get that stretch of the neck that you do in a backward roll.

What about hands if you're going to do a backward roll?

S: (unclear)

T: Right, where you just put them in that back arch, where your hands went underneath you in the back arch, that's where they go. Keep your elbows in, don't have them flying out to the side, elbows in, knees tucked to your chest and backward rolls.

Let's see, one at a time please, longways, along your mat. Don't have to tell you that you know that one already.

The text above begins with a set of statements which classify rolls into backward rolls and forward rolls and goes on to set up the criteria For successful backward rolls (normalisation, classification). In this case, the students are invited to recall (presumably from a previous lesson) what they already know about the execution of backward rolls (an opportunity for surveillance since the teacher can note who remembers and who doesn't). The teacher reiterates student responses in a linguistic form which is characteristic of this section of the lesson: that is, a rule-like statement realised grammatically by modulation (meanings of necessity and obligation). Such meanings are realised through the use of modal auxiliaries such as have to, must, got to, should, is in: 'you have to keep your head tucked in' and 'you've got to keep

your back rounded'. It is also realised in imperatives which encode correct procedures rather than demanding an immediate response, for example 'keep your elbows in', an enactment of a regulatory process by which certain rules of behaviour are invoked. In this way specific knowledge about the body is meant to be acquired through a process of learning which assumes that direct instruction together with appropriate teaching points drawn from exercise physiology and biomechanics are the best (and only) ways of learning socially valued skills.

The number of questions in this section is rather unusual for a typical physical education lesson and is indicative of the ways this particular teacher draws upon a movement education discourse, where students are expected to think about the elements of time, space, weight and flow in relation to their movements. A movement education approach is ostensibly intended to place more emphasis on student-centred learning and problem-solving. In Gore's terms it shifts more to mechanisms of the self. However, movement education classes still provide contexts for constant surveillance and for the processes of normalisation. What has changed is what is regarded as normal. In traditional physical education classes standardised performances are valued as normal; in movement education classes expressions of creativity and variance are valued.

Material ('doing') processes predominate, with the body or body parts as objects to be moved in particular directions, in a particular manner (circumstances of place) to achieve a specified skill. It would seem that the body is taken primarily to be a tool or instrument, whose skills can be honed in response to directions from the teacher/expert, but that learning and thinking about movement is generally not part of the physical education process.

It is clear from the analysis that it is the teacher who is primarily involved in the processes of regulating what can be done, how it can be done and where it can be done. She is embodied as the expert through her capacity to ask questions to which she knows the answer, to demonstrate skills, to assist others through directions and by supporting and moving bodies. Through her use of language, the teacher constructs particular notions of female embodied subjectivity, concerned with how one looks. On the one hand this is constituted in terms of male scrutiny and, on the other, in terms of the female body as an aesthetic object where close attention to the positioning of body parts is important.

The lesson illustrates those assumptions about the body, about physical activity and about bodies and gender that are taken-forgranted, that is, that are dominant/hegemonic. What we have in both gymnastics and sport more generally is adherence to the idea that there is a hierarchy of skills, with the basics having to be mastered before moving on to skills of a higher order. Not only is a hierarchy of skills assumed, but there is also a profound conviction that certain skills are valuable in themselves and need to be part of each student's repertoire, for example, the forward and backward roll in gymnastics. While this is rationalised by arguments of safety, the whole configuration, the way of thinking about the body, the existence of these activities and not others in the syllabus, speaks to a particular historical set of circumstances and not the universality of these activities and skills and the ways of acquiring them.

The analysis above demonstrates that, as Foucault points out:

. . . a relation of surveillance, defined and regulated, is inscribed at the heart of the practice of teaching, not as an additional or adjacent part, but as a mechanism that is inherent to it and which increases its efficiency.

But as Gore points out, inherent in Foucault's notion of power is its capacity to be productive to bring into being that which it names. This is of particular relevance to pedagogy, in which the exertion of power is inescapable. In physical education, the exertion of mechanisms of power on the body is particularly evident: the physical organisation of the lesson lends itself to constant surveillance of the students by the teachers, and vice versa; the knowledge and skills which constitute the content of the lesson are taken as given, with the teacher as expert. This provides a context in which the practices that regulate the body, and which determine normal and appropriate ways of behaving, are constantly reiterated. At the beginning of the lesson students are categorised in terms of different 'naturalised' characteristics. The students' practice of the set activities and their ability to judge their own rating in relation to the uniform requirement both speak to the successful operation of the various technologies of the self that are in keeping with their positioning as students and as students of a physical education lesson.

What this means for the teachers and students involved is that certain ways of thinking about the body and moving the body become naturalised and other ways remain hidden impossible and inconceivable. Students may, outside the school, encounter alternative ways of moving the body, such as yoga, as well as different discourses of femininity. They may not. There is no evidence of student resistance to the discursive regime in operation in this class, only the co-operative performance of required movements. Such compliance may indicate an only too successful outcome to bodywork as the means of production of feminised subjects according to dominant discourses.

11

Research Methodology, Literacy and Cultural Difference

Introduction

Method. An ugly word. And my Shorter Oxford concurs, simultaneously convincing me of my deepest fears, and confounding them, demonstrating as it does the necessary relationship between method, methodical and Methodist. 'Procedure for attaining an object', 'a way of doing anything, esp. according to a regular plan', 'excessive regard for methods'. Help. How can I turn my eclectic, eked-out-of-experience and necessarily experimental scribblings into procedures, plans, regularity? Can I write about what belies my own practice? Am I expected to lie?

Of course, I could hide behind professional platitudes and institutional commonplaces. That is, after all, what they are there for. 'Without the experience of fieldwork I could not have written this chapter. The immeasurable generosity, patience and intelligence of Lajamanu Warlpiri made this research possible'. And of course, these statements, like all discursively dominant ones, are necessarily true. And I don't for an instant want to underplay the enormity of fieldwork as a pedagogic, a life experience. Nor, worse, would I want to disavow particular Warlpiri individuals' efforts in both tolerating, and teaching me throughout the ongoing process of my 'fieldwork'.

But equally true, and far less easily uttered, is the artifice of writing itself. Writing can never simply capture or represent my own let alone Warlpiri experiences. And it is a deeply suspicious view of language, of writing particularly, that also informs this paper.

Alternatively, I could speak of the 'methodologies' of Jacques Derrida which, along with the exigencies of fieldwork, do serve to shape this chapter, at least in part. Only I am not convinced that Derrida's 'deconstruction' offers a clear-cut methodology. To outline as I might, as indeed, Jonathan Culler and Christopher Norris before me have, deconstructive 'approaches' and 'formulas' for reading a text, is, of course, possible. One could, undoubtedly, identify in my work certain 'deconstructive' propinquities: the identification and subversion of taken-for-granted ways of thinking about historically entrenched binaristic logics—speech and writing, orality and literacy, colonised and coloniser, Aborigines and Europeans; the tenacity of these ways of thinking, and the violence of their effects; the enactment of a systematic reversal and displacement of the assumed hierarchies between the terms while continuing to work in and through them or, as Spivak writes, quoting Derrida, the aim is 'to dismantle the metaphysical and rhetorical structures which are at work not in order to reject or discard them, but to reinscribe them in another way'. Yes, I could locate these types of operations for you throughout this chapter, ergo, I have done so by listing them here.

But to do so is to miss the point. Edward Said has called Derrida's work a 'technique of trouble' a phrase I love precisely because it gets at what is altogether too often overlooked in 'methodological' discussions about deconstruction—that is, as Cordelia Chavez Candelaria has noted, the profoundly anti-authoritarian nature of Derrida's project. This may also serve to explain why, when Derrida is taken-up by women theorists, they do so in terms of explicitly politicised, explicitly anti-authoritarian agendas, be these feminist, sexual, postcolonial or otherwise. Gayatri Spivak, Judith Butler, Barbara Johnson, Jane Gallop, Eve Kosofsky Sedgwick, Trinh T. Minh-ha and Elizabeth Grosz are names which come immediately to mind. Men who take-up Derrida tend to do so in more strictly philosophical and/or literary ways. Gasche and Rorty represent the former, Culler and Norris, the latter.

In other words, it is more an orientation, an attitude to my subject matter, that describes whatever 'Derridean' inflections and influences are operant here. If I may be so bold as to insert myself in this genealogy of feminist theorists, it is precisely these kinds of antiauthoritarian attitudes that coincide with, and inform, my own. And it is this which, above all else, from my perspective, typifies the 'method' at work in this chapter, if method I must call it. A refusal to accept the terms in which literacy, in which the alphabet and, in turn, Aboriginal difference itself, has been constructed and construed; a disregard for the supposed 'neutral' terms of writing combined with an imperative to rework the pernicious consequences of conceptualisation itself; a belligerent conviction that writing is a culturally specific material practice with no little effect.

The universal embracing of literacy cross-culturally makes the effects of writing particularly difficult to trace. Thus, the historically absented identity of the writing subject that is, (universalised) European cultural conceptualisations and practices is as much under interrogation here as are the terms of Warlpiri differences. In short, my paper works to enact what it seeks to describe: to find a form to figure cultural differences differently. Or because that sounds altogether too idealistic, too hopeful, given the immutable legacy of language as I have inherited it in semiotic and poststructural definitions at least to avoid reinscribing the same kinds of differences.

But I ask myself: can refusal be a method?; does irreverence count?

This chapter is an investigation into writing and cultural identity. It is concerned with the way in which alphabetical writing, as a culturally specific mode of representation, is actively involved in the production of cultural difference(s). Nowhere are the effects of writing more apparent, and simultaneously disavowed, than in the writing of a language and the teaching of literacy to people assumed to be 'without writing'. The dominant portrayal of Australian Aboriginal people as either pre-literate or illiterate a portrayal reinforced rather than countered by the contemporary heralding of traditional 'oral' Aboriginal practices is here refuted. I argue that it is not the case that Warlpiri Aborigines are pre- or illiterate but, on the contrary, Warlpiri use the alphabet in terms which not only demonstrate a profound appreciation of literacy, but ultimately the inadequacy of literacy, of the alphabet, to represent literate subjects.

I rely here on a specific conceptualisation of writing as a mimetic form of representation. As I explore below, the alphabet is commonly understood to represent speech. It purports to mimic to imitate, to copy, to liken—the sounds of speech. Even if unsuccessful, as I will argue, this purportedly mimetic relationship between graph and sound produces important social and political effects which this chapter seeks to discern.

In order to trace the mimetic effects of the alphabet as it moves to write, and to name, Warlpiri differences, I use a notion of mimesis derived from a number of sources. Adapting from Walter Benjamin and Michael Taussig , I argue that mimesis can be understood as 'effects produced by the copy'. It is the partial and virtual force mimesis produces as it moves to copy and reproduce European models and methods of writing and, in turn, Warlpiri mimetic responses, which I examine below. The attempt to create colonised subjects mimetically, through the use of writing and naming techniques, is shown to have both succeeded and failed. Following the work of Homi K. Bhabha, I examine the ways in which colonial mimicry produces an ambivalent authority. The colonised are kept at a distance, becoming only ever partial resemblances, partially reformed, both miming and menacing the colonial order or, as I explain below, 'almost the same but not quite'. Or, as Warlpiri might say themselves, same but different'. Mimesis, Paul Carter argues, while 'designed to minimise difference, exacerbates it'.

A proviso: the material under consideration in this chapter is of a highly sensitive nature. I have taken great care to limit potential offence by employing circumspect renderings of the proscribed or Kumanjayi names I refer to in order not to violate the taboo on their usage. When the actual sound of the name is important for the purposes of discussion, I have used International Phonetic Alphabet (IPA) letters. As I discuss below, it is the use of Roman alphabetic letters to write out a name in its entirety which is potentially taboo for Warlpiri. In my understanding, the use of IPA letters to represent a name in full, as I do here, is less likely to cause offence. Unlike the letters of the Roman alphabet, IPA letters are not a commonly held or utilised code; they are not recognised or identified as being 'names' as such. These variant renderings of taboo names will undoubtedly affect reader accessibility, and I apologise in advance. However, these variant forms represent my attempt to remain in keeping with taboo restrictions. I do not want to cause offence or 'sorry'.

In order to appreciate the use of literacy, of the alphabet, in Warlpiri figurations of the proper name, it is necessary to understand something of the complex system of personal appellation Warlpiri possess. But this is not easy. There are no generalisations without qualification here; no tendencies which aren't seemingly belied by others. The unassuming proper name is anything but simple. Nowhere are the 'bewildering' effects of mimesis that Taussig describes more evident than in contemporary Warlpiri names. The name is no mere signifier of identity. Nor has the name simply been one thing among others exchanged between Europeans and Aborigines in the ongoing attempt to encounter, to comprehend, the difference of the other. Both groups have moved and continue to move to rename the other throughout the colonial endeavour. The terms in which Europeans have re-named Warlpiri make definitive differentiations between contemporary European and Warlpiri naming practices difficult to sustain.

To make matters even more complicated, it is through the name itself that Aboriginal cultural specificity has been understood. Aboriginal societies are renowned for their intricate and varied naming practices. Numerous names for any one person are common, and a tacit principle of non-disclosure operates regarding personal names. An absolute quantification a typology of personal address and reference forms is perhaps impossible in Aboriginal context(s). As von Sturmer puts it, the use of names in Aboriginal societies is 'subject to extreme variability'. Dixon suggests, following Stanner, that Aboriginal peoples have so many names because there needs to be at least one or more name(s) available at any given moment which are not proscribed by prevailing taboos (kin-avoidance, polite deference, death). This is, however, a somewhat functionally reductive explanation, in that it assumes a singular identity which pre-exists and, in a sense, supersedes the very complex notion of identity that multiple nominal forms suggest.

The avoidance of the use of personal names is combined with a marked preference for the use of 'class' terms, that is, terms which indicate membership of socially determined groupings based on age, gender, kinship, moiety and country. This preference for the use of class terms over that of personal names is what Sutton calls the 'Principle of Generality'.

This Principal of Generality and the potential 'danger' of personal names has been understood as resulting from particular configurations of the Aboriginal social, primarily 'avoidance relationships' and the taboo on speaking the name of the dead. Circumspection with regards to others is something of a cultural imperative among Aborigines. The overt identification of others is eschewed. Identifying another too closely in a particular context—using a personal name may act, or enact, a certain identification of, and/or with, the name bearer and, in turn, serve to closely identify the name user. One should avoid 'presenting oneself too forcefully' and 'linking oneself too clearly with one's ideas', von Sturmer claims. Instead, a highly diplomatic tendency towards 'self-effacement', as Kendon describes it, prevails in many Aboriginal societies.

Personal names may also be considered dangerous because they do not specify identity in terms of publicly recognisable classificatory categories of 'being' and 'relating'. As Levi-Strauss argues, personal names threaten classificational systems because they push, and define, the limits of classification. Class terms may be privileged in societies like Warlpiri because they 'name' and group persons in terms of structured categories of kinship, age, moiety or gender. Thus, they prescribe and proscribe certain relationships—modes of behaviour accordingly. Class names are organised, and in turn organise, in terms of the external dictates of Jukurrpa, the Dreaming, Law: the regulatory body of Warlpiri society. By contrast, personal names are said to individuate and simultaneously de-differentiate because they do not encode in terms of the prevailing dictates of external authority. Personal names may be considered 'dangerous' because they do not entail the externalised authority that class names necessarily possess. They may, in turn, pose a certain threat to the Law because they do not necessarily circumscribe an order of relations and relating.

Here, distinguishing between types of personal names becomes important. For, while Lajamanu Warlpiri may concur with this Principle of Generality, there is also evidence of a more free use of European personal names than the literature maintains. That is, there appears to be a movement towards the favouring of the more sociocentric, stable names over those of the egocentric, situationally specific and necessarily variant, class terms (with due variation across the Warlpiri nation, as Dussart preliminarily outlines). Stanner, Sutton and von Sturmer seem to suggest that class terms always predominate over personal names. But, in my experience at both Lajamanu and Dussart at Yuendumu, European personal names are commonly used in both reference and address.

I want to suggest that this movement can be understood in relation to the dissemination of the 'proper' European name effects of writing in and on and by Warlpiri. In other words, there appears to be a growing correlation between the proper name and the actual terms of address and reference Warlpiri currently use. But not without a difference. Let me explain. Warlpiri currently hold names which are very like European proper names: first name, surname, and subsection term or skin name (with the skin name located in either 'middle' or 'last' name position). For example:

Michael Nelson Jakamarra
Jimmy Jampijinpa Robertson
Norah Nelson Napaljarri
Lady Nungarrayi.

Europeans imposed both first and last names on Warlpiri throughout the period of early contact for a variety of identificatory and administrative purposes. Warlpiri themselves currently confer European personal names on their children at birth, unlike the much later conferred Warlpiri personal names. The more unusual, the better, for example, Azaria, Lava, Basil and Attrina are names recently conferred. In my experience, the naming of children explicitly does not involve naming through inheritance practices as happens with Warlpiri personal names. In short, Warlpiri appear to have been diligent students of the lessons that the 'proper' name teaches, in their movement to employ the unique, highly individuated personal name.

The conjoining of the skin name in the making, the marking, of the proper Warlpiri name is significant. The sixteen 'skins' are one of the more complex systemic features of Warlpiri society and have been subject to much debate and commentary. Crudely formulated, skin names serve to define kinship relations between each and every member of Warlpiri society, structurally and, potentially, genealogically. They also position members of society in relation to one another in broader organisational terms by moiety (patrimoiety and matrimoiety), semi-moiety (patri-couple) and subsection. Skin provides terms commensurate, on the one hand, with both the egocentric kinship and the sociocentric classificatory dictates of Jukurrpa, the Dreaming, Law. On the other hand, skin provides terms which are simultaneously commensurate with the absolute terms required by the dictates of the proper European name—that is, names which can be used 'equally' in address or reference, which remain the same regardless of referent, addressee or propositus. Proper European names, like the skin names, are not circumscribed by speaker, topic, gender or social state, as are all the other names which Warlpiri potentially hold and use: kinship terms, age-mate and social status terms, nick-names, and Warlpiri personal names. Sutton and Rumsey provide detailed discussions of the enormous variation in usage of personal names and kinship terms.

Skin names have come to form part of the Warlpiri proper name. They occupy the space between the European first name and the surname and, consequently, have been used by Europeans as both. The ongoing presence of an 'Aboriginal' signifier has been maintained in the Warlpiri proper name. Skins are positioned as, and thus likened to, both European middle names and surnames, although the latter may be becoming the more common position. For example, Peggy Napaljarri Rockman has more recently been written as Peggy Rockman Napaljarri. So, too, Jimmy Jampijinpa Robertson is more recently found as Jimmy Robertson Jampijinpa.

Whether this Aboriginality is figured as middle or last name, the inclusion of the skin necessarily positions Warlpiri names ambivalently in relationship to European names, creating a recognisably similar but nevertheless different name from the proper name, a point I return to below.

The increasing standardisation of this form of the proper name is evident in the use of initials in both 'death taboo' and graffiti practices. One of the more serious offences, widely reported in the literature and witnessed time and again in my experience, is the speaking aloud of a recently deceased person's name. Warlpiri fervently avoid the presence of the recently deceased. Mortuary ceremonies and bereavement practices are organised by and around certain ritualised avoidances or 'erasures'. For instance, camp is moved from where the deceased has lived; places frequented by the deceased are avoided; clothing, shoes, blankets, mattresses, furnishings belonging to the deceased are burned; cars of the recently dead are dumped; photographs, tapes and videos showing the deceased are destroyed, covered or stored; ceremonial songs / dances associated with the person and / or their birthplace are not performed.

12

Creating Databases in Research Methodology

Introduction

The inception of the cross-grade service-learning program, the English teacher noticed that his students' grades improved each grading period and that the students' attendance was up, especially on days when they worked with the second grade. He also noticed an improvement in the comprehension of material on in-class projects and improvement of capitalization, punctuation, and grammar in writing assignments. As his students prepare to take the state writing assessment and a standardized test, he wonders if the student gains he saw in the classroom will transfer to the formal assessments. He is also interested in finding out if his students are doing better in other classes.

Similarly, the second grade teacher, whose classroom was selected based on the end-of-the-year reading scores from last year's first grade cohort, saw an improvement from the fall to winter reading assessment. She also noticed that attendance was better on days that the seventh grade class visits. She wonders if more of her students will be at grade level or closer to grade level on the spring assessment than they were the prior year. Both teachers think that participation in the cross-grade service-learning project made the difference and want the program to continue. They want to be able to show the impact of the program in terms of student grades and performance on standardized, district, or state assessments. They also would like to know if participation is really affecting attendance, and perhaps disciplinary referrals as well.

Student 11234 does not really exist in any school district, but millions of similar students do, and a story can be told about each one. There are thousands of schools and community organizations, each collecting various types of data. There are thousands of cross-grade reading programs and many other types of service-learning programs operating in schools and communities across the country that are collecting data as well. This information is often used to fill out forms or write reports. In many cases the data remain untouched, sitting in file cabinets or in computer files. However, when the information from the thousands of service-learning programs is organized and presented, it can tell stories to willing ears and serve an ally and guide for teachers, students, parents, youth workers, administrators, funders, and community members. Examining how to create and utilize such databases for the purpose of service-learning evaluation and research is the focus of this chapter.

Databases are organized collections of stored information on a defined subject area and are of importance in carrying out a mission or running a program. The database may contain information on single subject or discipline or can be multidisciplinary, problem oriented, mission oriented, or oriented toward certain types of transactions (Fortier, 1997). Large databases bring together data from many programs, projects, schools, and communitybased organizations.

Advancements in information sciences and computer technology have enhanced the means to create, access, and share large databases that were not available only a few years ago. Database software packages such as Microsoft®Access 2002, FoxPro®, and Paradox® provide new capacity to individuals to engage in evaluation and research activities through personal and professional computer use. Many database books, training, and resources are available and readily accessible in stores and on the Internet. Larger database packages, such as Oracle and Microsoft SQL Server have increased institutional and organizational capacity to use the data generated from their activities and programs to make decisions.

This chapter focuses on creating and utilizing large databases for the purpose of service-learning program evaluation and research. It is drawn from Pennsylvania service-learning evaluations from which large databases were created and used to evaluate the effectiveness of K-12 service-learning programs. The functions, design, and characteristics of large effective databases are investigated, along with the types of skills necessary for individuals to build their own local, large database using existing information (data) from their schools and communities. Finally, the chapter considers ways in which national databases can be used by researchers to enhance servicelearning evaluation and research.

Functions of a Service-Learning Database

Databases perform many functions within the educational system and during educational evaluations and research. Four functions of databases that are critical for service-learning research and evaluation and are important when constructing large databases are presented here. Any large database one might design would need to perform these functions.

First, databases provide a consistent and standardized format for data across program types, approaches, and models. The standard format provides a recognizable picture of the data. This allows the user to consistently compile, organize, preserve, and analyze large amounts of data. A uniform style of record keeping lets the user look back at the data to obtain a historical perspective. With a standardized format, there is a framework to inform decisions. With a standardized format comes the ability to test hypotheses and pose questions about service-learning activities and programs.

Second, databases serve as the basis for timely and accessible report generation. One frequently encountered challenge in educational evaluation and research is the task of efficiently distributing information to everyone who might need it. With databases at hand, information that teachers and school administrators might find useful to strengthen their service-learning programs can be distributed to all interested parties and stakeholders. Such data may include academic content areas, service foci (e.g., human needs, environment, public safety, and education), grade levels, and student demographic data (e.g., gender and age). Once a database is in operation, it can supply countless reports of various kinds to professionals, parents, community members, and students in school districts and counties who have a need for the information offered.

Reports can be tailored to match the unique needs of specific stakeholders. A major contribution of the current database software packages is their emphasis on reporting. For example, specific software packages such as Crystal Report focus exclusively on reporting. Mixes of data types (e.g., numbers, photographs, hyperlinks, calculations, and descriptions) from a database are easily shared. For example, the Service Star Report shown in Table 6.2 is a sophisticated report generated from the Pennsylvania service-learning database for school district administrators to show a number of program variables. Each school district can receive an individualized report. Such reports can be compiled into a statewide report along with an executive summary and aggregate statistics for the entire state.

Third, queries can be made in a database to answer specific questions. A query searches the database for specific fields, or sets of fields with specific features that have been selected. It provides access to specific pieces of information. For example, the user could query a large state service-learning database to identify: (a) middle schools (b) that provide cross-grade service-learning reading programs (c) for more than four hours of direct service per week. Such a query would provide a quick list of schools meeting all three criteria. Queries can be simple, identifying one or two fields of data, or more complex, identifying several fields of data. Queried data can be taken a step further and imported into a report format for quick and easy report generation.Fourth, databases serve as the basis for data analysis and management. Databases allow for easy record keeping, report generation, and queries, but their great strength lies in the user's ability to complete complex analyses of data quickly and easily. One of the challenges today in developing such information systems is in building the expertise of a data analyst into the systems so that the benefits of accurate and efficient analyses are available to those who require them. Database developers can try to anticipate the types of analyses that might benefit these people and make the results available to users.

Database Design

Databases hold the raw data for an evaluation or research project that will eventually be used for one of the database functions. Database design is contingent on the particular information needs of the user. Databases are only as good as the information they hold, so the design of the database is critical. When designing a database, large or small, three key elements need to be considered:

1. The data themselves
2. The relationships among the data, and
3. The database schema.

It is important to hire an information specialist to design the database since only the user can identify the information that will need to be collected and determine how that information will be used. Some knowledge of the particular software program to be used to implement and operate the database is necessary. Although similar in many aspects, each software program has unique characteristics and attributes that may influence the database design and use. In essence, the data that are collected and stored in a database are the sum total of all the information that has been collected to document program implementation and to answer evaluation or research questions. They are the raw material for all calculations and reports that are then used to lead to discussions and guide decision making.

If clarity of purpose or use of the data are uncertain, there is an increased danger in collecting too little data or the wrong kind of data to answer the questions of the stakeholders. Conversely, collecting large amounts of extra information with the hope that the data might be needed or useful is problematic as well. Collecting too little data is often the product of not sufficiently canvassing and involving stakeholders in defining the purpose of the database. Collecting excessive data is also an indicator of poor planning. In most instances, collecting too many data adds confusion and, if left unexamined and unused, raises questions and frustrations that can detract from the program or the evaluation being conducted. Once a database is operating it can be modified over time; however, the time and energy to make changes to the database can be considerable and costly. Being clear about how data will be used to answer specific questions lessens anxiety and resistance to participation.

As part of the design process, experts recommend working backwards. It often helps to think the content of the report. Preparing mock tables, charts, and a report framework with section headings and explanations of how the data will need to be analyzed helps ensure that all the necessary data are identified.

Another suggestion to help identify data that need to be collected is to take time to talk to all the stakeholders and assess their areas of interest. In most cases program implementation and impact is shared with a variety of stakeholders, each having their own idea of what is important and what they would like to know about the program. Their ideas about what is important and what they want to know also provide guidelines for identifying which data to collect.

Once all the data are identified, the relationships among the data become important. Relationships refer to a correspondence among data items. It is important to remember that within the database, each data item has its own field. Fields are organized into tables. Individual fields within a table can be selected to run a query, or individual fields between tables can be selected (linked) to run a query. Knowing the relationships among data is essential when identifying what fields go into what tables. Clarity of the relationship between data items is critical so that the user will be able to query and manipulate the data in whatever fashion is necessary. When each data item is identified, in their own field and organized logically in tables, data items can be selected and linked in any combination. When each data item is not given its own field, or is not organized correctly by table, data analysis is more problematic.

A schema describes the organization and the relationships among data within the database. Another term for schema is point of view. In the Pennsylvania database the organizing schema was the school. Data were reported at the school level. These data helped users keep consistent records of what was happening across the state. Without this agreed-upon schema the data can become unclear. A schema provides a unit of measure or analysis.

A database in a school district related to a program might include data on student demographics, family information, grades, attendance, participation levels, teacher notes, and standardized district and state assessment scores. Each data item would be related to a student and placed together in the student's record. Student records could be organized into classes and then grades (schema). Teachers and principals could then use the database to answer the questions posed in the opening scenario.

A larger statewide service-learning database presents the opportunity to expand the schema from the individual student, classroom, and school to many students, classrooms, and schools. By adding information about the school, community, and service-learning project, the database user has the ability to compare and contrast projects and programs. Interested stakeholders can move from questions about individual service-learning project implementation to examine questions related to service-learning best practices, program effectiveness and outcomes, cost and benefit analysis, and policy.

There are other factors that need to be considered as the database is being designed. They include accessing the database and security issues. A database may be shared among several users. The database design should allow people to access and use the data, while providing protection of the data. Determining who and to what degree individuals will have access to the database is also critical in its design. For example, some users may only have access to input or update data; others may have access to run queries, analyze data, and produce reports; whereas others may only be able to view data, queries, or reports. Protecting data from unauthorized disclosure, alteration, or destruction is a security issue that needs to be addressed early by a database administrator. This decision is usually based on the usefulness and sensitivity of the data with respect to the needs of the person wishing to have access privileges.

Once the database is established, a user's guide is developed. A user's guide typically includes descriptions of the research for which the database is prepared, data collection instruments and sources, sample design and implementation, data collection, management, and processing. The final section is information on the data files, codebook, and analyses. In the guide's appendices are copies of the instrumentation. If scores from statewide educational assessments are a data item, the assessment probably would also be included. A user's guide is critical for large database operation. It sets the database parameters and concretely sets the expectations and outcomes for the database.

Users' guides are written detailed descriptions of the database that can be shared. Although they have the potential to be quite overwhelming, they do not have to be. User's guides simply describe the database and help users navigate the database. The guides detail the relationships among the data. Ideally, for each report, table, and chart, a description of the data items and any calculations or manipulations of the data are included. Presentation options may be considered; for example, whether to use pie or bar charts.

Effective Databases

Ensuring that data are current and accurate is another critical task. The Pennsylvania database developers learned how time consuming and difficult this task can be. The process was dynamic, influenced by the stakeholders, reporting requirements, funding requirements, and questions being asked. Over time, with changes in the field of information management, the data available changed in both quantity and quality.

In the beginning the task was simply to document what was happening in terms of service-learning across the state of Pennsylvania. The task required collecting service-learning program data that was beneficial and useful to individual programs in schools while being able to use the information for statewide evaluation reporting. Database developers began by collecting general program and school demographic information such as participating schools, program contacts, telephone numbers, e-mail addresses, fax numbers, and brief program descriptions of services being provided.

With this information developers created a program directory for the state. This directory report format was easy to formulate and proved to be very useful to the state service-learning coordinator, the evaluators, and even the individual districts. It provided a snapshot of what was going on in the state and served as an excellent resource and reference for participating districts. In addition to the individual district entries, it also provided a listing of districts by several topics including region of the state, county, and even type of service being provided. Districts used the guide to network and find support and resources as they built their service-learning programs.

The database also organized program implementation information. Early on the interest focused on what was actually occurring, who was participating, and to what degree. Data collected included the number of classrooms, projects, and reflection hours students accrued; how well integrated the service was into the curriculum; the types of service that were occurring; the number and type of collaborating agencies; the ways in which parents were involved; the amount and types of training teachers received; how active the advisory board was; and if any products were produced. The database could be queried to produce individual district reports, or queried by topic, to provide a local, county, or statewide snapshot of that topic.

Data were also collected as part of the evaluation process. Each school received at least one onsite visit during the grant cycle. During the visit the evaluator had a chance to observe or participate in one or more of the components of service-learning and had the opportunity to interview administrators, program coordinators, teachers, students, and sometimes parents and advisory board members.

School and program demographic information, program implementation data, and information collected during site visits all became a part of the statewide evaluation database, and the data were used to produce several types of brief reports as well as the yearly evaluation report.

In an attempt to collect consistent data across the state, instruments were created. These instruments were completed by hand by service-learning site coordinators. The information was then entered into the central evaluation database and various directories. Brief reports and evaluator reports were produced from the queried data. A hard copy of the reports was sent to the district. If the district personnel wanted the report distributed to interested parties, they had to photocopy it. The data belonged to the state. Districts received the final results. Although district personnel could use the information provided to them for decision making, they did not have direct access to the raw data; however, they showed little interest in using the data for any purpose than what was required for evaluation.

By providing the data collection instruments and reviewing them at meetings and during onsite visits, database administrators hoped to increase the chances of receiving accurate data. But, service-learning coordinators, like other school personnel, are busy and often wore more than one hat. To reduce their workload and increase the accuracy of the data received, the data collection instruments were placed on diskettes. This allowed districts to update their data electronically, saving them much time. However, it was very time consuming for the database administrators because every district had different computers (Mac vs. PCs), software packages, and the like, and data still needed to be entered into the database once the diskettes were received. There still could be errors in the data, it was still time consuming, and districts still received only completed district data.

By the mid 1990s all districts were required to have Internet access in order to submit certain data to the state Department of Education in Pennsylvania. This factor alone changed the way evaluation data could be collected and the accuracy of those data. The evaluator could now house the database on a website, and districts could access the website through whatever Internet access they had within the district, thus eliminating different computer or software difficulties. All security access issues could be addressed and built into the database system. Additionally, each data field parameter could be explicitly defined, almost eliminating errors in data entry, assuring increased accuracy in the data submitted. Service-learning coordinators, instead of providing data on the diskettes, would now enter them directly into the database via the Internet. Individual spreadsheets or filing systems were no longer needed to track individual program data.

Building Your Own Local, Large Databass

The advancements in technology have provided service-learning practitioners, evaluators, and researchers with a major tool for managing their own data. Although the statewide evaluator can still run queries and produce whatever type of report necessary, districts can now be trained to query their own data and produce their own individual reports. Having access to their own data enables districts to go beyond documenting and reporting program implementation to addressing program impacts. To illustrate this power, consider the scenario presented at the beginning of the chapter. Locally, the coordinator knows the students who participate in the cross-age service-learning program. He or she may decide to answer questions related to attendance, grades, disciplinary action, standardized tests, and state assessments. At first, the coordinator might think all this information would need to be added to the service-learning database that was created to evaluate the program. This would be a huge task, and far beyond the scope or job description of any service-learning coordinator or even state evaluator. However, after doing a little research, exploring a few database packages and their capabilities, and speaking with an information development specialist, the coordinator would learn that it is not necessary to develop a new database, or even update an existing one, but rather the coordinator can import or export data, run queries and conduct data analysis using the data that are currently maintained by the district, teachers, or buildings.

Regardless of how narrow or vast the scope of the data analysis or the linking of data fields between databases, the same simple principles of identifying the data fields and the queries apply. Although this can be an expensive endeavor, the results can go far beyond the impact of service-learning especially when one remembers that one can link, sort, and generate data reports using data from any or all of the existing databases.

This is not to say that districts need to write large technology grants; buy expensive database packages with its accompanying training, technical assistance, or reports outputs; or hire expensive information development consultants to integrate the databases and create the designated queries or data analysis. Districts can be creative and can partner with companies that provide this service. Many companies have community service as part of the organization and may want to forge some type of exchange, for example, interns for services. The district develops the database it needs (and perhaps also provides a site for a senior project or service-learning project for an advanced computer programming course or interested student), and the company gets free interns. A partnership may also be developed with a college course or professor. Often a real-life project for college students, especially for upper-level students preparing for an internship, is preferred. The purpose here is not to offer a way to undertake this task, but to let the reader know that the technology and knowledge is available to perform such a task.

This district level example can be extrapolated to the statewide level. A person conducting a statewide evaluation could work with each of the state's participating districts to develop the same type of database system that would import district data to be queried with data in the service-learning database. When developing a comprehensive information management system as described previously, the database developer may seek existing reports that highlight the data or review existing databases to see how similar or related indicators are identified, collected, and reported. This is necessary if the database user wants to compare and contrast these data with other local, state, or national data. Furthermore, with a database reflective of existing educational and servicelearning evaluations and research data, the potential to contribute to broader service-learning theory and knowledge is possible.

Utilizing National Databasee

Large national databases exist that can be accessed and utilized in local service-learning evaluations and research. With little effort, it is possible to access and link to national and regional databases to compare and contrast district, state, and national data. Exploration of these databases has the additional advantage of providing models for evaluation and research.A number of databases at the national level can assist in locating potential linkages for service-learning data sources. There are two national clearinghouses that serve as central locations for collection and dissemination of information about education and service-learning programs, resources, events, participants, and organizations involved in the field. The two clearinghouses, while not providing data on service-learning implementation, research, and evaluation, are excellent sources in which to locate and link to appropriate databases. A third source of educational databases is the Washington, DC- based nonprofit The Education Trust. In addition to these sites for information, there are many databases available at the national level that are applicable directly to the field of education and to service-learning. It is important to note that there are also a large number of national topical databases available in such fields as health, human services, agriculture, and criminal justice that are appropriate to utilize with service-learning projects focused in these areas. One excellent national database for service-learning evaluators and researchers to access is the National Center for Educational Statistics (NCES), which is a part of the U. S. Department of Education. The NCES conducts surveys, maintains data, and publishes reports intended to inform educational policymakers, teachers, researchers, those in the media who write about education, and the general public. There are 15 available NCES databases. Each database with its surveys has its own homepage that can be accessed through the Survey and Programs Area listed on the NCES homepage.Four of the NCES databases most relevant to service-learning are: the Common Core of Data (CCD), the National Education Longitudinal Study, the National Household Education Survey (NHES), and the National Assessment of Educational Progress (NAEP).

1. Common Core of Data. The CCD is a set of five surveys sent to State Departments of Education as a means of gathering information about all United States public elementary and secondary schools, local education agencies, and state education agencies. The CCD contains three categories of information: general descriptive information on schools and school districts, data on students and staff, and fiscal data. The descriptive information includes names, addresses, telephone numbers, and types of locale; the data on students and staff include demographic characteristics; and the fiscal data cover revenues and current expenditures.
2. The National Education Longitudinal Study. Beginning with an eighth-grade cohort in 1988, NELS began to explore trends in data concerning critical transitions experienced by young people as they develop, attend school, and embark on their careers. Data were collected from students, parents, teachers, high school principals, and existing school records (such as high school transcripts). Cognitive tests (in math, science, reading, and history) were administered during the base year of 1988, with follow up data collection in 1990, 1992, 1994, and 2000. The fourth follow up collected in 2000 is scheduled to be published in 2002.
3. National Household Education Survey. The NHES is a data collection system of the National Center for Educational Statistics (NCES), and is designed to address a wide range of

education issues, such as early childhood education, participation in adult school safety and discipline, school readiness, and school safety and discipline. In 1996 data collection focused on civic involvement and participation among adults and children in Grades 6-12. The 1999 survey added more questions about youth service activities. The NHES will be repeated in 2003.

4. National Assessment of Educational Progress. This survey is designed to continually monitor the knowledge, skills, and performance level of the nation's children and youth. NAEP provides objective data on student performance at the national and regional levels in reading, mathematics, science, writing, civics, U. S. history, geography, social studies, art, music, literature, computer competence, and career and occupational development.

The NCES produces many different types of information from the databases it maintains. A report from each survey citing major findings, analysis reports, and methodological/technical reports are some of the publications that NCES produces. Learning About Education Through Statistics is an NCES publication that provides information about NCES surveys and how to access information from NCES. The Mini-Digest of Educational Statistics and The Condition of Education are produced from survey data.

Programs and Plans of the National Center for Education Statistics is a publication that summarizes NCES's existing statistical programs, publications, and plans for future work. Included are descriptions, timelines, and plans for all of NCES data collection programs. Also included are descriptions of NCES center-wide programs and services: customer service, technology, and training.

While these NCES databases are friendly, and will walk users through the steps they need to take to conduct their studies, they are primarily used by the experienced researcher. Exploring them, however, can give the novice a comprehensive view of how data are identified, collected, analyzed, and reported. It is equally helpful that all of the computerized databases presented have user guides that explain all aspects of data collection and analysis, and include copies of the instruments used for data collection. Although assistance is provided and user's guides are available, negotiating through large databases and becoming familiar with them does take time and practice.

The greatest asset in learning how to use these large national databases is not just being able to identify, compile, analyze, and report data or use existing data to conduct additional studies, but to gain the ability to integrate exiting databases into one's own work, and thus be able to compare and contrast data.

Conclusion

Service-learning evaluators and researchers have the opportunity to design and implement comprehensive information management systems (databases) and make use of an extensive quantity of current data readily available locally and nationally. The capacity exists to utilize in our evaluations and research a range of data and data analyses. These are powerful tools in advancing servicelearning and positive student outcomes.

13

Design and Evaluation of Research Methodology

Introduction

Numerous studies point to the positive benefits of engaging students in service activities. Benson found that students who serve their communities are less likely to engage in risky behaviors. Cohen and Duckenfield and Swanson found that service-learning is an effective strategy for the prevention of substance abuse and dropping out of school. Conrad and Hedin found that students engaged in service gain in social and personal responsibility and in academic performance. Calabrese and Shumer reported that students engaged in field work have few discipline problems and lower levels of alienation. Newmann and Rutter found an increase in problem solving skills and improved communication skills, particularly with adults. For a more complete review of the research.Despite these findings, establishing direct links between service-learning program objectives and outcomes for students has been difficult. One reason has been that service-learning practitioners have not always connected program design and evaluation to existing developmental and learning theory. This theme was echoed at the Service-Learning Summit, sponsored by the W. K. Kellogg Foundation. Their Wish List for service-learning research included: (a) studies that go beyond the Conrad and Hedin scale; (b) longitudinal studies; and (c) the development of better tools for assessing civic attitudes, civic problem solving, critical thinking, and other key dimensions of personal development. The research questions might be put this way:

- Are there reasons, based on accepted developmental or learning theories, for asserting that service-learning will have positive impacts on K-16 students?
- If there are, what do developmental or learning theories suggest about the design and evaluation of service-learning programs?
- How would the use of developmental or learning theories help practitioners better understand the links between program design and program outcomes?

The last question is particularly important. Research suggests that experiential learning, such as the kind embodied in service-learning, may be one of the best ways to invite and encourage movement from one stage to the next. However, whether movement through developmental stages occurs is dependent upon a number of factors, including the level of cognitive development and the level of social perspective taking.

One way of accounting for the discrepancies between intent and action is offered by Person-Environment Interaction Theory. This theory suggests that an individual's behavior (B) is a function if) of the person (P) and his or her interaction with the environment: B =/ {P x E}. The environment is made up of various internal variables, such as the level of cognitive and moral development, learning style, concern for others, commitment to prosocial values, self-esteem, and personality type; and external variables, such as opportunity to work with people from diverse backgrounds; quality of program design; cultural, school, and peer norms about helping others; and experiencing positive relationships with others. These variables interact in ways that complicate the relationship between program design and program outcomes. Theory-based research can help clarify these relationships and give practitioners more guidance in designing high-quality service-learning programs that have a high probability of achieving the desired outcomes for participants.

This chapter examines three theories of development and the two learning theories that could be used, either individually or in combination, to design and evaluate the effectiveness of service-learning programs: (1) psychosocial development Erikson and Chickering; (2) cognitive development; (3) personality type and (4) multiple intelligences.

Using theories in the design and evaluation of service-learning programs can serve practitioners in two ways. First, theories can provide a rationale for designing particular service-learning activities. For example, research in the field of cognitive and moral development indicates that movement from one stage to the next requires repeated exposure to an issue over an extended period of time. Although a single visit to a homeless shelter may convey important information about homelessness, it is not likely to change student attitudes or behaviors toward the homeless. Multiple visits over an extended period of time are needed.

Second, theories can act as filters or lenses through which anticipated and actual program outcomes may be assessed. In the preceding example, a research question based on moral development might focus on whether the service activities were appropriate for participants in relation to their ages, the duration of the project, and learning styles. Research studies resulting from the use of development and/or learning theories would focus on program outcomes in relation to levels of psychosocial, cognitive, and moral development and /or the learning styles of participants.

Perspective of Psychosocial Development

Psychosocial theory describes the content or issues with which individuals may be dealing during a given period in their lives. Two theories are examined here: Erik Erikson for K-12 youth and Arthur Chickering for college age youth.

Erikson: The Elementary School Years

According to Erikson, children face two main tasks in elementary school. The first, occurring typically during Grades K-3, is for children to develop a sense that there are things they can do for themselves and be supported in the necessary exploration. Children's curiosity about how things work and what impact they can have on their world leads to seemingly endless questions about what, why, how, and when. If children are led to believe that their curiosity is pointless or that their questions are a bother, Erikson suggested they may emerge from this stage of life with an excess of guilt. Children who are encouraged to try a wide variety of activities and explore their inner and outer worlds are likely to emerge from this stage with a sense of initiative.

During Grades 4 and 5, the developmental task typically is to see how quickly abilities and skills in broad areas of life can be learned. If children's efforts to initiate and complete projects, to establish relationships, and to explore new interests on their own are perceived by adults as mischief or wasted effort, children may emerge from this stage with a sense of inferiority. If children are supported in their efforts, they are likely to emerge from this stage with a strong sense of inferiority.

Erikson: The Middle School Years

The main developmental task typically facing youth in Grades 6 through 8 is to begin putting together a coherent, unified idea of the self out of a bewildering array of possible identities: child, student, friend, and sexual being. Younger adolescents take their first hesitant steps to move away from the various identities given to them by parents, teachers, and others toward an identity they choose for themselves.

Identity confusion typically results when the tasks associated with the previous stages have not been adequately resolved or when the negative messages young teens receive from others, such as "You're no good! You can't do anything right!" outweigh positive messages. The result is often a heightened sense of isolation, an overall sense of shame, and a general sense of not knowing who they are or where they fit in. A positive sense of identity is most likely to develop when teens are surrounded by adults who affirm them and encourage them to discover their own identities.

Erikson: The High School and College Years

High school students must prepare themselves for transition into the adult world. Resolution of two psychosocial tasks predominates during this stage. The first task is finishing work on Identity versus Identity Confusion. The second focuses on issues related to intimacy and isolation. In this stage adolescents begin to develop a sense of their own unique identity. This makes it possible for them to begin to explore meaningful, healthy, and intimate relationships with those around them and to share with and care about others without undo fear of losing themselves in the process.

To assist children and youth in successfully resolving the developmental tasks associated with each of Erikson's stages, Duckenfield and Swanson suggested that curriculum-based service-learning programs be designed with very specific needs and opportunities in mind. These design criteria also suggest research questions relating to the appropriateness of service activities for each age group.

Chickering

Arthur Chickering divided Erikson's stages of Identity and Intimacy into seven vectors or developmental tasks associated with the college years. Each vector rises to prominence at a certain time during a person's life, taking from one to five years to resolve. Like Erikson, Chickering believed that resolution can be positive or negative, affecting future vectors. Successful resolution of each vector depends on offering opportunities to explore tasks associated with each vector. The seven vectors and possible curriculum-based service-learning activities are shown in Table Research by Chickering and others suggests that tasks associated with the first three vectors are typically addressed during the freshman and sophomore years of college; tasks associated with the fourth vector during the late-sophomore year or junior year of college; whereas tasks associated with the last three vectors are not typically resolved until the senior year of college or beyond.

Perspective of Cognitve Theory

Stages of Cognitive Development

Stages of cognitive development follow a hierarchical, invariant sequence first identified by Piaget, with each successive stage building on previous ones. Earlier ways of reasoning are not lost, but are integrated into the reasoning process of later stages. Movement from one stage to the next is not like learning how to do something faster (e.g., speed reading) but like learning how to read in another language. In designing service-learning programs appropriate for K-16 youth, two of Piaget's stages of are involved.

Concrete Operational Stage, which first appears at about the age of six in most children, involves the ability of the child to solve conservation problems. Logical operations are developed, thereby allowing the child to solve problems involving concrete situations or data by a process of serialization. Research suggests that 50% to 70% of adults never progress beyond this stage of thought.

Formal Operational Stage, which may appear at about the age of 10, represents a qualitative change in the approach to problem solving. The individual is no longer limited by concrete details and experiences. Abstractions are now possible, enabling the individual to reason out possible explanations and weigh their consequences.

An example of the difference between these two forms of thought and their implications can be seen in the story of two little girls who were playing with scissors. The first girl, Marie, wanted to give her mother a nice surprise by cutting out a piece of sewing; however, she did not know how to use the scissors properly and accidentally cut a big hole in her dress. Another girl, Margaret, took her mother's scissors and accidentally cut a little hole in her dress.

Marilene, age six, was asked which child should receive the greater punishment. "The one who made the big hole." When she was asked "Why?" she replied, "because she made a big hole." When Julie, age eleven was asked the same questions, she replied that neither child should be punished because "they made the holes accidentally and not on purpose." These comments illustrate the difference between concrete operational and formal operational thought.

Simons suggested that service-learning activities reinforce the following Piagetian concepts.

1. Learning, particularly for young children, needs to be experientially based, and is more effective when the classroom is expanded into the real world.
2. Cognitive development relies not only on physical and mental interactions with the environment, but also on social interactions, centered in relevant experiences with others, that help children gain a better understanding of others and recognize the shortcomings in their own thinking.

3. Children learn best through self-initiated activity, in which they have the freedom to explore, discover, choose their own tasks, construct knowledge, and direct their own behaviors and learning experiences.
4. Reflection enhances learning by bridging the gap between the abstract and the real, identifying common elements, and building new more mature understandings.

Levels of Social Development

Research by Rosen indicates that the transition from concrete operational thought to formal operational thought is influenced by the individual's ability to see things from another's point of view, that is, by the individual's level of social perspective-taking. Questions about why service-learning activities appeal to students of one age but not students of another may, therefore, be related to student levels of social perspective-taking. Selman outlined five sequential stages in the development of social awareness and understanding. Research into the implications of Selman's work for the design and evaluation of service-learning programs has been published by Woehrle.

Stages of Moral Development

Research by Kohlberg and Lickona suggests that the development of moral reasoning passes through distinctive cognitive structures or stages that determine: (a) what a person sees, (b) how a person organizes information, and (c) the judgments a person makes about what someone should do under carefully prescribed circumstances. It is important to note here that Kohlberg's theory is not about what a person actually does.

Kohlberg's theory suggests fours stages of moral development encompassing the K-16 years. According to this theory, the underlying reasons for participating in school-based service-learning activities will vary according to the student's stage of moral development.

Gilligan proposed an alternate model for moral development, based on her work with women facing real-life, rather than hypothetical, dilemmas involving moral issues. At Level 1 (girls, Grades 4 to 8), goodness is defined by a pragmatic focus on the self. There is a feeling of powerlessness that often makes relationships painful. The transition from Level 1 to Level 2 is characterized by moving from selfishness to a sense of responsibility for others. There is an increasing ability to see one's limitations and oneself realistically that makes relationships with others less painful.

At Level 2, characteristic of many young women of high school and college age, society's values are adopted and goodness is defined as sacrificing self for others. Fear of abandonment makes acceptance by others increasingly important, often resulting in an avoidance of self-assertion. The transition from Level 2 to Level 3 involves shifting the focus from goodness to truth, with an increasing tendency to question the logic of self-sacrifice. At Level 3 goodness is defined in terms of nonviolence and caring for others.

From Gilligan's perspective, motivation for participating in servicelearning activities would be: Level 1, pragmatic self-interest; Level 2, desire to protect the less fortunate; and Level 3, a sense of caring for others (while caring for self)-

William Perry's model of intellectual development is based on his work with college students but can be extrapolated backward to include high school students. His model includes three broad positions dualism, relativism and commitment that tend to guide the individual's perception, organization, and evaluation of knowledge and values.

The position of dualism, which would include almost all high school students and most college freshmen, is characterized by a belief that all information is either right or wrong. Where uncertainty seems to exist, there are only three possible explanations: (1) the authorities are playing games with me, (2) the authorities have made a mistake, or (3) the authorities do not have all the answers yet, but someday they will. The position of relativism, which would include most college sophomores and juniors, is characterized by a belief that knowledge and questions of personal identity are either uncertain or valid only within the context of non-absolute criteria for making judgments. The position of commitment, not achieved by most college students until their senior year or later, is characterized by attempts to reflect on and define one's identity in terms of commitments made and lived out, with actions and beliefs being fully integrated.

Design and Evaluation of Service-Learning Programs Erikson's theory of psychosocial development contributes to the design and evaluation of service-learning programs by describing the predictable developmental challenges children and young people feel and have during their years in school. Knowledge of these challenges can be used to guide decisions about the kinds of service activities that are most appropriate for each age group and also to frame research questions regarding observed student outcomes.

Unfortunately, assessing the relationship between program design and student needs from the perspective of psychosocial development is not straightforward. One instrument, Measures of Psychosocial Development, is available to assess positive and negative resolution of tasks associated with Erikson's stages. However, there is no similar instrument for assessing resolution of Chickering's vectors. Instead, a combination of instruments is needed, including: (a) the Erwin Identity Scale; (b) the Interpersonal Relationship Inventory; (c) the Omnibus Personality Inventory and (d) the Developing Purposes Inventory-2;

The developmental theories of Kohlberg, Gilligan and Perry contribute significantly to the design of service-learning programs by describing the process people use to perceive and make meaning out of what they experience. Kohlberg provided service-learning practitioners with a model for understanding how students view what is right and their reasons for then doing it. Gilligan raised important gender issues and reminded program designers of the importance of caring.

Perry's unique contribution may be his description of the alternatives to moral development: temporizing, escape, and retreat. These alternatives may result when there is either an overload or a prolonged absence of challenge within the environment. In addition to the original Perry oral interview, one written tool exists to assess development along Perry's model, Measures of Epistemological Reflection.Problems exist in assessing the actual relationship between program design and impact from the perspective of moral development. The first relates to the tools used to assess levels of moral development. The original assessment tool, Kohlberg's Moral Judgment Inventory, requires subjects to be interviewed using a set of standardized moral dilemmas. Responses are taperecorded, transcribed, and then scored by a trained rater, a process that is both time consuming and expensive. Two alternatives exist, both using Kohlberg's dilemmas. One is Rest's "Defining Issues Test"(DIT). Subjects are offered multiple responses to each question and are asked to select the response that is closest to their current way of thinking. The second, the Measure of SociomoralMoral Reflection, is a paper-and-pencil instrument that requires subjects to generate their own responses to each question.Research on moral development indicates that individuals can recognize a response before they can spontaneously produce it on their own. This means that scores on the DIT are typically about one stage higher than an individual's true level of moral development. Related to this is the fact that the DIT does not really measure moral development, but rather levels of what Rest called "principled reasoning. "A second problem is that research in moral development indicates that movement from one stage to the next can take anywhere from six months to three years. Given the fact that most school-based service-learning programs last less than nine months, detecting significant pre-to-post changes in stages of moral development may be problematic at best. The third issue has to do with the fact that both the DIT and the SMRM require at least a middle school reading level, thus making assessments of middle school and at risk students difficult.Additional factors influencing development, and therefore, student outcomes, include:

- The degree to which the individual cares about the issue related to the service activity. There are two issues to consider in this regard:

1. When students are personally involved in selecting the service activity, they are far more likely to buy into the program and care about what happens; and
2. When there are clear connections between the classroom and the service activity, students are far more likely to see the importance of what they are doing and more likely to invest themselves in the program.

- Opportunities for reflection are included throughout the service activity, enhancing the likelihood of positive impacts from the service. Without reflection, they are likely to view their service experience negatively.

- How often the challenge is repeated. Service experiences need to be repeated many times and in many different ways to maximize potential positive learning impacts.
- Whether the level and kind of challenge associated with the service activity is balanced by an appropriate level of support from teachers and other adults who care about what the student may be experiencing.

In simple terms, if students are involved in a service activity, such as working with the homeless, they may perceive their experience to be extremely challenging to their world view and sense of how things are. If no adults are present to encourage them to continue their involvement in this service activity and to help them reflect on the meaning of their experiences, the students may feel overwhelmed and quit. On the other hand, if students are involved in service activities only with people like themselves, they may find their experiences to be too supportive. There is no challenge and hence, no reason to examine their current world views. Well-designed service-learning programs seek to balance developmentally appropriate challenge with appropriate levels of personal support in order to invite and encourage student risk-taking and growth.

Design and Evaluation Questions Based on Stages of Development

The following is a list of design and evaluation questions resulting from use of these theories that can be used to guide service-learning research and practice.

- Were service activities designed from the perspective of one or more developmental theories? If so, what assessments were made? In what

Perspective of Learning Styles:

Personality Type: The Myers-Briggs Type Indicator.Another way of approaching the design and evaluation of service-learning activities is through the use of learning styles. Two approaches are considered in this section: Jung's theory of psychological types and Gardner's theory of multiple intelligences.

According to Jung, there are four basic mental processes sensing, intuition, thinking, and feeling used by everyone but not equally preferred and developed. Individuals tend to use the processes they prefer most and, through repeated use, develop expertise in the kinds of activities associated with these preferences, resulting in characteristic habits, attitudes, and behaviors associated with that type. Jung suggested that, as individuals move into mid-life and beyond, they are increasingly challenged to appreciate and make appropriate use of their less preferred learning styles.

Jung's theory was operationalized by Myers in the Myers-Briggs Type Indicator and by Meisgeier and Murphy on the Murphy-Meisgeier Type Indicator for children (the MMT1C). The MBTI, which assumes a high school reading level, identifies four basic personality dimensions: (1) extraversion-introversion, (2) sensing-intuition, (3) thinkingfeeling, and (4)judging-perceiving.

The MMTIC, which has a reading level appropriate for Grades 3 through 6, adds an additional scoring category; classifying children who do not demonstrate clear preference for one side of the E-I, S-N, T-F, or J-P scales as undetermined, based on the assumption that psychological type is a developmental phenomenon and that some children may not be fully developed in terms of their type.

The extraversion-introversion preference indicates a person's preferred way of interacting with the world. Extraverted individuals, designated by the letter E, prefer to spend most of their time and energy interacting with the world of people, events, and things. Introverted individuals, designated by the letter I, prefer to spend most of their time and energy being alone with their thoughts. Extraverts typically need to experience something before they can understand it, whereas introverts usually need to understand something before they will risk doing it.

The sensing-intuition preference has to do with basic differences in how people become aware of what is going on in their world. Sensing individuals, designated by the letter S, are primarily interested in facts and details and in what is going on here and now. They focus their time and energy on collecting information with their five senses. Intuitive individuals, designated by the letter N, use this information to speculate on meanings and future possibilities.

The thinking-feeling preference has to do with how people make decisions and commitments. Thinking individuals, designated by the letter T, prefer to make decisions and commitments logically and impersonally, based on a careful analysis on the potential consequences of various courses of action. Fairness is defined as impersonal adherence to rules and principles; treating everyone the same. Feeling individuals, designated by the letter F, prefer to make decisions and commitments based on a prioritized set of personal values, including how they feel about the issue in question. Because consideration for the needs of others is important to them, they define fairness as standing up for the rights of the individual, regardless of what the rules say.

The judging-perceiving preference has to do with the kind of world in which people prefer to live. Judging individuals, designated by the letter J, prefer to live in a decisive, orderly, planned way and are oriented more towards controlling life than experiencing it. In contrast, perceiving individuals, designated by the letter P, take a more flexible, adaptable, tolerant approach to life, preferring to experience life rather than control it. Differences related to gender and ethnic background have also been observed.The existence of four different preferences, resulting in 16 different personality types (no one type better than another), is supported by a growing body of empirical evidence. There is also a growing body of research supporting the hypothesis that these preferences are linked to visible and measurable differences in preferred learning styles. These preferences would also result in potentially different learning experiences and outcomes for participants.

Multiple Intelligences

Howard Gardner suggested that intelligence has more to do with the capacity for solving problems and fashioning products in a context-rich and naturalistic setting than with looking at how a student does when taken out of his or her natural learning environment and asked to do tasks he or she will probably never have to do again (e.g., taking a standardized test such as the SAT or ACT). The eight intelligences identified by Gardner and curriculum-based service-learning and reflective activities that might be related to them. Research by Armstrong and Campbell indicated that teachers can use the theory of multiple intelligences in a variety of ways.

- As an instructional process that provides numerous entry points into lesson content;
- As a reason to develop each student's talents early in life;
- To organize classroom learning stations;
- To teach students self-directed learning skills; or
- To establish apprenticeship programs with community experts to teach students real-world skills.

Concluding Comments

The purpose of this chapter has been to show how developmental and learning theory may be used, alone or in combination, in the design and evaluation of age-appropriate, curriculum-based service-learning activities. It is hoped that this theory-based approach will contribute to a better understanding of the connections between service-learning programs and resulting student outcomes. As these connections become clearer, service-learning programs can be designed to maximize the probability of achieving positive academic, personal, interpersonal, ethical, and vocational impacts for each and every student who participates in service-learning.

14

Teacher Research in Research Methodology

Introduction

Studies have shown effects for service-learning on a range of outcomes including grades, motivation to learn, social and personal responsibility, self-esteem and attitudes toward diversity. To date, however, servicelearning investigations in P-12 classrooms have primarily been the domain of those external to the classroom (i.e., college and university researchers or evaluation specialists interested in its effects). Studies by the teachers who actually design and implement service learning projects have been notably absent.

The exclusive emphasis in the field of service-learning on researchergenerated studies stands in contrast to developments in the larger field of research on teaching. For almost 20 years, educational researchers have acknowledged the difficulty of establishing generalizable laws about teaching and learning given the multivariate world of the classroom and the contextualized nature of these processes. In response, many have adopted qualitative forms of inquiry such as ethnography in order to obtain a more textured understanding of the ways in which particular curricula or techniques are experienced by participants. Teacher research is consistent with this recognition of the indeterminacy, complexity, and tenuousness of educational findings. Proponents of this point of view argue that teachers, as insiders to a classroom community, are in the best position to articulate the frameworks within which members apprehend classroom life. Interest in teacher research has also been stimulated by concerns about the marginalization of teacher knowledge and the desire to add teachers' power and voice to the field of educational research.

The purpose of this chapter is to suggest an increased role for teacher research on service-learning. Teacher research can provide insight into the situational variables that mediate service-learning, as well as into the lived experiences of participants. Encouraging teachers to contribute to the dialogue on service-learning is consistent with the democratic and emancipatory purposes of this approach. Conducting teacher research can enhance teachers' autonomy in analyzing and solving the problems of designing, implementing, and improving service-learning in their classrooms. Finally, investigations by practitioners may be more accessible to teachers, increasing the likelihood that they will apply the results of service-learning research to their own practice.

Definition

Although teacher research is a family of approaches rather than a single method, definitions share some agreement about its nature, goals, and agents. According to Hopkins, teacher research is "research in which teachers look critically at their own classrooms primarily for the purpose of improving their teaching and the quality of education in their schools". Carr and Kemmis defined teacher research as

a form of self-reflective enquiry undertaken by participants in social situations in order to improve the rationality and justice of practices, their understanding of these practices, and the situations in which these practices are carried out.

Noffke noted that teacher research is "at once a set of things one can do, a set of political commitments that acknowledges that... lives are filled with injustice and a moral and ethical stance that recognizes the improvement of human life as a goal.

The literature on teacher research reflects disagreement over issues such as the appropriate focus of inquiry or level of collaboration between teachers and university researchers. However, there seems to be agreement that formal investigations of teaching and teacher research differ in several key epistemological principles including their assumptions about the sources, purposes, and use of knowledge about teaching. Formal investigations, even those concerned with problems of learning and instruction, tend to address theoretical or methodological questions, many of which derive from disciplines other than education, such as anthropology and psychology. In contrast, the questions for teacher research studies originate from teachers' own experiences. Thus, the questions for teacher research projects are highly reflexive, and typically concern immediate classroom problems.

Results of formal research typically take the form of propositional knowledge about teaching and learning, whereas those of teacher research assume the shape of practical knowledge, such as procedural knowledge or narrative. By meeting scientifically established standards for proof, the results of formal research are characteristically intended to generalize beyond the research setting, while the results of teacher research are intended mainly to exert influence on one or several teachers' practice.

History of Teacher Research

Most authors trace the origins of teacher research to action research, a method pioneered by Collier and Lewin. Collier, a Commissioner of Indian Affairs, assisted Native-American communities to conduct research on local problems. Lewin, a social psychologist, defined action research as "research on the conditions and effects of various forms of social action and research leading to social action". He proposed a cycle of "action-research-action" that would yield both the advancement of knowledge and also social change.

The leading early figure in the application of action research to education was Corey. Corey and teachers associated with Teachers' College Columbia conducted numerous research projects on curriculum and instruction.

In the late 1950s and 1960s, as support for a formal science of education housed in universities and research and development laboratories increased, acceptance of teacher research waned.

Proponents of teacher research, such as Taba, continued to promote the activity, not as an instrument for education reform but as a tool for teacher change.

In the 1970s, Lawrence Stenhouse, at the Centre for Applied Research in Education, advocated teacher research in order to include teachers in the processes of curriculum development and evaluation. Reacting against the outside-in nature of contemporary curricular reform, Stenhouse argued that curriculum was a set of hypotheses to be tested and revised by the teacher. Teacher research was also viewed as a means to professional emancipation, allowing teachers, rather than external evaluators, to control their professional development.

Teacher research achieved additional momentum in the 1980s. CochranSmith and Lytle pointed out that the several movements that contributed to its renewal collectively rejected a view of the teacher as technician rather than creator and mediator of knowledge. In many cases, too, proponents of teacher research shared a commitment to altering the fundamental social and political organization of schools.

In the field of language arts in the 1980s, an emphasis on process models of learning led to a view of reading and writing as active, personal, and meaning centered. Literacy performances were understood as holistic efforts, inseparable from the student's membership in a language community and from family and social influences. In order to grasp the complexity of students' literacy acts, the teacher him or herself needed to become a "RE-searcher."

The 1980s also marked the integration of teacher research with critical social theory. Critical social theorists encouraged teachers to analyze the ways in which educational practice could perpetuate the race and gender-based inequities of the broader society and to collaboratively seek the transformation of schools.

In the 1990s, teacher research gained broad acceptance in schools and in teacher education programs as a component of professional development and programmatic reform initiatives. However, during this period, teacher research was also subject to increased scrutiny on both epistemological and methodological grounds. Proponents argued that teacher research permitted the elaboration of a unique form of knowledge about teaching: practical knowledge or understandings gleaned from experience and grounded in the contingencies of specific teaching situations rather than formal knowledge. However, Fenstermacher noted that, "There are serious epistemological problems in identifying as knowledge that which teachers believe, imagine, intuit, sense, and reflect upon". As with the formal science of teaching and learning, the claims of teacher researchers needed to be supported by epistemic warrants that, ideally, render them objectively reasonable.

Teacher research was criticized on methodological grounds. For example, Huberman argued that the closeness to the classroom enjoyed by the teacher researcher can provide unique opportunities to generate interpretations, observe events as they unfold, and revise one's understandings. However, he also cited the difficulties of conducting research as an intimate participant. As Huberman stated, "caught up in our limited milieus filled with complexities, we can seldom make out, much less reflect on the rational and nonrational forces acting on those milieus". According to Huberman, to guard against distortion and bias there must be "a body of research, some robust methods, and a set of plausible constructs".

Conceptual Frameworks in Teacher Research

McCutcheon and Jung argued that teacher research studies can be based in different epistemological frameworks, each of which makes particular assumptions about the nature of reality, the relationship between the researchers and the objects of knowledge, and the goals of research. One potential source of teacher research projects is the informal epistemology of the classroom teacher (i.e., theories, scripts, etc., about students or classroom events constructed out of practical experience). Alternatively, teacher research can be grounded in formal epistemologies.

One such epistemology, positivism, assumes that there is an objective reality that exists separate from the observer and that the nature of this reality can be determined through rigorously controlled observation. Positivist researchers also assume that phenomena are governed by general laws and that the goal of science is to discover these relationships. Teacher researchers investigating service-learning from a positivist perspective might ask questions such as, "What is the impact of service-learning on students' mastery of standards and benchmarks?" "What correlations exist between the number of hours students have spent volunteering prior to this project and their attitudes toward service-learning?"

A second model of knowing is the interpretivist perspective. Interpretivism does not presuppose an external knowable reality. Instead, knowing is personal and involves the interaction of features of situations and the cognitive structures of their participants. The purpose of research in the interpretivist framework is to determine the nature of the meanings assigned by insiders to a social situation. A teacher conducting an interpretivist study of service-learning might ask questions, such as, "How do students understand the meaning of servicelearning?" "How do students construct the causes of social problems or the individuals they are seeking to serve?"

A third perspective is the critical theory perspective. Critical theorists such as Carr and Kemmis reject the positivist model of teacher research and discount interpretivism as well because of its failure to empower participants to alter their situations. Critical theorists assume that social behavior, including teaching and research, reflects social, political, and economic categories. From the critical perspective, the goal of teacher research is to liberate teachers and students from oppression based on race, gender, or other aspects of personhood through praxis—a cycle of action and reflection. Praxis is viewed as the means by which practitioners can uncover their own and others' biases and create more just practices. Teachers conducting investigations of service-learning within a critical theory framework would view themselves as agents of social change. They would be concerned about the effects of service-learning on students' critical social consciousness and on problems such as inequity and discrimination. These teachers would also want to ensure that the servicelearning project itself not perpetuate differences in power and status between participants and those they sought to serve.

Rationales for Teacher Research in Service-Learning

There are several rationales for promoting teacher research on service-learning. Conducting research on servicelearning has the potential to be an effective tool for preparing teachers to use this approach. Current perspectives on teacher thinking suggest that practitioners actively construct knowledge about students and teaching situations. Teacher knowledge appears to be in the form not of declarative prescriptions, but of personal theories, scripts, and metaphors. Further, recent research suggests that teaching itself is not the routine application of empirically derived generalities, but a complex cognitive activity involving planning, interpretation, and decision making. Finally teacher change appears to be self-directed, a natural response to the need to create more workable practice, rather than the result of externally mandated training. The implication of these findings is that if teachers are to incorporate service-learning into their practice, they must be actively involved in the conceptualization, design, and assessment of service-learning activities. This view is supported by the results of the curriculum development efforts of the 1960s and 1970s, which indicated that teachers seldom directly replicate innovations in their classrooms, but interpret, modify, or abandon them according to their perceived fit with their beliefs about practice. Opportunities to conduct their own classroom research may facilitate teachers' adoption of service-learning. In addition, teacher research may help teachers become more effective in their use of service-learning. For example, Bennett found that "teacher researchers viewed themselves as better informed as experts in their fields who were better problem solvers and more effective teachers".

Conducting research on service-learning may also empower teachers to act as agents of educational and social change. Several authors have argued that servicelearning is consistent with more holistic, authentic, socially constructed, and responsive educational practice. To articulate the linkages between servicelearning and district or school improvement, however, teachers need to have a thorough understanding of this approach. Conducting teacher research studies can be one route to understanding. In addition, teacher research can help teachers acquire the "communicative competence" to structure district discussions of service-learning to include their concerns. Conducting teacher research on service-learning can also enhance teachers' awareness of the degree to which schooling is coextensive with historical and political problems. Such awareness may strengthen teachers' willingness to act as public advocates for learning and for children and families and to reflect on the ways in which they create the conditions for social justice or injustice in their own practice.

Finally, findings from teacher research can be an important addition to the knowledge base on service-learning. Dewey argued that teachers should be producers as well as consumers of educational research, stating, "A constant flow of less formal reports on special school affairs and results is needed". Existing research in service-learning has identified several variables that mediate the impacts of service-learning, such as opportunities for structured reflection; integration of service and academic goals; and characteristics of individual students' experiences. By tapping into teachers' extensive practical knowledge of students and the conditions under which particular teaching approaches work, teacher research studies can contribute information about how, why, and for whom service-learning is effective. Teacher research studies can also provide a body of case studies about service-learning.

Cochran-Smith and Lytle argued that teacher research can contribute to two general knowledge bases: local and public. In addition, they have identified several types of knowledge that can be generated by this research. Locally, teacher research can contribute to the teacher's professional development. For example, it can inform teachers about how a particular curriculum is constructed in their classrooms, or how students learn. In addition, teacher research can contribute knowledge to the local community of teachers (i.e., it can inform teachers about the ways in which a particular method is being implemented across classrooms or contribute to decisions about district reform). Publicly, teacher research can contribute case studies to the educational research community and questions for further research.

Teacher research on service-learning has the potential to contribute similar information to local and public knowledge in education. However, because service-learning involves the integration of local or public social problem solving with academic learning, it has the potential to contribute insights and questions and to influence decision making in local and public knowledge communities beyond those concerned with educational practice. Table 10.1 on the next page illustrates the knowledge domains to which teacher research on service-learning can contribute and examples of the knowledge such research could provide:

Teacher Research in Service-Learning

The following example illustrates a teacher research project in servicelearning. Between 1993 and 1994, researchers from Central Michigan University, Michigan State University, and Alma College directed a project in which four K-12 teachers conducted teacher research studies of servicelearning. In the first session of the project, the teachers articulated concerns about their students or their teaching that they felt might be addressed by service-learning. Using the technique of graphic representation, they created maps identifying these dependent variables, as well as antecedent variables and possible mediating variables. From these representations, the teachers were able to formulate researchable questions for teacher research projects. For example, Jeri, a third-grade teacher, was interested in the effects of a project that paired elementary students who needed special attention with at risk middle school "buddies" on participants' attitudes toward school and attendance. Linda, a middle school teacher, wanted to engage all the students in her team in a community restoration project at a local opera house. She was concerned about the impacts of the project on students' self-esteem and attitudes toward their class and their community. Warren, a high school social studies teacher, wanted his students to become more active, self-directed learners. He developed a research project in which students investigated the consequences of a proposal to locate a low-level radioactive waste facility in their community. Warren was curious about the consequences of the research project for students' engagement (e.g., participation, being prepared for class) and meaningful learning.

The second session of the teacher research training focused on methodology. The differences between formal and teacher research in goals, audience, and methods were discussed. Teachers were introduced to the steps in the action research process. The session addressed research ethics, constraints on teacher research, and techniques for enhancing the validity of teacher research findings such as triangulation. The majority of this session was devoted to data gathering techniques. Each teacher developed a data collection matrix for his or her project that listed the research questions for their project and three data gathering techniques appropriate to each question. For homework, teachers were given additional readings on data collection methods and asked to prepare a detailed design for their project for the next session.

In the third session, teachers shared the methods they had chosen. They had selected a range of methods such as teacher and student journals, observation, standardized and teacher-developed questionnaires, interviews, and student work. For example, Jeri created two questionnaires to assess the attitudes of the middle school and elementary children toward school. In addition, she had students complete evaluations of each buddy session. Linda decided to ask the school counselor to administer a standardized self-esteem index to students. Their parents were also asked to complete the same survey to reflect their perceptions of their children. Linda also used a teacher log, interviews, and photographs. Warren decided to use to use two of his traditional classes as a comparison group. The primary data source for his study was self-report sheets on which students recorded the types and settings of learning tasks they engaged in each day. Warren also used a teacher journal, interviews, student work, and video recordings.

Over the next several months, teachers implemented their projects and collected data. The next phase of the project that involved data analysis and report writing was the most difficult. Teachers received a manual on data analysis in teacher research created by the project directors. In the next group session, the teachers discussed and practiced techniques for analyzing their narrative data, such as coding, thematic analysis, and creating maps. Warren, for example, developed a system for coding the level of intrinsic motivation for learning apparent in students' questionnaires. After the session, the teachers continued analyzing data and writing and occasionally meeting individually with researchers to clarify questions.

The teachers presented the results of their projects at a national servicelearning conference. The results of Jeri's project showed no change in self-esteem for the students; however, both middle school and elementary students showed improved attitudes toward school. Linda found that the community restoration project required a much greater investment of time than expected and was not able to give the self-esteem post-test before the end of the year. However, interviews with a subsample of her students indicated that the project had caused them to have more positive feelings toward their classmates and their town. Warren found that the self-reports of students involved in the service-learning research project more frequently indicated intrinsic interest in learning than did the self-reports of learners in his traditional classes. For example, participants were more likely to describe learning tasks in terms of task-internal features, such as the types of cognitive activity involved, rather than external features, such as grades. They were also more likely to report working on and thinking about the project outside of class.

In each of these cases, the teachers were able to use teacher research to arrive at conclusions about the effectiveness of service-learning in the context of their specific classrooms and to modify their classroom planning and practice based on these conclusions.

In summary, as these cases suggest, teacher research offers several potential benefits:

1. Although formal research can provide normative information about the effects of service-learning and mediating variables, a body of teacher research cases is needed if we are to gain a more precise understanding of the influence of contextual variations and the specific processes involved in designing and implementing servicelearning activities effectively.
2. Curricular innovations and research-based principles are not implemented directly by teachers, but interpreted, or modified based on their consistency. Knowledge about teachers' models of practice suggests that a different perspective on teacher training in servicelearning is needed. Specifically there is a need for training programs that actively engage teachers in the conceptualization, design, and evaluation of service-learning experiences. Teacher research projects can be a key component of such training programs.
3. One goal of service-learning as a curricular method is to enhance students' capacities for productive citizenship. Although most teachers accept some responsibility for promoting the personal and moral development of their students, a concept of teaching as a "bounded, " technical activity has dominated the profession. Conducting inquiry

on the effects of service-learning may heighten teachers' awareness of their responsibilities in civic education and public advocacy. Involvement in teacher research may also make teachers more cognizant of injustices in their own teaching.

The potential effects of teacher research on service-learning are recursive and multidimensional. Engaging in spirals of action, research on practice, and new action can provide teachers with a continuously improving knowledge and pedagogy in service-learning. Teacher research can simultaneously bridge the gap between service-learning theory and practice by adding to the knowledge base in service-learning the voices and concerns of teachers themselves.

15

Subset Principles in Research Methodology

Introduction

The goal of an acquisitional study is to examine the compatibility between a linguistic theory and acquisitional data, the study should be submitted to at least two tests. First, it must be established that the learner data actually do reflect knowledge of the phenomena under investigation; and, second, it must be established that the linguistic constructs under investigation are theoretically sound and defensible, given the current state of a theory's development. If the study fails either one of these tests, its results cannot be considered a valid contribution to SLA theory construction.

In this chapter I apply these two tests in evaluating SLA studies that have explored a possible role for the Subset Principle (SP) in SLA. Although the SP has been offered as a general learning constraint on first-language acquisition, the few SLA studies that have examined the SP have generally concluded that the SP does not apply in SLA. Using the two tests of a study's validity, I demonstrate that the arguments offered to date against application of the SP in SLA cannot be considered valid. I show that, in some instances, the SLA studies have design problems and that, therefore, the L2 data offered as evidence do not accurately represent knowledge of the phenomenon under investigation. In other instances I argue that current developments within linguistic theory motivate a reanalysis of the constructs under investigation and that, consequently, the studies' conclusions have no relevance to the SP.Establishing that existing arguments against application of the SP in SLA are not tenable does not, of course, demonstrate that the SP applies in SLA. In this regard, I offer an analysis of relative clause formation along with arguments that the SP in fact applies to relative clause acquisition. On the basis of existing L2 relative clause data, I then provide evidence that the SP does apply in SLA. The approach to research methodology taken in this chapter incorporates the assumption that successful theory construction in SLA requires careful scrutiny of both the appropriateness of task design and the soundness of theoretical proposals.

The Subset Principle

Berwick promoted the SP within a computational approach to language acquisition as a general learning constraint guiding much of language acquisition. Referring to a broad range of acquisitional phenomena, Berwick demonstrated how the SP guarantees that, where one hypothesized language is properly contained within another, the acquisition procedure will always guess the smallest language compatible with the positive evidence so far encountered. Because it is generally assumed that language learners have no access to negative evidence, the SP protects a learner from hypothesizing a language larger than the target language, given that there would be no way to retreat subsequently to the correct smaller language without negative evidence. Wexler and Manzini and Manzini and Wexler interpreted the SP more narrowly within a parametric theory of language acquisition. They viewed the SP as an independent learning principle that interacts with principles of Universal Grammar (UG) during acquisition to guide the setting of UG parameters. They formulated the SP as in (1) and illustrated its application to their Governing Category Parameter (GCP) in (2), a parameter of binding theory determining the interpretation of anaphors and pronominals.

(1) The learning function maps the input data to that value of a parameter which generates a language:

a.compatible with the input data; and

b. smallest among the languages compatible with the input data.
(2)y is a governing category for á iff ã is the minimal category which contains á and
a.has a subject, or
a.has an Infl, or
b.has a TNS, or
c.has an indicative TNS, or
d.has a root TNS

The GCP was formulated on the basis of the actual domains within which anaphors and pronominals in various languages are interpreted. English happens to have GCP value (2a) for both anaphors (e.g., himself) and pronominals (e.g., him).Crucially, in order for the SP to determine every value of the learning function, that is, to guide the acquisition of parameter values, Wexler and Manzini argued that the languages generated by the various values of a parameter of UG must lie in a strict subset relation to one another. This restriction, their Subset Condition, is given in (3).(3) For every parameter p and every two values i, j of p, the languages generated under the two values of the parameter are one a subset of the other, that is, $L_{(p(i))} C L_{(p(j))}$ or $L_{(p(j))} C L_{(p(i))}$ .In those instances where a parameter's values yield languages that do not lie in subset relations to one another, the SP does not apply. Wexler and Manzini demonstrated that the languages generated by the five values of the GCP do in fact lie in a subset relation to one another. Each of the five values in (2) defines a successively larger syntactic domain within which an anaphor requires a c-commanding antecedent and within which a pronominal disallows a c-commanding antecedent, in accordance with Chomsky binding principles. In accordance with Binding Principle A, an anaphor is bound in its governing category, and in accordance with Binding Principle B, a pronominal is free in its governing category. In the English sentences represented in (4), the labeled bracketing corresponds to those values of the GCP in (2) that are relevant to English.

(4) a. [e John knows that [c Bill wants [b Tom to discuss [a Mike's criticism of himself

b. [e John knows that [c Bill wants [b Tom to discuss [a Mike's criticism of him

Because English has GCP value (2a) for anaphors, Mike in (4a) binds himself as the only possible c-commanding antecedent within the governing category labeled a. Because English also has value (2a) for pronominals, Mike in (4b) is the only noun phrase (NP) that cannot serve as the antecedent for him, because him must be free in its governing category. In this case, any of the NPs Tom, Bill, John, or some sentence-external NP referent could serve as the antecedent of him, because all are outside of the governing category labeled a. Thus, (4b) actually represents four sentences of English, one for each interpretation of him, whereas (4a), with its one interpretation of himself, represents only one sentence of English.

Where the Subset Condition holds and the SP applies, Wexler and Manzini defined markedness hierarchies on the basis of the subset relations among the languages generated by a parameter's values. The parameter value that yields the smallest language is the unmarked value, and each successive value yielding a larger language is more marked than the preceding value. As Wexler and Manzini illustrated, the markedness hierarchy for anaphors is the opposite of the markedness hierarchy for pronominals. For anaphors, GCP value (2a) is unmarked because it defines the smallest language, and values (2b), (2c), (2d), and (2e), in that order, are progressively more marked. On the other hand, for pronominals, GCP value (2e) is unmarked because it defines the smallest language, and values (2d), (2c), (2b), and (2a), in that order, are progressively more marked.

From the learnability standpoint, a child learning English will require minimal positive evidence to set the GCP at the unmarked value (2a) for anaphors, because that value defines the smallest possible language. In setting the GCP for pronominals, however, a child learning English will require considerably more positive evidence to arrive at value (2a), because (2a) is the most marked value with respect to pronominals, the one defining the largest language.

Psychological Reality of the Subset Principle

Berent and Samar provided independent psycholinguistic evidence in support of the learnability predictions of Wexler and Manzini SP. A 56-item pencil-and-paper test in which half of the items were sentences containing the English anaphor himself and half were parallel sentences containing the English pronominal him was administered to 35 prelingually deaf college students and to a control group of 19 hearing college students. The sentences, which exhibited a variety of syntactic structures similar to those in (4), were constructed to determine the subjects' GCP values for English anaphors and pronominals.

Each test sentence was followed by a series of yes/no questions that probed subjects' interpretations of possible antecedents for the anaphor or pronominal contained in that sentence, including the possible selection of an external antecedent. In answering the questions about possible antecedents, subjects were instructed to consider a variety of interpretations for any given sentence. A sample test item is shown in (5).

(5) Jack learned that Don voted for himself.

a. Can himself = Jack?	YES	NO
b. Can himself = Don?	YES	NO
c. Can himself = another person?	YES	NO

Subjects' responses to the composite of the structures used in the 56-item test would reveal which of the GCP values in (2) had been set independently for anaphors and pronominals.

The deaf subjects comprised two separate groups that did not differ significantly in age, degree of hearing loss, age of onset of deafness, hearing status of parents, or sign language proficiency. They did differ, however, in their overall English language proficiency as measured by the Michigan Test of English Language Proficiency. The High Proficiency group had a mean score of 77.3 (SD = 1.2), and the Low Proficiency group had a mean score of 51.3 (SD = 1.4). Previous studies of prelingually deaf students' English language knowledge have revealed that deaf students often have greater knowledge of the unmarked properties of English but lesser knowledge of the marked properties of the language.

Therefore, Berent and Samar hypothesized that the subjects who tend to exhibit a more restricted knowledge of the marked properties of English might also have restricted knowledge of the marked values of UG parameters, in this case, the GCP. Specifically, it was predicted that both the Low Proficiency group and the High Proficiency group would show evidence of having set the GCP for anaphors at the correct unmarked value (2a), which defines the smallest language and which, from the standpoint of learnability, requires the least evidence to set. However, it was further predicted that, in view of their more restricted knowledge of the marked properties of English, the Low Proficiency group would also exhibit evidence of the unmarked, but incorrect, GCP value (2e) for pronominals because it, too, defines the smallest language and requires the least evidence to set. In contrast, the High Proficiency group, with its greater knowledge of the marked properties of English, was expected to approximate the correct marked value (2a) for pronominals.

These were precisely the results obtained. The High Proficiency group, along with the hearing control group, showed evidence of the unmarked value (2a) for anaphors and the most marked value (2a) for pronominals. The Low Proficiency group also showed evidence of the correct value (2a) for anaphors but indeed approximated the unmarked, but incorrect, root TNS value (2e) for pronominals. These parameter values were verified in a separate analysis of spontaneous writing samples from the two deaf groups. Thus, in the acquisition of a first language under conditions involving a severe restriction of positive (auditory) language evidence, individuals with lower general English proficiency appear to select grammars characterized by parameter values that generate a smaller set of sentences.

The results of Berent and Samar provided independent psycholinguistic evidence in support of Wexler and Manzini parametric theory of learnability. In verifying the markedness predictions of the SP, these results supported the SP as a determinant of the learning function for parameters of UG whose values conform to the Subset Condition.

Second Language Acquisition

Although the SP has been offered as a learning constraint on language acquisition from positive evidence, it was motivated by the learnability considerations of first-language acquisition. In the context of SLA, empirical support for the SP has not been readily forthcoming. In fact, most investigations of a possible role for the SP in SLA have offered evidence against it.

In the context of SLA, White summarized three presumed parameters of UG—the Adjacency Parameter, the Configurationality Parameter, and the Governing Category Parameter—and reviewed arguments against the role of the SP in SLA in the (re)setting of these parameters by L2 learners. In what follows, I address the arguments against the SP in SLA, and for each parameter I suggest an alternative analysis or cite problems with task design on the basis of which these arguments might be refuted. Finally, I review an analysis developed in Berent that supports the role of the SP in SLA.

The Adjacency Parameter

Stowell proposed the adjacency condition on the assignment of (abstract) Case to NPs, which requires an object NP, for example, to be adjacent to a governing verb, as in (6a) or (6b).

(6) a. Paul quickly opened the door.
b. Paul opened the door quickly.
c. *Paul opened quickly the door.

Stowell noted that the adjacency condition varies among languages. Whereas (6c) is ungrammatical in English because the door is not adjacent to opened, the equivalent French or Italian sentence is grammatical despite the intervening adverb. Stowell concluded, therefore, that the adjacency condition in its strict form applies in English: Even an intervening adverb is sufficient to block Case assignment.

In Berwick computational approach to the SP, strict adjacency was interpreted as the most restrictive assumption, therefore the unmarked case. Because adjacency violations like (6c) will never be encountered in English, the assumption of strict adjacency will never be dropped. However, when positive examples equivalent to (6c) in a language like French or Italian are encountered, indicating that adjacency is violated, then the most restrictive assumption is loosened.

Drawing on this interpretation, White explored the Adjacency Parameter in the context of SLA, using as subjects French speakers learning English as a second language (ESL) and English speakers learning French as a second language (FSL). Because English has the unmarked value [+ strict adjacency] of the Adjacency Parameter whereas French, admitting sentences analogous to (6c), has the marked value [- strict adjacency], it is possible to determine whether the SP guides ESL learners' acquisition of English relative to adjacency.

White considered two hypotheses, the subset hypothesis and the transfer hypothesis. According to the subset hypothesis, the French-speaking ESL learners should assume the unmarked value [+ strict adjacency] for English despite the fact that their first language has the marked value [- strict adjacency]. Therefore, they should not accept or produce adjacency violations as in (6c). According to the transfer hypothesis, the ESL learners should allow adjacency violations as in (6c), transferring the marked value from French. This result would provide evidence that the SP is not operative in SLA.

With respect to the English-speaking FSL learners, the subset hypothesis predicts that they will reject adjacency violations in French, that is, reject grammatical French sentences analogous to (6c). However, the transfer hypothesis predicts the same result because, in this case, the FSL learners would be transferring the unmarked English value onto French. Therefore, evidence for or against the SP in SLA hinges on the performance of the ESL learners.

The subjects completed two types of grammaticality judgment task and one sentence preference task in the target language. The results revealed that the FSL learners rejected many of the (grammatical) adjacency violations, applying strict adjacency to French. Because both hypotheses predict that the unmarked value [+ strict adjacency] should be assumed initially, the FSL learners' performance supports neither hypothesis. The ESL learners' performance, on the other hand, revealed that many of them accepted (ungrammatical) adjacency violations, assuming that English, like French, has the marked [- strict adjacency] value. This result supports the transfer hypothesis over the subset hypothesis. White concluded, therefore, that the SP fails to apply in SLA.

Actually, a more recent proposal in linguistic theory provides a new perspective on the distribution of adverbs in English and French and suggests a reinterpretation of adjacency phenomena that renders the preceding arguments against the SP vacuous. Pollock attributed a broad range of word order differences between English and French with respect to adverbs, sentence negation, questions, and quantifiers to a parameter of UG affecting thematic role (È-role) assignment.

The sentences pertinent to the current discussion are given in (7).

(7) a. John kisses often Mary.
b. Jean embrasse souvent Marie.
c. John often kisses Mary.
d. Jean souvent embrasse Marie.

Pollock proposed that the differences within minimal pairs (7a, b) and (7c, d) stem from a difference between English and French in verb-raising. Within the barriers framework of Chomsky, the relevant structures are as in (8).

(8) a.>$[_{CP}[_{IP}[_{NP}$John] [I' INFL $[_{AgrP}$AGR $[_{VP}[_{ADV}$often] $[_{V'}[_{V}$ kisses] Mary]

b.$[_{CP}[_{IP}[_{NP}$Jean] $[_{I'}$ embrasse $[_{AgrP}\, t_i [_{VP}[_{ADV}$souvent] $[_{V'}[_{V}\, t_i$] Mary]

UG requires that verbs assign both Case and È-roles to their NP arguments. In the barriers framework, when V raises to INFL (= I), it transmits its Èroles to its NP arguments from its raised position. Pollock maintained that the differences in (7) derive from the fact that verb movement to I is obligatory in French but is blocked in English. In French, V (embrasse) in (8b) must move out of VP first to AGR, leaving a trace, ti, in its original position, and then to INFL, leaving another trace in the AGR position. The resulting structure leaves the adverb (souvent) between the verb and the object NP, as in (7b). In English, V (kisses) in (8a) remains within the VP between the adverb and the object NP.

Pollock's explanation was that French AGR is transparent to È-role assignment because it is morphologically "rich" but that English AGR is opaque to È-role assignment because it is not rich enough morphologically to transmit a verb's È-roles. Accordingly, all lexical verbs in French raise to I, whereas lexical verbs in English cannot raise to 1. The only verbs in English that raise to I are those that do not assign È-roles, namely, be and have. This is evident from the position of always in John is always happy and in John has always been happy.

Assuming Pollock analysis, strict adjacency is simply a consequence of the opacity of AGR in English. Given this Opaque/Transparent AGR Parameter, if it were the case that French, relative to English (or vice versa), had a wider distribution of adverb positions—for example, if both (7b) and (7d) were grammatical options in French but only (7c) were grammatical in English then it would appear that the opaque value was marked, because it would generate a larger language than the transparent value relative to potential adverb positions. However, this is not the case; the relevant pairs in (7) are in complementary distribution. Accordingly, the two values of the AGR parameter do not define languages that satisfy the Subset Condition (3), and so the SP does not apply to determine the learning of this parameter.

Under these circumstances, the argument offered in White against the SP in SLA is untenable. Configurationality Parameter Zobl explored the possible role of the SP in guiding SLA in the context of Hale Configurationality Parameter. With respect to this parameter, [+ configurational] languages like English have argument positions that are structurally governed by a verb, whereas [- configurational] languages like Walpiri have argument positions that are not structurally governed but are instead associated with a verb via coindexing. Structural government in configurational languages results in relatively strict word order, whereas the lack of structural government in nonconfigurational languages results in relatively free word order.

Zobl considered the [+ configurational] value the unmarked value of the Configurationality Parameter. From the computational perspective, Berwick claimed that the narrowest language is one in which thematic and syntactic units are strictly aligned, for example, where agent-action-patient parallels subject-verb-object. If a language also allows the order patient-actionagent (as in passive sentences), it constitutes a larger language. Berwick therefore argued that, in accordance with the SP, the learner's first hypothesis will be strict thematic-syntactic alignment. Then nonconfigurational languages, which do not maintain a strict thematic-syntactic alignment, would reflect the marked value [- configurational] of the configurationality parameter.

Some linguists have described Japanese as a nonconfigurational language, although others have not. Zobl assumed that it is. As a test of the SP's applicability to SLA, Zobl conducted a study using as subjects adult Japanese speakers learning ESL. These subjects were given an "adjacency judgment" task consisting of eight sentences, including those in (9):

(9) a. I washed the glasses (carefully).
b. The girl cut her birthday cake (with a knife).
c. She asked me what I was doing (in a loud voice).

Subjects were required to mark the best location in each sentence for the portion given in parentheses. Zobl hypothesized that if the subjects committed certain adjacency violations, for example, if they inserted with a knife directly after cut in (9b), this would indicate that they were treating English as [- configurational] like Japanese by allowing constituents within the VP to appear in any order. This result would provide evidence against the SP because these L2 learners would not be assuming the unmarked [+ configurational] value of the Configurationality Parameter as their initial hypothesis.

Zobl's results revealed that, with increasing English proficiency (as measured by an in-house placement measure), his subjects made fewer adjacency violations in their judgments. Zobl concluded that the adjacency violations admitted by the subjects with lower English proficiency indicate that their hypothesized grammars do not exhibit structural government within the VP and that they therefore are viewing English as a nonconfigurational language. In contrast, the lower frequency of adjacency violations of the more advanced subjects implies structural government within the VP, characterizing a configurational language. This situation indicates an initial assumption of the marked value [- configurational] for English and the subsequent resetting to the unmarked value [+ configurational], in contradiction to the learnability predictions of the SP.

However, Zobl also reported production data from the same subjects that contradict the results of the adjacency judgment task. In journal entries and English compositions, the subjects committed very few adjacency violations, and there were essentially no differences in adjacency violations according to English proficiency level. These results imply an initial assumption of the unmarked value [+ configurational], in full accordance with the SP.

White pointed out certain design problems with the study reported in Zobl, for example, the lack of a native English-speaking control group and the fact that the stimulus materials consisted of one token each of only eight sentences. I add to these criticisms, arguing that the SP does not pertain to the phenomena investigated.

More recent developments in Japanese linguistics indicate that Japanese is in fact a configurational language, that NP arguments are governed within the VP, and that the relatively free word order of Japanese results from NP-movement under certain conditions. Given these developments, if there were a Configurationality Parameter, English and Japanese would reflect the same unmarked value [+ configurational].

With regard to the free word order among Japanese argument NPs, subject, object, and oblique NPs may generally appear in any order before the verb. The sentences in (10) illustrate three of the six possible word orders for the same Case-marked NPs.

(10) a. John ga hon o Bill kara nusunda. John NOM book OBJ Bill OBL stole 'John stole a book from Bill.

b. Hon o Bill kara John ga nusunda.

c. Bill kara John ga hon o nusunda.

In each sentence, ga unambiguously reflects nominative Case (NOM), o unambiguously reflects objective Case (OBJ), and kara unambiguously reflects oblique (OBL) Case. Now if there were a Configurationality Parameter and if the Japanese speakers in Zobl study initially assumed the marked [- configurational] value for English, as claimed, then, in addition to the kinds of adjacency violations targeted in Zobl's study, the subjects at the lower proficiency levels should be expected to accept and to produce in English, as in Japanese, any of the constituent orders in (11), as well as three other possible orders.

(11) a. John stole a book from Bill.

b. A book stole from Bill John.

c. From Bill stole John a book.

The marked value of the Configurationality Parameter would generate a language including all of these sentences. However, in describing his subjects, Zobi characterized those at the lower proficiency levels as exhibiting SVO word order and a phrase-initial head position in their English interlanguage, properties of a [+

configurational] language and, specifically, properties of English. Therefore, it is theoretically impossible that these subjects would accept or produce sentences like (11b) or (11c), treating English as [-configurational].

There are other grounds on which the word order differences between Japanese and English are not comparable in any way relevant to the SP. The two languages differ fundamentally in their Case-marking devices. Case in Japanese is reflected essentially through morphology; Case in English is reflected essentially through word order. With respect to this difference, there is no one-to-one correspondence between the Japanese and the English sentence in each of the pairs (10a)-(11a), (10b)-(11b), and (10c)(11c). In other words, sentence (11a) could be considered a subset of the three sentences in (10) only if English not only associated NOM Case with the preverbal subject position but also marked NOM Case morphologically. The fact that English does not mark Case morphologically is precisely why sentences (11b) and (11c) are ruled out independently by the Case filter of Chomsky (198 I). Thus, the sentences of (10) and the sentences of (11) comprise two disjoint data sets.

From the standpoint of thematic-syntactic alignment, the two sets are also disjoint. As noted earlier, Berwick assumption was that the learner's first hypothesis will be strict thematic-syntactic alignment, as reflected in canonical SVO word order in English, for example. This implies that Japanese, with its free word order, is not characterized by a strict thematic-syntactic alignment. But if the alignment entails, as Berwick maintained, that agent = subject and patient = object, then Japanese also instantiates this alignment, but in a typologically different manner. In Japanese, the alignment is a strict thematic-morphological alignment. If the learner's first hypothesis is in accord with the SP, then a strict thematic-syntactic alignment and a strict thematic-morphological alignment are equally restrictive assumptions. They are merely two typological dimensions of the same phenomenon.Given the foregoing discussion, there appears to be no basis for the existence of a Configurationality Parameter with respect to which English carries the unmarked value and Japanese carries the marked value. Furthermore, as noted, there were problems with task design in Zobl and contradictions between the judgment and production data. Therefore, the results of Zobl cannot be viewed as offering any evidence against the role of the SP in SLA.

The Governing Category Parameter

The GCP of Wexler and Manzini, defined in (2), remains the only UG parameter under discussion whose values have been shown to generate languages that satisfy the Subset Condition and to which the SP therefore must apply. It is also the only parameter for which the SP's learnability predictions have been verified in an independent learnability experiment for firstlanguage acquisition under crucial test conditions of restricted input. However, research on the GCP in SLA appears to provide some of the strongest legitimate evidence against the SP in that context. White provided a summary of much of the SLA research on the GCP. She discussed the results of Finer and Broselow, Finer, Hirakawa and Thomas. All of these studies, and more recently, Thomas and Lakshmanan and Teranishi (this volume, chapter 10) have investigated, through picture-identification or multiple-choice tasks, L2 learners' acquisition of the English anaphor himself/herself. The structures that these studies focus on include sentences like those in (12).

(12) a. Mr. Fat thinks that Mr. Thin will paint himself.

b. Mr Fat asks Mr. Thin to paint himself.

In accordance with Binding Principle A, and under the English value (2a) of the GCP, himself must be bound within the that-clause in (12a), namely, by Mr. Thin, because the that-clause is the minimal category that contains the anaphor and has a subject. Similarly, in (12b), Mr. Thin binds himself because here the minimal category containing the anaphor and a subject is the infinitival clause.

Collectively, the SLA studies examine interpretations of English sentences containing anaphors by speakers of Spanish, Korean, Japanese, and Chinese. Although English and Spanish share value (2a) of the GCP, the other three languages have governing categories larger than that defined by (2a), specifically, value (2e). Therefore, these studies could reveal whether L2 learners assume the unmarked value of the GCP, transfer to English the more marked GCP value of their first language, or adopt some other GCP value for English.

Generally, the results of these studies suggest that L2 learners do not initially assume the unmarked GCP value (2a) for anaphors. This finding militates, of course, against the role of the SP in SLA. In particular, Finer and Broselow and Finer found that local antecedents are favored in sentences with an embedded finite clause (i.e., Mr. Thin in (12a)), but that the assignment of nonlocal antecedents is quite frequent in sentences with an embedded infinitive clause. This pattern of results suggests value (2c) of the GCP, which is intermediate between English value (2a) and value (2e) of the Korean- and Japanese-speaking subjects who participated in those studies.

However, Hirakawa, Thomas and Lakshmanan and Teranishi reported somewhat higher incidences of nonlocal antecedents chosen in sentences like (12a) (though local antecedents are still preferred). This result is consistent with value (2e), the value associated with Korean, Japanese, and Chinese, rather than with a "compromise" value (2c). It would be reasonable to assume that subjects were transferring the GCP value of their first languages to the L2 if it were not for the fact that Thomas' Spanish-speaking subjects also showed evidence of adopting value (2e) for English. This rules out the transfer hypothesis, because Spanish has value (2a).

Overshadowing this entire theoretical discussion is the fact that all of the studies exploring the GCP in SLA suffer from methodological problems concerning task design (cf. the discussion in Lakshmanan & Teranishi). The study of binding theory and associated parameters is by nature more complicated than, say, the study of word order and associated parameters. Word order is a more salient feature of language than is the invisible association of two or more nominal expressions through coreference. Given the formidable task of developing reliable measures for assessing coreference in emerging grammars, the results of many child language studies that address binding theory have been held suspect.

Studies of the application of binding principles and the acquisition of GCP settings in SLA are susceptible to many of the same methodological problems to which child language studies are susceptible. Thomas argued that L2 coreference judgments may reflect subjects' preferences rather than actual grammars. She noted that Finer and Broselow speculation that Korean-speaking subjects assume GCP value (2c) in their grammars cannot be confirmed unless the subjects actually disallow nonlocal antecedents for sentence type (12a), rather than just show what may be a preference for local antecedents.Clearly, intricacies of task design can influence subjects' responses. For example, in explaining her task procedures, Thomas provided three sample task items, including.

David could see that Bill was looking at himself in the mirror. Who did Bill see in the mirror?

a. Bill

b. David

c. Either Bill or David

In this multiple-choice task, subjects are required to read the sentence and the following question and to circle one of the three possible choices of antecedent for the anaphor. Thomas explained that choices for the local antecedent, in this example, (a), and the nonlocal antecedent, (b), are listed in random order throughout the task, but that choice (c) always appears last.

There are problems with this design. First, one cannot take for granted that subjects at all proficiency levels will appropriately process the wh-question to which choices (a), (b), and (c).pertain. Processing this particular question, in which who is the object of see, presumes the acquisition of English whmovement and do-support. In this example, moreover, the same verb, see, occurs both in the matrix clause of the target sentence and in the question as a substitute for looking at in the embedded clause of the target sentence. Second, having thought through choices (a) and (b) as possible antecedents of the anaphor, subjects must rethink the associations for choice (c) after they have, most likely, decided between (a) and (b). Therefore, (c) choices should be artificially low, if only because they are always last. Furthermore, the disjunction either or is acquired late in first-language acquisition, and this may also be the case in SLA, so that choice (c) may not be fully understood. These disjunctions, moreover, are actually ambiguous, having an inclusive meaning (either p or q, or both) and an exclusive meaning (either p or q, but not both). Combined, these factors severely weaken the reliability of a subject's responses.

Similar task design problems occurred in Lakshmanan and Teranishi. The sample item they provided from their English interpretation test is given in (14), where subjects were to read the sentence and think about each of the following statements separately when indicating whether they agreed or disagreed.

(14) John said that Bill saw himself in the mirror.

1. 'Himself' cannot be John. agree disagree
2. 'Himself' cannot be Bill. agree disagree

Although this design solved problems by avoiding wh-questions and by not requiring subjects to rethink options after making choices, it introduced other problems. Specifically, the negative statements employing cannot followed by positive and negative agreement options place a heavy cognitive load on subjects (e.g., agreeing requires a negative response to a negative statement). Assuming that this cognitive load in the L2 is alleviated somewhat as English proficiency level increases, it is not surprising that, as Lakshmanan and Teranishi noted, their subjects at the lower proficiency levels gave the highest percentage of incorrect responses.

The task design employed in Berent and Samar to establish the GCP settings of prelingually deaf adults avoided the problems noted in the previous discussion. As illustrated in (5), there are no wh-questions for subjects to process, only simple yes/no questions in equation form, presented randomly. Furthermore, subjects were instructed to consider a different possible interpretation for a given sentence for each yes/no question. Finally, a procedure was employed that identified responses motivated by pragmatic bias and eliminated them from the statistical analysis.

Methodological problems notwithstanding, suppose that the results of all of the SLA studies pertaining to the GCP were accurate characterizations of English interlanguage grammars. How could they be explained, and what would be their implications for the SP in SLA?

In Berent, I provided an explanation for the results of existing SLA studies of the GCP that suggested that those results, even if accurate, do not constitute evidence against the application of the SP to SLA. Although Wexler and Manzini defined the GCP as in (2), Manzini and Wexler elaborated a more detailed definition of the GCP that incorporates Chomsky notion of accessible subject. Under this definition a governing category for an anaphor must contain an accessible subject, which includes the subject of an NP, infinitive, or small clause, but not the subject NP of a finite clause. In the case of a finite clause, the subject is the agreement element AGR, which is coindexed with the lexical NP and is responsible for subject-verb agreement and the assignment of nominative Case to the lexical subject.Because of the significant role of AGR in the Principles and Parameters Theory and, in particular, its role as an accessible subject, reasonable questions from the acquisitional perspective are: How and when is AGR acquired in SLA and how does its acquisition influence the setting of GCP values? Errors in phenomena like tense, agreement, and question formation persist for very long periods in SLA. All of these phenomena depend on AGR, either in its role in verb-raising or in its capacity to transmit È-roles and agreement features and to assign Case. Therefore, the lack of AGR in an interlanguage grammar, or its incomplete development, might have far-reaching consequences.If, in fact, the full instantiation of AGR occurs very late in SLA, then accessible subjects in finite clauses will also be a late development. Under this supposition, the results of the SLA studies of the acquisition of GCP values have a logical explanation irrespective of the SP. Where L2 learners bind anaphors in the root sentence, they do so by virtue of the absence of an accessible subject. Indeed, Aoun has demonstrated with respect to binding theory that a root sentence is the governing category for a governed element that lacks an accessible subject.Consider now the sentences in (12) from Finer and Broselow, repeated in (15) with structural detail added.

(15) a. Mr. Fat AGR thinks that [Mr. Thin will AGR paint himself]
b. Mr. Fat AGR asks Mr. Thin [PRO to paint himself]

If AGR in the embedded clause in (15a) is available to the L2 learner, then this AGR is an accessible subject for the anaphor and defines the embedded clause as the governing category under GCP value (2a). Therefore, himself should be bound by Mr. Thin in accordance with the SP. But if neither AGR in the embedded clause nor AGR in the matrix clause is available to the learner, then there is no accessible subject for the anaphor and the root sentence serves as the governing category. Accordingly, himself may be bound by either Mr. Fat or Mr. Thin. Pragmatic or semantic considerations should guide the selection of an antecedent, especially in forced-choice tasks requiring judgments on sentences out of context.

In (I 5b), the presence of the PRO subject of the infinitival clause introduces other acquisitional factors. As noted earlier, the subject of an infinitive is an accessible subject. Therefore, the embedded clause in (15b) is the governing category for himself and himself is bound by PRO (= Mr. Thin), which receives its reference in accordance with both binding and control theory. If L2 learners at certain stages have not acquired the nonlexical category PRO, then there will not be an accessible subject within the infinitival clause in (15b) and the governing category will again be the root sentence as in (15a). Equating the acquisition of AGR with the acquisition of PRO is a reasonable approach inasmuch as Chomsky considered PRO and AGR to be identical: They are both nominal elements that carry person, number, and gender features.With respect to the acquisition of the English GCP value in SLA, I noted earlier that the results of Finer and Broselow, Finer, Hirakawa, Thomas and Lakshmanan and Teranishi purportedly provide evidence against a role for the SP in SLA. However, the absence of AGR and PRO as accessible subjects in SLA permits a principled alternative analysis of the results obtained so far in SLA studies of the GCP. The SP would not be expected to apply to the setting of GCP values in SLA until AGR and PRO are acquired. Given this analysis, the results of these studies cannot be taken as evidence against the SP in SLA.

Evidence for the Subset Principle in Second Language Acquisition

In the preceding discussions of the Adjacency Parameter, the Configurationality Parameter, and the GCP, I have provided arguments to refute claims in the literature that the SP is inapplicable to SLA. In what follows, I provide evidence in support of the SP's applicability to SLA.In Berent, I reinterpreted Keenan and Comrie noun phrase accessibility hierarchy (NPAH) as a parameter of UG associated with the UG principle pertaining to operator-variable binding. This principle states that an operator is licensed by binding a variable. Within the barriers framework, in the sentences of (16), the whoperator who moves to the specifier position of the complementizer phrase (CP), leaving behind a coindexed trace, t_i, which is a variable.

(16) a. We saw the girl $_i$ [$_{CP}$ who $_i$ [$_{IP}$ t $_i$ [$_{VP}$ bought the book]]]

b. We saw the girl $_i$ [$_{CP}$ who $_i$ [$_{IP}$ the boy [$_{VP}$ knows t $_i$]]]

c. We saw the girl $_i$ [$_{CP}$ who $_i$ [$_{IP}$ the boy [$_{VP}$ took the book [$_{PP}$ from t $_i$]]]]

Since who c-commands and is coindexed with t in each sentence, it binds a variable as required by the principle of operator-variable binding. Also relevant to the binding requirements of relative clause formation is Safir R-binding, which is binding by the head NP of a relative clause. In (16), the girl R-binds the wh-operator who (as well as the variable t). These binding relationships must hold in order for relative clause sentences to be interpreted.

The NPAH reflects the fact that, in a given language, certain NP positions participate in relative clause formation whereas others do not and that patterns of relativizable NPs define an implicational hierarchy, wherein relativization of a given position on the hierarchy implies relativization of all higher positions on the hierarchy. For example, the positions of the traces in (16a)(16c) indicate relativization of an NP subject (SU), direct object (DO), and object of preposition or oblique NP (OBL), respectively. In accordance with the NPAH, if a language relativizes OBL it will also relativize DO and SU, and if it relativizes DO it will also relativize SU, but the reverse implications do not hold.

In associating these options with operator-variable binding in Berent, I reinterpreted the NPAH as a Relative Clause Parameter (RCP) with values based on the number of maximal projections an R-bound wh-operator crosses in order to bind a variable. In (16a) the operator crosses one maximal projection, IP; in (16b) the operator crosses two maximal projections, VP and IP; and in (16c) the operator crosses three maximal projections, PP, VP, and IP. I demonstrated that the values of the RCP define languages that satisfy the Subset Condition (3), and that therefore the SP will apply to determine the acquisition of these parameter values. A language with only SU relatives has the unmarked RCP value defining the smallest language; this value is predicted to be the easiest to learn. A language with SU and DO relatives has a more marked RCP value defining a larger language; this value is predicted to be harder to learn. Finally, a language with SU, DO, and OBL relatives has the most marked RCP value defining the largest language; this value is predicted to be hardest to learn (with respect to the structures in (16) under discussion). English exhibits the most marked value of the RCP.

The learnability predictions of the SP for the RCP were tested in Berent in an experiment involving prelingually deaf college students as subjects. As in Berent and Samar with respect to the GCP, I hypothesized that language acquisition under conditions of restricted auditory input associated with prelingual deafness should suppress the positive evidence required to set the marked English value of the RCP successfully. This hypothesis was confirmed. Subjects with lower general English proficiency showed knowledge of the unmarked SU value of the RCP but little knowledge of the more marked values. Overall, subjects' performance supported the learnability predictions of the SP for the RCP by correlating with the NPAH.

With regard to SLA, if L2 learners' acquisition of English relative clauses also correlated with the NPAH (reinterpreted as the RCP), this would provide evidence that the SP did in fact apply to SLA to determine the learning of RCP values. Indeed, the SLA literature includes several studies that demonstrate that L2 learners acquire English relative clauses in an order that correlates with the NPAH. For example, Gass, Gass and Ard and Fuller reported results that reveal that L2 learners, despite language background, produce, judge, and avoid English relative clauses in a manner consistent with the accessibility predictions of the NPAH. Furthermore, in instructional experiments, Gass and Eckman, Bell and Nelson provided results showing that, when L2 learners are taught relative clause formation on the more marked NPAH positions, they generalize this knowledge to the less marked positions, even without instruction on the less marked positions.

Given the reinterpretation of Keenan and Comrie NPAH in terms of the RCP in Berent as a parameter of UG associated with operatorvariable binding, the results of these L2 studies of English relative clause acquisition provide support for the application of the SP in SLA. Despite language background, L2 learners of English generally exhibit mastery of the unmarked SU value of the RCP but relatively less knowledge of each of the more marked values. Consistent with Wexler and Manzini parametric theory of learnability, where the values of a parameter define languages that lie in a strict subset relation to one another in accordance with the Subset Condition, the SP appears to predict the learning of English RCP values in SLA.

Conclusion

The goal of this chapter has been to review and evaluate studies that address the applicability of the SP to SLA. In carrying out this goal, I have employed a methodology that involves two tests of a study's validity—one that assesses the appropriateness of task design and one that assesses the soundness of theoretical linguistic proposals. I hope to have shown that attention to both concerns is essential for successful SLA theory construction.

Although the case is by no means closed on the extent to which the SP might apply in SLA, the methodology employed here reveals that arguments levied to date against the SP's application to SLA cannot be accepted as valid and that, furthermore, arguments in support of the SP's application to SLA can be developed on the basis of existing theoretical constructs and existing L2 data. Much further research is required both to identify other UG parameters to which the SP might apply and to determine whether the SP guides the setting of these parameters in SLA.

16

Constructs and Measurement in Research Methodology

Introduction

The chapter deals with theory construction rather than theory evaluation and so assumes that SLA does not yet have any full-fledged theories I want to call attention to a few troublesome theoretical, methodological, and empirical problems that parameter models will have to work out. The first of these has to do with syntactic theory itself. I point to some problems raised by non-GB theories like Generalized Phrase-Structure Grammar or Head-Driven Phrase-Structure Grammar, theories that have not received the attention they deserve in SLA research. Parameter models have so far taken the GB framework for granted, even though alternative accounts of some of the phenomena handled by parameter models have been developed in these other theories.

Second, I discuss measurement procedures in parameter models. Generative-based research in SLA sees itself as a branch of psychology, yet it differs from other branches in that it has virtually no coherent program of measurement research of its own. This has left it vulnerable on a number of fronts, two of which I deal with directly in this chapter. The first is a problem that Eckman characterizes as "endemic in all of the research reported thus far on L2 binding and much of the research attempting to test UG principles in SLA"; that is, "research in this area has reported aggregate results rather than results for individuals," and "principles of UG have been interpreted directly with respect to data instead of with respect to IL grammars." The second problem is that, the generative tradition recognizes a distinction between implicit knowledge of grammar and explicit or formal knowledge, yet no such distinction is taken into account in the methods that have been used in SLA research to date. Because implicit knowledge alone is the object of inquiry in parameter models, any systematic effects of explicit knowledge on measurement can contaminate the data.

In the latter part of my chapter, therefore, I describe methods of data analysis that (a) allow for generalizations across IL grammars without confounding differences between individuals, and (b) gauge the effects of explicit knowledge on grammaticality judgment tasks. I discuss three principles in order to illustrate how these methods can be put to use. The first is reflexive binding (r-binding), a proposed universal, by which a regular relationship between subjects and reflexive pronouns (r-pronouns) holds in all natural languages. The second has to do with parametric variation or has at least been treated as such in some generative-based SLA work. Some pronouns are proclitic in French but either enclitic or proclitic in Spanish. The third involves a language-specific characteristic of English that falls beyond the scope of parameter theory: The morphologies of English reflexive pronouns are distinct from the morphologies of their nonreflexive counterparts. In the study I describe, data on grammaticality judgments and response times from English- and Spanish-speaking learners of French were gathered via a computer-driven program and then analyzed using a factor procedure and a repeated-measures ANOVA. After discussing some of the advantages of the methods used, I argue that the results suggest that neither parametric variation nor r-binding accounts for the observed differential responses on grammaticality judgment tasks.

Sla and Linguistic Theory

Let us begin with a general definition of a parameter model, one that I hope is not too distorted. A parameter model is supposed to explain why certain structures in certain nonnative grammars (NNGS) are acceptable but others are not. Models of this sort should allow for three kinds of rules or principles that explain NNGS. First, there are "nonviolable universal principles of a quite abstract sort that account to a large extent for the similarities across all languages". These principles are part of what the learner "brings to the language learning task". The Specified Subject Constraint, which requires that r-pronouns be bound by specified antecedents, is an example of such a principle. Second, "associated with some of these principles are sets of parameters that define possible variations across languages, the setting of each parameter being determined on the basis of experience with the input". In addition to the pro/enclitic parameter, a head-initial/head final parameter, a topicalization parameter and an adjacency parameter have all been cited as examples of parameters in SLA research. Third, particular languages may have purely parochial or incidental properties that fall beyond the scope of parametric variation. For instance, both Spanish and French have morphologically distinct masculine and feminine definite articles in the singular (el/la and le/la, respectively), but only in Spanish does the distinction hold in the plural (los/las, compared to les/les in French). Although this may very well have a bearing on French as an L2 for Spanish speakers, it is doubtful that anyone would choose to construe this difference as a consequence of parametric variation.

Parameter models are parsimonious insofar as they account for what Chomsky characterized as the "chasm" between the complexity of a language and the limited amount of relevant linguistic data to which the learner has access. Parameter models need to postulate considerably less acquisition in language competence, which seems to be consistent with observations of first languages even if it seems somewhat less so as far as adult second languages are concerned. In any event, if learning the L1 is a matter of setting parameters, then learning an L2 is a matter of resetting parameters.

It should be emphasized that this line of SLA research has its origins in one of many theories (GB) and has in fact come to be dependent on that theory to the exclusion of all others. For instance, in the third section of Berent there is a review of a GB-internal debate regarding the parameter that is responsible for adverb placement in French and English. GB theory itself and its various tenets, however, are taken for granted throughout. In one sense this may be beneficial, inasmuch as GB has become a reasonably homogeneous theory, and its broad dissemination means that a growing number of SLA linguists are familiar with its scope, its terminology, and its methodology. But there will inevitably be some collateral risks to such a restricted view of syntactic theory.

Because we examine r-pronouns and binding later in this chapter, let us look at one relevant study involving first-language acquisition of anaphors and pronouns in order to illustrate some potential difficulties. Wexler and Chien tested children's sensitivity to two well-known principles of Chomsky Binding Theory:

(1) (A) An anaphor is bound in its governing category. (B) A pronominal is free in its governing category. They reported that: (a) children older than 5 years, 6 months know that antecedents must c-command reflexives, (b) children in the same age range do not know that a pronoun cannot have a local c-commanding antecedent, and (c) children's performance on tasks involving the c-command property of reflexives increases continuously from chance level at age 2 years, 6 months to almost perfect performance at 6 years, 6 months.

It is implicit here, as in all SLA research on parameters, that SLA hypotheses can be construed to test the psychological reality of particular formulations of UG principles. Non-GB formulations, however, have so far been roundly ignored. For example, Pollard and Sag gave an account of r-binding that differs considerably from the one assumed in Wexler and Chien. Pollard and Sag's account relied on an array of metarules and feature-passing principles that have no homologues in GB theory. They claimed that their analysis explains "facts involving reflexive pronouns in dislocated constituents (e.g. in cleft, pseudo cleft and topicalization constructions) which stand as blatant counterexamples to current, widely-accepted treatments within Chomsky's 'binding theory'". As far as I can tell, none of the stimuli in Wexler and Chien present any special problems for either GB or GPSG. The only obvious advantage in couching experimental research in the language of GB, in this case, is in the familiarity of the terminology. But if terminology rather than anything of substance is at issue, then clearly this line of research loses much of its interest. Unless one is prepared to test one theory against another, the jargon of traditional pedagogical grammars would serve equally well and might even reach a wider audience.

Moreover, it may be that GB or GPSG will have to be altered or perhaps even rejected entirely, perhaps for reasons that touch only marginally on whatever syntactic phenomenon one is researching. If one is interested in r-binding in second languages, for example, it is important to keep in mind that, were it shown that GPSG's assumptions about monostratal grammars could not account for certain types of dependencies or multiple extractions in some languages, then its account of r-pronouns in clefts and dislocations would have to be reworked entirely, because that account depends crucially on the distribution of the SLASH feature.

Of course, the same fate could befall GB. For instance, one hallmark of GPS/HPS grammars is the extraction of linear precedence from immediate dominance. Pollard and Sag argued, "it is a well-known fact (though little acknowledged in most recent syntactic theorization) that the linear order of sister constituents in a given language is not an idiosyncratic property of particular classes of phrases but rather is determined by general constraints which have force across the whole language". Without going into too much detail, let us recall that GPS/HPS grammars make use of immediate dominance (ID) rules of the form A ,B, C. A comma indicates linearly unordered constituents, so that a rule of this sort is compatible with the following structures:

(2) a. A B C
b. A C B

Traditional phrase structure rules like A * B C, on the other hand, are compatible with (2a) only. The linear order of nodes in a local tree is determined by independent principles. This permits generalizations about constituent order across the entire grammar of a language (e.g., that verbs in English are phrase-initial, that determiners and complementizers are phrase-initial even though they are not heads, that English has prepositions rather than postpositions. This immediate dominance/linear precedence (ID/LP) format, however, is possible only for grammars that have the Exhaustive Constant Partial Ordering property (ECPO). If a grammar possesses this property, "the set of expansions of any one category observes a partial ordering that is also observed by the expansion of all other categories". Gazdar pointed out that many hypothetical but plausible-looking phrase-structure grammars cannot be put into ID/LP format. Thus, simply to incorporate the ID/LP format into a theoretical framework is to claim that ECPO holds universally for natural languages. If it does, then GB will have to be reworked, because it fails to capture the generalizations expressed by the ID/LP format. It is not difficult to foresee adverse consequences for some work already done in SLA. For example, Flynn and Hulk research on head initial/head final parameters, as well as Berent's account of adverb order in French, would be rendered vacuous because they would presuppose an inadequate theory.

The standard position in the GPSG/HPSG camp has been to ignore the whole question of parameters because it is not yet clear what sort of evidence counts as proof for or against the claims being made. In fact, Gazdar rather bluntly dismissed "reference to questions of psychology, particularly in association with language acquisition" as "packaging and public relations". Chomsky also made some interesting remarks:

Suppose that we have two theories of the states of knowledge attained by a particular person and suppose further that these theories are "extensionally equivalent" in the sense that they determine the same E[xternalized]language in whatever sense we give to this derivative notion. It could in principle turn out that one of these grammars incorporates properties and principles that are readily explained in terms of brain mechanisms whereas the other does not. Although results of this sort are remote in the current state of understanding, they are possible.

Here we are jumping ahead to matters that concern the neurolinguist, but Chomsky's comments carry over to SLA research. It is possible in principle to develop two distinct generative theories that are descriptively equivalent in that they allow the same class of possible natural languages and disallow the same class of impossible natural languages. Under such conditions, SLA research could perhaps demonstrate by its methods that one of the two grammars incorporates principles that can be conveniently explained by certain psychological postulates in a way the other does not. A perusal of existing research on parameter models will clearly show that SLA is not so well developed at the present.

In fact, the preceding discussion itself begs important questions, because it is not at all certain that adult second languages abide by the sort of principles governing first languages. There is, moreover, neither widespread agreement nor adequate research on the methods of data analysis appropriate for SLA research. In this section I hope to make a little progress on both fronts by focusing on r-binding in second languages. As a convenient point of departure, let us begin with a familiar version of the general concept of interest (the Specified Subject Constraint), without committing to any particular theory:

(3) Specified Subject Constraint: A pronoun must be free in the domain of its nearest subject, and an anaphor such as each other must be bound in this domain.

As far as first languages are concerned, any theory of syntax will allow for some variation among speakers of a language, but not so much variation that this relationship between subject and r-pronoun holds for some speakers but not for others. In fact, because it evidently holds for all speakers of all languages, it is "presumably a principle of UG, or a consequence derived from principles of UG, perhaps with parameters set", insofar as it cannot be explained in terms of learning or experience alone (following the familiar arguments regarding poverty of stimulus, lack of corrective feedback, and so on). As far as SLA is concerned, research is at a considerable disadvantage because it has to live with far more inter- and intraspeaker variation, variation due to factors like first language, age at onset of acquisition, and type of exposure to the L2.

Still, uncovering any generalizations that may hold for all speakers is methodologically desirable in both first-language and second-language research. In theoretical syntax, for example, GB, GPSG, and HPSG all rely on one general principle to do the bulk of the work involved in r-binding: the Foot Feature Principle in GPSG, c-command in GB, and o-command (oblique command) in HPSG. Moreover, it is taken for granted in generative grammar that, given two accounts of some phenomenon in a language, the one that generalizes across a wider range of data is the better, other things being equal. Suppose some theory A proposes one principle to explain the relationship between an r-pronoun and its antecedent in local binding examples like (4):

(4) Do youi know yourself$_{i}$ / *himselfi?

A second principle explains the relationship in long-distance binding examples like (5):

(5) He, is going to make up his mind one of these days to try to control himself$_{i}$ / *herselfi

A different theory B, on the other hand, proposes a single principle to take care of both cases. The latter would win out, other things being equal. Then again, suppose the single principle in theory B turned out to be too broad in scope for instance, if examples like (6) were well formed in some language (6) *Voting for each other is not something Al and Bob are likely to tell Carl to do.((6) is interpreted as meaning, "Al is not likely to tell Carl to vote for Bob, and Bob is not likely to tell Carl to vote for Al.") then theory A would be vindicated, other things being equal.This same methodological criterion regarding the scope of principles should apply to SLA research as well. But if one is to come up with a satisfactory account of r-binding as an SLA construct, one needs first to uncover all of the relevant facts about the relationship between subject and r-pronouns in the NNGs under investigation. Any number of questions come to mind: Does the relationship hold in extractions and topicalizations as it does in L1's? Does it hold in embedded VP complements like (5)? And what about adjunct VPs like the following?(7) Do you have a cup of coffee before washing yourself?Does it hold at all stages and at all levels of L2 acquisition? In short, how general can one be about binding in L2s, given such a degree of interspeaker variation? Suppose we set out to measure a construct like r-binding in French as an L2 by comparing grammaticality judgments from English and Spanish speakers for sentences like those in (8):(8)

a. a. Elle se lave. She herself bathes. 'She's bathing.'
b. b. Je me lave. I myself bathe. 'I'm bathing.'
c. c. Elle me lave. She me bathes. 'She bathes me.'
d. d. *Je se lave. I oneself bathe.

In the first place, it would not do to point to one or two speakers who incorrectly judge (8d) to be grammatical, as a counterexample to a supposedly universal trait. There are many plausible explanations. Perhaps the reflexive se is unfamiliar to certain speakers/learners, who thus assume some nonreflexive interpretation of the sentence. Perhaps English morphology plays a role; English speakers may reject examples like (8b) because me is perceived to be an inherently nonreflexive morpheme like its orthographically identical English counterpart. Thus for some, se may be lexically an idiosyncratic, highly underspecified reflexive pronoun meaning nothing more than "self." I raise the issue now because, as has been reported elsewhere, apparent r-binding violations like (8d) from nonnative learners of French are not that uncommon. Interestingly enough, such violations seem to be somewhat more frequent in long-distance examples like (5) and (7) than in local examples like (8b).But I am reporting anecdotes; let us pursue the matter more rigorously, starting with a few more observations about the Engiish, French, and Spanish pronominal systems. We have already noted that in English, every reflexive pronoun has a morphologically distinct nonreflexive counterpart (e.g., me/myself, you/yourself). This is not the case for French and Spanish, however: me/myseff are me/me in both languages. It is reasonable to suppose that this will be a source of error for English speakers. In fact, let us propose this as a first hypothesis:(9) H1: The morphological identity of reflexive and nonreflexive pronouns in French is a source of error for English-speaking learners of French (but not for Spanish-speaking learners).Next, recall that Spanish has a pro/enclitic parameter that does not hold in French:(10)

a. a. ¿Te lavo? antes de tomar una taza de café. Yourself wash before having a cup of coffee 'Do you bathe before having a cup of coffee?'

b. b. éTomas una taza de café? antes de lavarte. You-have a cup of coffee before of to wash-yourself 'Do you have a cup of coffee before washing yourself?'

c. c. Tu prends une tasse de café avant de te laver.

d. d. *Tu prends une tasse de café avant de laverte.

Thus let us also propose the following:(11) H2: The pro/enclitic parameter in Spanish is a source of error for Spanish-speaking learners of French (but not for English-speaking learners).Here we do not suggest that English speakers will never err when giving grammaticality judgments for French infinitival phrases with pronouns. Rather, we are claiming that they are neither more nor less likely to err in, say, adjunct-infinitival VPs than in base VPs. Thus those who reject preverbal clitics in (10c) should also reject them in examples like (12):(12) Tu te laves avant de prendre une tasse de café. 'You wash yourself before having a cup of coffee.'In fact, if we knew reliably that English speakers did not give the same judgments for reflexive pronouns in, say, base VPs and adjunct VPs, then we would conclude that r-binding is not a monadic or unitary construct as it is in theoretical syntax because it does not hold for the same broad set of grammatical structures. This would be an unexpected outcome, given the assumptions of UG, because notions like base-VP binding, as opposed to adjunct-VP binding, play no coherent role in any generative theory. Although it is unexpected, it is not to be ruled out a priori. Thus consider (13):(13) H3: For all second-language speakers, r-pronouns in NNGs are bound in base VPs as they are in adjunct VPs, by virtue of a nonviolable principle. Now we have to decide how to test such hypotheses. For purposes of exposition, let us focus on the first hypothesis. Imagine a test in which three English-speaking learners of French (call them A, B, and C) were asked to complete VPs like those in (14) with forms like me, se, moi, or moi-même.(14)

a. a. Je _____ lave.

b. b. Tu _____ laves.

Eckman made an astute observation regarding data gleaned from tests of this sort: "One cannot determine whether UG constraints have been violated simply by examining the errors. This is true because the principles and parameters of UG do not directly make claims about utterances, but instead make claims about grammars." Thus in the case of (14), notice for example that HI does not say whether some particular speaker will reject the use of me in (14a) or in (14b). We have already pointed out the obvious similarity between the French me and the English me, which suggests that (14a) is more likely to be accepted. But the opposite scenario is possible as well. Certain common and useful expressions like je m'appelle 'my name is', je me lève 'I get out of bed' are usually presented early on in adult foreign language courses, well before any general presentation of cliticization. This suggests that reflexives like me in (14a) will be acquired at some stage si, so that nonreflexives like me in (14b) become unacceptable at a subsequent stage s_{i+n}.

Whatever the case, if subjects tend to accept one morpheme as a firstperson singular reflexive and another as a first-person singular nonreflexive, there will be three possible outcomes, illustrated in (15) (1 indicates a correct response, 0, an incorrect response):

(15) F2 speaker	Stimulus/Response	REFL+	REFL-
A	Je me lave.	1	0
	*Tu laves moi.		
B	*Je lave moi-même.	0	1
	Tu me laves.		
C	*Je lave mio-même.	0	0
	*Tu laves moi.		

On the other hand, if language learners tend to accept a single pronoun as both a reflexive and a nonreflexive, as we might expect of Spanish speakers, then they will either get both (14a) and (14b) right or get both wrong:

(16) F2 speaker	Stimulus/Response	REFL+	REFL-
D	Je me lave.	1	1
	Tu me laves.		
E	*Je lave moi.	0	0
	Tu laves moi.		
F	*Je lave me.	0	0
	*Tu laves me.		

Even a cursory review of these data will show quite distinct patterns of responses between the group in (15) and the group in (16). Yet, as Eckman pointed out:

If a study reports that [an L2 group] gave local responses on English rellexives in 80% of the cases this result does not tell us whether the principles of

UG are being obeyed unless we know how those responses are distributed across subjects. Clearly, the case for UG can be made it all of the subjects scored 80%. If, on the other hand, the 80% group result is a composite of subjects compiling many different scores, some of which indicate systematic adherence to UG principles and others which either are unsystematic or indicate non-adherence to UG, then the case for UG governing SLA is not at all clear.

Thus, were we to calculate means for the groups in (15) and (16), we would get an uninformative 33% in each case, and the relevant distinctions would be lost, just as Eckman predicts.

On the other hand, were we to calculate phi-coefficients for these data, we would get magnitudes of 0.50 for (15) and 1.0 for (16). In other words, differential responses on variables where a single morpheme is required tend to suppress correlation coefficients of measures of grammaticality judgments. This in turn may show up in the form of distinct latent variables when the data are factor-analyzed. Such a method would have two additional advantages over the method Eckman used in his study. First, it would not require some arbitrary threshold of systematicity (two out of three, three out of four, or whatever) as did Eckman's study. Any lack of systematicity would merely deflate correlation coefficients and therefore lower factor loadings. Adherence or nonadherence to whatever principle one is investigating would conversely increase factor loadings. Second, it would permit tests of statistical differences. (Eckman did not report such tests in his study.) Typically, in factoranalytic studies, eigenvalues of 1 or greater are taken as indicators of reliable factors.

To give the reader some idea of what sort of results might come from a larger data set, Table 16.1 shows part of a factor matrix from Hagen. In that study, 178 adult English-speaking learners of French gave grammaticality judgments on French pronouns in a wide array of contexts. A factor analysis of the results yielded what was essentially a taxonomy of French pronouns closely aligned with the English pronominal system, with only a few rough edges. Table 16.1 shows one factor for judgments on French me and te in reflexive VPs and a distinct factor for me and te in nonreflexive VPs. Incidentally, Table 16.1 also shows that contexts in which me and te are used with feminine referents do not load on a factor distinct from contexts in which they are used with masculine referents. This makes sense intuitively, since neither French nor English has morphologically distinct pronouns meaning 'my-feminine-self' or 'your-masculine-self'. By the same token, we should not expect distinct loadings for locally bound as opposed to distantly bound reflexives because r-binding, as a universal, holds across arbitrarily long distances in French and in English. In other terms, a factor procedure should not be able to divide r-binding into local binding and long-distance binding because r-binding is not supposed to be a divisible construct. Indeed, no such factors show up in Table 16.1.

TABLE 16.1 Factor Matrix of Grammaticality Judgments of French Reflexives and Nonreflexives

Label	Referent	PRO-type	Local?	Case	Factor[a] 1	2
ME1	FEM	REFL	NO	DAT	.75	.22
ME2	FEM	REFL	NO	ACC	.79	.19
ME3	FEM	REFL	YES	ACC	.76	.29
ME4	FEM	pro	YES	ACC	.37	.64
ME5	MASC	pro	YES	ACC	.18	.72
TE1	FEM	REFL	NO	DAT	.81	.12
TE2	FEM	REFL	NO	ACC	.84	.11
TE3	FEM	REFL	YES	ACC	.80	.16
TE4	FEM	pro	YES	ACC	.43	.63
TE5	MASC	pro	YES	ACC	.19	.75

The primary goal of the study I discuss in the next section was to sharpen and expand the measurement procedures used in Hagen. One way of doing so was to introduce Spanish-speaking learners of French into the design in order to uncover, if possible, the sort of differential responses between base and infinitival examples that did not turn up in Hagen's study, and to see if they could be attributed statistically to first-language parameter differences. At the same time, one other concern needs to be dealt with. Recall that we have left open the possibility that two distinct mental faculties explicit and implicit knowledge come into play when one gives grammaticality judgments. For example, a trained linguist who neither speaks nor understands a word of French could perhaps plod through a test with items like (14) and get a respectable score. Were we to follow suggestions in Gregg and "establish the domain of a theory of second-language acquisition so that it is confined to the acquisition of linguistic competence", then we would necessarily want to exclude all data having to do with explicit grammatical knowledge. On the other hand, if we were to follow the advice in Eckman and "be reluctant to ignore any data" such as these, then it might prove worthwhile to incorporate explicit knowledge into some more comprehensive view of second-language behavior. Any number of plausible theories can be imagined. For example, it may turn out that UG is not available to certain types of adult learners of second languages but that information not supplied by UG is nonetheless available via explicit knowledge or monitoring.

In any case, it would not be worthwhile simply to study data from secondlanguage speakers casually and declare a particular utterance to be an example of implicit or explicit knowledge. Eckman has wisely reminded us that issues like these are empirical and need to be settled on empirical grounds rather than on a priori considerations. Thus let us take a few tentative steps toward the resolution of this particular problem by assuming, as Krashen does, that "it takes a real discrete-point grammar-type test to meet the conditions for Monitor use and encourage significant use of the conscious grammar", and that "in order to think about and use conscious rules effectively, a second language performer needs to have sufficient time". This suggests that resorting to explicit knowledge may have an effect on response times during grammaticality judgment tests. To be precise, it may be the case that (a) explicit knowledge is functional but not effective, (b) explicit knowledge is functional and effective, or (c) explicit knowledge is not functional. In the case of (a), problematic items will result in longer response times and a corresponding decrease in the likelihood of a correct response. Put simply, the subjects spend more time mulling over difficult items but still get them wrong because neither explicit nor implicit knowledge is adequate to meet the challenge. We would then predict some negative correlation between response times and the number of correct answers. In the case of (b), longer response times would be positively related to correct responses because the subjects would access conscious grammar whenever their implicit knowledge was insufficient to solve a problem posed by a test item, and their conscious grammar would then supply the missing information. Finally, under (c), more difficult items will neither speed up nor slow down response times because the subjects do not resort to formal knowledge, so that there is no correlation between response times and number of correct answers.

Let us conclude this section by noting that (a) is essentially the position taken by Krashen over the years, and that only (b) casts any doubt on the viability of using grammaticality judgment tasks in parameter research, because (b) alone allows for the possibility of confounding implicit and explicit knowledge.

Method

Let us summarize before going further. We intended to measure three phenomena: (a) the possible effects of English reflexive morphology on the grammaticality judgments of English-speaking learners of French, (b) the possible effects of the Spanish pro/encliticization parameter on the grammaticality judgments of Spanish-speaking learners of French, (c) the effects of r-binding, which is said to be a universal property of natural languages and so presumably not a source of error for any L2 speakers. At the same time, we intended to track response times in order to look for evidence that L2 subjects access explicit grammatical knowledge in the course of completing grammaticality judgment tasks, because such monitoring of grammatical forms would introduce a systematic nuisance variable that precludes generalizations about linguistic competence based on data gleaned from grammaticality judgment tasks.We start with four sentence types, each of which is treated as a variable:

(17) a.V1: Reflexive pronouns in base VPs, for example: Avant de prendre une tasse de caf5e le matin est-ce que tu te laves? Antes de tomar una taza de café ¿te lavas? Before having a cup of coffee in the morning do you bathe yourself?.

b.V2: Reflexive pronouns in adjunct VPs, for example: Est-ce que tu prends une tasse de café le matin avant de te laver? ¿tomas una taza de café? antes de lavarte. Do you have a cup of coffee before bathing yourself?

c.V3: Nonreflexive pronouns in base VPs, for example: Avant de prendre une tasse de café le matin est-ce que je te lave? Antes de tomar una taza de café ¿te lavo? Before having a cup of coffee in the morning do I bathe you?

d.V4: Nonreflexive pronouns in adjunct VPs, for example: Est-ce que je prends une tasse de café le matin avant de te laver? ¿Tomo una taza de café? antes de lavarte. Do I have a cup of coffee in the morning before bathing you?

In every case words have been neither added nor subtracted; they have merely been rearranged to create the desired distinction between reflexive and nonreflexive VPs and between base and adjunct VPs. We obtained grammaticality judgments on four items of each sentence type. Having taken the additional methodological step of recording response times on all items, we had a total of eight variables, shown schematically in (18):

(18) Label	PRO-type	VP-type	Method
$V1_{gj}$	REFL	BASE	G-judgment
$V2_{gj}$	REFL	ADVP	G-judgment
$V3_{gj}$	~REFL	BASE	G-judgment
$V4_{gj}$	~REFL	ADVP	G-judgment
$V1_{rt}$	REFL	BASE	R-time
$V2_{rt}$	REFL	ADVP	R-time
$V3_{rt}$	~REFL	BASE	R-time
$V4_{rt}$	~REFL	ADVP	R-time

The subscript in the first column is just a convenient way of indicating the method used to gather data. For instance, $V1_{gj}$ indicates grammaticality judgments gathered on items of the first sentence type shown in (17), and $V1_{rt}$ indicates the corresponding response times.

A total of 101 first- and second-year university students of French were tested. Of these, 47 declared English to be their first language, 29 named Spanish, and 25 named another language. This last group was excluded from the study, leaving a population that was 62% English speaking and 38% Spanish speaking. In addition to declaring "the language first learned as a child," all subjects were asked to indicate, on a scale of 0 to 6, how often they spoke Spanish at home (0 = never, 6 = always). A point biserial correlation between this variable and first language yielded r = .92; hence there was good evidence that Spanish was both a native language and a dominant language for the Spanish-speaking group.

All were tested on a computer-generated battery that included four items from each sentence type shown in (17). Verbs and pronouns were deleted from sentences, and the subjects were to select the appropriate verb-pronoun pair from a field of six to complete the sentences. The choices included preverbal and postverbal pronouns. As soon as a test item was displayed, a timer using 1/60th-second increments was activated. When the mouse was clicked in response to the test item, the timer stopped, and responses and response times were recorded.

Some controls were added to minimize the effect of potential nuisance variables. First, all items from all variables were generated randomly for all subjects to avoid carry-over effect. Second, the total number of characters per variable was held constant to within 2% difference so that response time was not affected by reading time. Finally, the correct response appeared in the same position among distractors for all items so that its positioning would not affect response times. Means and standard deviations for variables $V1_{gi}$ through $V4_{rt}$ are shown in Table 16.2.

TABLE 16.2 Means and Standard Deviations for Responses and Response Times

English L1 (n = 47)

Label	VP-type	REFL	Measure	Mean	SD
$V1_{gj}$	BASE	+	G-judgment	1.87	1.44
$V2_{gj}$	ADVP	+	G-judgment	1.26	1.17
$V3_{gj}$	BASE	-	G-judgment	1.30	1.56
$V4_{gj}$	ADVP	-	G-judgment	0.87	1.01
$V1_{rt}$	BASE	+	R-time	4015.38	1697.99
$V2_{rt}$	ADVP	+	R-time	4052.74	1969.83
$V3_{rt}$	BASE	-	R-time	3903.74	1416.09
$V4_{rt}$	ADVP	-	R-time	4267.62	1491.69

Spanish L1 (n = 29)

Label	VP-type	REFL	Measure	Mean	SD
$V1_{gj}$	BASE	+	G-judgment	3.00	1.13
$V2_{gj}$	ADVP	+	G-judgment	1.66	1.26
$V3_{gj}$	BASE	-	G-judgment	2.34	1.40
$V4_{gj}$	ADVP	-	G-judgment	1.45	1.45
$V1_{rt}$	BASE	+	R-time	3626.83	1328.84
$V2_{rt}$	ADVP	+	R-time	4912.03	1806.53
$V3_{rt}$	BASE	+	R-time	3788.07	1142.06
$V4_{rt}$	ADVP	-	R-time	4271.66	1364.57

As an initial step the data were factor analyzed much as they were in Hagen. Four factors were requested, allowing one for each method (grammaticality judgment/response time) and one for each syntactic feature we manipulated in (17) (REFL/~REFL and BASE/

ADVP). The best fit of the data came from a Harris-Kaiser rotation, which produced oblique or correlated factors. The results are shown in Table 16.3. In a factor matrix like the one in Table 16.3, we expect to find some variance due to method alone. Indeed, Factor I shows its highest loadings on grammaticality judgment variables, and Factor 2 shows its highest loadings on response time variables.

TABLE 16.3 Rotated Factor Matrix of Correct Answers and Response Times

				Factor[a]			
Label	VP	REFL	Measure	1	2	3	4
$V1_{gj}$	BASE	+	G-judgment	.26	-.05	.95	.36
$V2_{gj}$	ADVP	+	G-judgment	.98	-.08	.29	.47
$V3_{gj}$	BASE	-	G-judgment	.39	-.16	.64	.83
$V4_{gj}$	ADVP	-	G-judgment	.45	-.22	.26	.92
$V1_{rt}$	BASE	+	r-time	-.19	.82	-.34	-.20
$V2_{rt}$	ADVP	+	r-time	-.12	.84	.11	-.09
$V3_{rt}$	BASE	-	r-time	-.01	.87	-.10	-.30
$V4_{rt}$	ADVP	-	r-time	-.10	.84	.02	-.23

We should also expect to find some variance corresponding to the hypothesized first-language effects postulated in (9) and (11). This too is supported somewhat by the factor matrix in Table 16.3. Factor 3 has by far its highest loadings on grammaticality judgments of base VPs, whereas Factor 4 has its highest loadings on grammaticality judgments of nonreflexive pronouns (though note as well the moderate loadings on $V2_{gj}$). Recalling what was said earlier about explicit knowledge and negative correlations between response times and grammaticality judgments, on Factor 3, $V1_{gj}$ and $V3_{gj}$ show some signs of an inverse relation with their corresponding response times. That is, the highest magnitude negative loadings on response times correspond to the highest magnitude positive loadings on grammaticality judgments. The same is true of V39 $_{gj}$, $V4_{gj}$, $V3_{rt}$, $V4_{rt}$ in Factor 4, consistent with Krashen's claims about monitoring. However, considering the relatively low-magnitude loadings overall on response times for Factors 3 and 4, the relationship is not compelling. At any rate, there are no indications of adverse effect of explicit knowledge or monitoring on the grammaticality judgment tasks in Table 16.3. On the contrary, if Factor

3 represents the Spanish-as-L1 effect postulated in (11), and if Factor 4 represents the English-as-L1 effect in (9), then our hypotheses are right on target so far.

The matrix from the factor analysis in Table 16.3, however, is not nearly as perspicuous as the one in Hagen, most likely because the subjects in Hagen's study were quite homogeneous with respect to Ll background, whereas those in the present study were not. Thus, let us consider another method of analysis. The experimental design is illustrated in (19):

(19)	V1	V2	V3	V4
$L_{English}$	S1	S1	S1	S1
	S2	S2	S2	S2
$L_{Spanish}$	Sm	Sm	Sm	Sm
	Sn	Sn	Sn	Sn

We have dependent samples, and a simple ANOVA is thus inappropriate. We use instead a repeated-measures ANOVA and a General Linear Models procedure for unequal group size.

There are three sources of variance in this design: (a) group effect, (b) treatment effect, and (c) group-treatment interaction. The first will tell us if, setting aside differences between the sentence types in (17), the two L1 groups represent the same distribution of means. Similarly, the second will tell us if, setting aside L1, the results from the four sentence types represent the same distribution of means. Finally, the third will tell us if the two L1 groups respond in a significantly different fashion to the different sentence types. Variance due to group effect is of only marginal interest because it is amenable to too many explanations (e.g., the Spanish speakers are somewhat more proficient, they take research projects more seriously, or they study more). Variance due to treatment is of some interest because it tells us whether or not we have gained anything at all by manipulating syntactic features in the manner shown in (17). However, it alone will not reveal a great deal more than the factor analysis in Table 16.3. In short, testing for statistically significant differences of means between groups or between treatments will not in itself surmount the problems of confounding aggregate results and individual results that Eckman discussed in his study.

Variance due to group-treatment interaction, on the other hand, will tell us whether or not Spanish and English speakers differ significantly in their grammaticality judgments for base/adjunct VPs and reflexive/nonreflexive pronouns. With this in mind, let us repeat our original hypotheses and spell out what sort of results will support them:

H1: The morphological identity between reflexive and nonreflexive pronouns in French is a source of error only for English-speaking learners of French (predicting treatment effect for English speakers only on a comparison of REFL/REFL variables, thus significant treatment by group interaction).

H2: The pro/enclitic parameter in Spanish is a source of error only for Spanish-speaking learners of French (predicting treatment effect for Spanish speakers only on a comparison of BASE/ADVP variables, thus significant treatment by group interaction).

H3: For all second-language speakers, r-pronouns in NNGs are bound in base VPs as they are in adjunct VPs, by virtue of a nonviolable principle (predicting no treatment effect for English speakers on a comparison of BASE/ADVP variables, thus significant treatment by group interaction).

Results

The results of the repeated measures ANOVA are shown in Tables 16.4 and 16.5. There is overall significance (p = .0001) for treatment or sentence type effect on grammaticality judgments but none for interaction (p = .1055); Spanish and English speakers responded in essentially the same fashion to the different sentence types.

Table 16.5a shows that when a pronoun is reflexive, there is a statistically significant difference between the variable measuring adjunct VPs and the one measuring base VPs. Table 16.5b shows the same sort of statistical significance when the pronoun is not reflexive. This holds for both L I groups. By the same token, Tables 16.5c and 16.5d show statistically significant differences between reflexives and their nonreflexive counterparts, and again this is true for both L1 groups. Although we had expected the REFL/

REFL distinction to be a source of error for English speakers only, the pairwise comparisons show no signs of interaction. The comparison of reflexives to nonreflexives among base VPs is significant for all subjects (p = 0.0001), but the F value for interaction is not (p = 0.8222). The same comparison among adjuncts shows nearly the same results: Treatment effect is marginally significant (p = .0573), but the F value for interaction is well short of significance (p = 0.566).

TABLE 16.4 Comparison of Means: Grammaticality Judgments

df	Type III SS	Mean Square	F	p
3	65.03	21.68	19.82	0.0001 *
3	6.78	2.26	2.07	0.1055
222	242.76	1.09		

*Significant when á = .0001.

TABLE 16.5 a Adjunct VPs Compared to Base VPs When a Pronoun is Reflexive

df	Type III SS	Mean Square	F	p
1	69.02	69.02	27.51	0.0001*
1	9.49	9.49	3.79	0.05555

*Significant when á = .0001

TABLE 16.5 b Adjunct VPs Compared to Base VPs When a Pronoun is Nonreflexive

df	Type III SS	Mean Square	F	p
1	31.35	31.35	18.38	0.0001*
1	3.98	3.98	2.33	0.1309

*Significant when á = .0001.

TABLE 16.5 c Reflexives Compared to Nonreflexives When a VP is a Base Clause

df	Type III SS	Mean Square	F	p
1	27.12	27.12	11.80	0.0010*
1	0.12	0.12	0.05	0.8222

*Significant when á = .001.

(Contd.)

TABLE 16.5 d Reflexives Compared to Nonreflexives When a VP is an Adjunct Clause

df	Type III SS	Mean Square	F	p
1	6.24	6.24	3.73	0.0573
1	0.56	0.56	0.33	0.566

All of this means that neither L1 nor UG offers an especially good account of the data. The pro/enclitic distinction, whether or not it is considered a matter of parametric variation, predicts differential responses among Spanish speakers only. Similarly, the reflexive/non reflexive distinction in English morphology should be a source of error for English speakers only. The significant within-subject variance that turns up in the grammaticality judgment tasks is not due to L1 differences: English speakers are as likely as Spanish speakers to respond differentially across-the-board. In other words, r-binding does not extend into adjuncts in the NNGs of the English speakers. Thus there is no support for any of the hypotheses in (9), (11) and (13).

Now let us sum up the major points of this study. We set out to identify those aspects of parameter models of SLA that are likely to be problematic as the details of theory construction are worked out. I have focused on three aspects.

First, these models have so far taken for granted that the constructs to be studied have already been laid out correctly in GB theory. There are, nonetheless, counterclaims from other theories that have a direct bearing on the issues raised in SLA research and that need to be taken seriously. Newmeyer made this point some time ago:

The dominant trend [in SLA] has been to adopt the assumptions of GB, paralleling the fact that within linguistic theory itself, GB has considerably more supporters than the other models. But still a lingering, and entirely understandable, feeling persists that if so many questions about linguistic theory are still up for grabs, then the results of an allied field which are based on a specific set of assumptions internal to one particular theoretical framework can hardly be secure.

Admittedly, Newmeyer's tone was more optimistic than that in the present discussion. In any event, regardless of whether one prefers GB or GPSG as a point of departure, SLA theory construction will require a thorough accounting of the facts regarding NNGs through systematic data gathering. There is no reason why anyone cannot or should not construct a general account of those data quite apart from any prepackaged theory from generative syntax. Surely any points of convergence between SLA and theoretical syntax would be all the more compelling if they were motivated independently of one another.

Second, even in cases where there is essential agreement among competing syntactic theories as to the nature of L1s, SLA research needs to sharpen its research methods if it chooses to do reliable empirical data analysis involving NNGS. With some modifications and improvements, the methods presented in this chapter show promise for measurement validation as well as for hypothesis testing. Factorial ANOVAs like the one used here permit greater precision in pinpointing differences between L1 groups, as Flynn research has already demonstrated. However, the computerdriven format has the additional merits of permitting (a) repeated-measures designs, and (b) measurement of response times. Repeated-measures designs have the advantage of allowing the researcher to control for within-subject differences while substantially reducing the number of subjects required in experiments. Traditionally, they have been used sparingly because they are susceptible to carry-over effects when "treatments administered earlier in the sequence continue to affect the behavior of subjects while they are being administered a subsequent treatment". Latin Square Designs circumvent this problem by alternating the order of presentation of experimental treatments for all subjects, so that any inherent ordering effects will merely inflate the error term. Complete randomization of stimuli by computer accomplishes the same objective more thoroughly while doing away with a slew of logistical problems involved in staggering the order of many stimuli for many learners and reassembling the results afterwards. Once an experiment is moved into computer format, it is easy enough to keep track of response times, which, as we noted earlier, allow for hypothesis testing regarding the use of conscious or explicit grammar rules during grammaticality judgment tasks.

Third, the results of the study discussed here show that neither parametric variation nor the parochial first-language principles that were investigated worked as explanations for errors in grammaticality judgments for the stimulus sentences. Among other things, this means that the rather strong claim in Hagen that the structure of pronominal systems in NNGs can be explained by first-language principles is wrong. In fact, not even the "nonviolable" principle of r-binding worked well as an explanatory construct in this study, because the judgments of English speakers regarding the acceptability of locally bound reflexives did not extend to adjunct VPs. Thus the results point to an issue of substance that has already come up in work by Clahsen, Bley-Vroman and others: "UG principles available to L1 learners are not available to adults". If further research supports this proposal, an explanation of this fundamental difference between L2s and L1s will be in order

17

Promise and Challenges of Research Methodology

Introduction

Researchers have been collecting and describing quantitative and qualitative data about service-learning programs for several years, but many people in the field feel that current studies have been ineffective in capturing the richness and complexity of what they experience and observe. In 1996, in response to this reality and a growing interest in service-learning stories and to help meet this perceived need, The Service-Learning 2000 Center at Stanford University decided to try to adapt the research approach of portraiture developed by Sarah Lawrence-Lightfoot and Jessica Davis at Harvard University. Center staff believed that their portraiture theory held great promise for creating compelling narratives to engage readers and help inform the service-learning field.

Center staff began this effort by contracting with Lissa Soep, a colleague of Jessica Davis at Harvard University's Project Zero, to translate central portraiture methodologies into a set of concepts and practices to guide Service-Learning 2000 Center research and writing. From 1996 to 2001, Center staff coordinated the research and writing of service-learning portraits for three secondary schools, two middle schools, and six service-learning teacher education programs in California. In addition, two staff members led an institute at Clemson

University in South Carolina in July 2001, to help launch a major portraiture project for professors and K-12 teachers from the southern region of the U. S. who shared a common interest in creating powerful narratives about their service-learning work.

This chapter begins by describing the general conceptual framework used in four portraiture projects. Examples are drawn from three Service-Learning 2000 projects to illustrate the framework in action. More attention is focused on the teacher education project because it departed from the Lightfoot-Davis model by asking professors to write about their own work. Faculty members serve not as outside researchers but as key actors in the projects. These professors were, in many respects, portraiture pioneers who tested the possibility that action research could be successfully adapted for portraiture. In addition, they experimented with the value of forming a collegial learning community connecting six teacher education institutions across the state of California. The chapter concludes by describing a fourth portraiture effort centered in South Carolina. Although participants in the South Carolina project received training in the Lightfoot-Davis model, they further adapted the model to serve their unique purposes.

Characteristics of Portraiture

Portraiture shares much of its approach with other forms of qualitative research. Ethnographic case studies, for example, assemble details in a similar manner. Whereas the writer's voice is normally absent or masked by the veil of objectivity in a case study, a portrait is marked by the voice of the writer.Portraiture, like all qualitative research, must be grounded in the data that lead to authentic description via an intense analysis process. The description, like a portrait painting, should capture the essence of the subject. Creative fiction has no place. Portraiture researchers also take a different stance toward their subject than many traditional researchers. They adopt what LawrenceLightfoot described as a generous regard for what you study. Instead of probing intentionally for failures from an autopsy lens, portraiture seeks to focus more on process and unashamedly cares about what is being studied and represented. This stance does not mean sugar coating reality but rather means a commitment to uncovering potential goodness.

Doing Portraiture Research

Using portraiture research to study service-learning requires the following components:

- Agreeing on a central guiding question for research;
- Identifying a small number of dimensions to serve as organizers for data collection and project analysis;
- Identifying from data analysis a small number of themes that guide the writing of a portrait;
- Triangulating data from a variety of sources; and
- Using an outside-in writing strategy that effectively brings the reader into the context of the project.

Portraiture also involves stressing the importance of creating a compelling narrative that uses vivid language and includes multiple voices and perspectives. Portraiture shows rather than tells a story.

Guiding Question

The central guiding question for portraiture research is similar to traditional research or evaluation questions. Agreeing on a central guiding question for this portraiture research was both crucial and difficult. Many hours of debate focused on fine-tuning questions so that they offer potential both to drive data collection and lead to results that will matter for the service-learning field. Careful attention was directed to reaching agreement on the definition of each word.

The resultant questions were simple and almost self-evident. The middle school portraits focused on the strategies and challenges of integrating servicelearning into academic curriculum. The teacher education portraits researched how service-learning impacts the teaching and learning of program participants. One would never guess how much heated discussion and experimentation with alternatives preceded the final decision. Few would disagree, however, that this discussion time was well spent. Portraits need to be grounded in a serious question that matters, that limits the scope of data collection, and that informs the selection of themes.

Central guiding questions made important contributions to ServiceLearning 2000 portraiture work. The teacher education project began by inviting professors from seven schools to attend a workshop on portraiture that concluded by identifying a common guiding question for their research. This workshop was followed by Service-Learning 2000 staff support that included one-on-one coaching, conference calls on different aspects of portraiture research, a second workshop to share progress and obtain further training, and a two-day writing retreat with personal writing conferences. Throughout this collaborative work and coaching, the guiding question provided a constant and common focus. In addition, having this common guiding question facilitated cross-portrait analysis at the end of the project and gave the resulting analysis more credibility.

Dimensions

Organizing the collecting, sorting, and analysis of data for portrait writing is similar in many respects to other forms of research. Data collection is organized in a small number of conceptual categories called dimensions that are selected to inform the central guiding question and to reveal themes. Because the culminating goal is to craft a portrait that brings the multidimensional context of a service-learning experience to life, special attention is directed to collecting insightful quotes and examples across dimensions and from a variety of sources and voices.Research in each of the three projects began by agreement on a small number of dimensions that offered promise for sorting data for analysis and shaping theme selection. Dimensions function much like a temporary storage bin for related data. The high school portraits used four dimensions to collect data.

- The journey of the program defined as origins and future vision;
- The service activity defined as the nature of service provided;
- The environment in which the program operates defined as relationships with and nature of the school and surrounding community; and
- The program structure defined as leadership, funding, and buy-in.

The dimensions for the six teacher education portraits were similar but they included change over time, with an emphasis on flexibility involved in implementing reform within institutions.

Themes

The most important and difficult challenge of service-learning portrait research is to select two or three themes that capture the drama and reality of a project while providing valid insight into the guiding question. Looking across dimensions for powerful themes is where art and science collide. As a researcher aiming for scientific objectivity, one analyzes all data, looking for generalizations that might explain what was observed, experienced, and reviewed. After reading and rereading interview transcripts, observation and focus group notes, student work, surveys, and other kinds of school and community documentation, the researcher begins to create possible themes to test for explanatory power. When four or five tentative themes emerge, the researcher must then test the capacity of these themes to work as the organizers for the actual writing of a portrait. It is here where the artist meets the scientist. Sometimes promising themes simply do not work they fail to generate the kind of vivid writing demanded or initial writing efforts gradually reveal that a theme is less powerful and insightful than originally thought.

There is no set way to identify an effective portrait theme. The limited experience at Service-Learning 2000 suggests that themes often emerge from conversations where the researcher talks with one or more colleagues at some length about possible themes and, in a sense, listens to ideas being reflected back and questioned. Final themes often surface at the last moment. Although the process of theme search is grounded in intense, concentrated analysis of data, the final selection has the feeling more of an artistic "aha" experience. Experience here suggests that researchers consider five questions or criteria to determine the authenticity and power of a potential portrait theme.

1. Are there patterns in the evidence that lead to and support the theme as distinct from single occurrences?
2. Is the theme something that simply appeals to you or does it really emerge from the data? Researchers need to avoid the temptation to settle on a theme that they think they can find data to support rather than something that the data compel.
3. How useful is the theme in generating description? Does it serve as an effective catalyst for your writing?
4. Does the theme make sense and convey authentic insight to

people involved in the project? If it does not, the researcher needs to return to start over.

5. How well does the theme fit with the guiding question? Does it have clear potential to inform?

Service-Learning 2000's portraits have used a variety of themes. Some researchers have used quotes from participants to describe a theme; other researchers have created their own language to describe a theme. Although listing some of the themes used in this service-learning portraiture research will reveal little about the identification process, it will, perhaps, offer insight into the range of possibilities that may emerge. Themes from this service-learning portrait research include:

- The Gift of Community Life on the Sidelines
- Service-Learning as Instigator of Empowerment and Transformation Gentle Infiltration
- Weaving Connections
- Sowing the Seeds of Humanity
- Multiple Hurdles

Portraits use themes to organize the presentation of narrative data. For example, Gelenian in a portrait, Service-Learning in Multicultural Settings, described a project at California State University, Humboldt. He identified the Gift of Community as one of his themes. He introduces this theme directly. "As I examined and reexamined my students' work and listened to site personnel talk about their students, I repeatedly read or heard comments about community and the importance of caring". He proceeds to cite several examples of community through the words of participants. "The Mural Project required many hands and talents. It also fostered a sense of community among everyone involved". In his journal, Gelenian had this to say about one project:

The project was teen-centered. It brought together students from various backgrounds and communities who had a chance to talk together. There were no assignments, no grades, and no obligations. Students choose to come, decide what they want to work on, and how long they can work. Tammy (project director and credential candidate) guided the teens by organizing work dates and activities. Teens have designed the mural, raised money for it, and did it. This sense of ownership is extremely motivating for them. Parents seem to be very proud of their teens that are participating, which add to the positive atmosphere. The project is also very open. Anyone can come to help, and this seems to create a cooperative atmosphere.

A second theme in Gelenian's portrait, Life on the Sidelines, provided a conceptual coherence for sharing a rich array of data in gallery pieces at the end of his Multicultural Education course. For example, one student composed a song to illustrate his observations and insights:

Well look at me I'm sittin in the back again I'm the one that never volunteers I just sit and try to figure out what you want Why can't you see I do care? You ask me questions that I don't understand You interrupt me when I speak You tell me what I say has just about nothing to do with what It is you want me to say Well I can't tell you how many times I've tried to tell you What it is I mean But I don't speak like you, and you don't speak like me Isn't there someplace we can meet?

It is hard to read the first stanzas of this poem without recognizing and feeling the reality of the Life on the Sidelines theme.

Outside-in Writing

In order for a service-learning portrait to achieve its overarching goal of helping K-12 teachers and university professors better understand the promise and problems of service-learning pedagogy, it must succeed in engaging the reader and bringing the project context to life. A major strategy for meeting this challenge is what portraiture calls outside-in writing. The portrait writer works extraordinarily hard to find language and images that bring the reader up close and into the world of the service-learning experience depicted—to help the reader sense the smells, sounds, and tensions like a participant. In the words of Lissa Soep:

The narrative begins with a setting of the scene; the reader encounters the site of the study from the outside-in- a picture of the geographic, demographics and ideological setting that helps shape the experiences portrayed. Portraiture makes no attempt to present these experiences through the anonymous, disembodied voice typically associated with research documents. The writer is present in portraiture, in every detail included and omitted, in the themes explored, and sometimes (but not always) in first person accounts that run through the narrative.

The carillon from St. Vincent's peals the evening melodies. Birds of many species sing their varied songs above in the exotic old trees as I walk toward the classroom buildings for my elementary education methodology class. Pulling my cart of books, handouts, videotapes, and assorted teaching materials, I wonder what I have forgotten. I take a few breaths to draw in the peacefulness, and nod to students clustered for a quick before-class meal at outside tables. The low drone of freeway traffic is almost lost to consciousness. The is the Doheny campus of Mount St. Mary's College, located in the heart of Los Angeles, two blocks from the busiest LA freeways, clogged bumper to bumper.

The Doheny campus is a pond of tranquility within the complex, pulsing energy of central Los Angeles. Its history is entwined in the rise of millionaires. A square bloc of Victorian homes surrounded by plantings collected from around the world. The campus was home to the Dohenys, their relatives, and friends. Today it serves the college mission: preparing multiethnic, multilingual students to become leaders in a diverse and changing world. The splendor of past, isolated wealth has been adapted for 21st century work to empower those who have historically been ignored. As I continue toward class I mull over my student's incredibly diverse stories and experiences. One group of students in my class describes themselves as "two Catholics, two Protestants, and one Hindu. We speak English, Spanish, Hindi, Tagalog, and Vietnamese. Two of us are graduate students, three are undergraduates. One has taught for 10 years, one for two years, one has been a teacher's aide, and two of us have never taught.

This outside-in description paints a picture of the campus while providing introductory background to the themes of Weaving a Team Tapestry and Flexibility is Essential that the author develops in the portrait.

Portraiture: A Collaborative Approach

As part of the W. K. Kellogg Foundation funded Learning In Deed(LID) national service-learning initiative, several districts in South Carolina are working interdependently and with the state

Department of Education to integrate servicelearning into the core education experience of K-12 students. This goal encouraged the LID districts to create collaborations with local postsecondary institution education programs, ensuring that current K-12 teachers gained the necessary competencies to engage students in service-learning, and helping the next generation of teachers gain corresponding knowledge and skills during their collegiate experience. These efforts built on the National Service-Learning in Teacher Education Partnership (NSLTEP) focusing on professional development and integration of service-learning into the core teacher education curriculum.The initiative in South Carolina is focused on a central guiding question: "How are we moving toward the institutionalization of service-learning into our educational programs?" Each of the K-12 and teacher education collaborations, after training from Service-Learning 2000 professionals, embarked on the portraiture process to share their experiences, document progress, and improve service-learning practice. The training included:

- A basic understanding of the portraiture process and benefits, through formal training, stories, and resources;
- The development of a realistic timeline for completion;
- A commitment to take the risk to try something new;
- Knowledge of appropriate data collection methods, checklists, and formats to effectively implement the portraiture process.

At the conclusion of the training, participants understood that:

- There is a benefit of including multiple voices in analysis of student performance, school cultures, and collaborations;
- Frequent data collection, analysis, and reflection are critical to documenting and improving service-learning practice and programs;
- Regular meetings within the organizations and within the collaborations are critical to utilize the information in a timely manner;
- There should be a focus on equity in the process; and
- The portraiture process would be a catalyst for enhancing K-12 and teacher education (higher education) collaborations.

Participants also identified the following audiences for the portraits.

- Teacher education faculty;
- School and district administrators;
- Service-Learning practitioners;
- Peers (teachers and faculty); and
- Community members.

The South Carolina portraiture process covered 12 months. The coordinators requested the writing teams be composed of members from both higher education institutions and K-12 whenever possible. The teams agreed to a series of working meetings and conference calls to report on their progress, seek assistance, and provide support for one another. They also shared their early drafts via a listserv.To facilitate the writing process, the coordinators gave the portraiture teams a checklist to help them to conceptualize and begin their writing. This checklist was very effective in assisting the higher education partners, in particular, in moving away from the traditional academic writing style to the more engaging portraiture process. In addition, at a face-to-face workshop, the checklist was used as a tool to critique shared writings, assessing how they could bring more art into their fledgling portraits. As this group of participants engaged in the portraiture process, they encountered other novel experiences besides the change in writing style. They began to:

- Understand that portraiture is a process(someone needs to keep participants on task and time—they need to be motivated and supported with feedback);
- Focus on showing what occurred rather than telling what happened;
- Wrestle with the issue of the authenticity of portraiture so that it is acceptable by peers in the higher education world;
- Be patient with the data collection, avoiding the temptation to settle on a theme that has one or two compelling illustrations without rigorous triangulated analysis; and
- Learn to talk to each other as they were collecting the data ensuring all the perspectives of the partners were in the portrait.

Over time, the majority of portraiture participants found the process exciting and appropriate for capturing their efforts, outcomes, and improvements. They discovered that the process enabled them to reflect constantly within their partnerships on their progress toward institutionalization. The following is an example of an early effort to create an outside-in introduction to a forthcoming portrait. The University of South Carolina is a partner with Richland School District Two in Columbia, South Carolina, in the Learning In Deed national initiative.

By introducing some of the key actors from the university, sharing their comments, and describing actual events, the authors bring the reader into their world to better understand the context of what follows. This introductory piece also introduces what will likely be a stronger theme of this portrait—serving and learning together.

Another portrait clearly shows the powerful connection between a college and its neighborhood and how service-learning enhances that partnership. Benedict College, a historically black college located in Columbia, South Carolina, is a NSLTEP partner.

In this portrait, readers are introduced to this community, gaining an understanding of the institution and its role in the neighborhood. The team of authors shows, from both the cultural and historical roots of the institution and the words of the president today, that the environment for nurturing service to the community is an especially rich one at Benedict College.As is evident from both portrait introductions, the authors bring the reader into the setting of the project, creating an understanding that will serve as the foundation for the stories that will follow. The uniqueness of this technique is that the authors are key actors, responsible for establishing the process and caring about what is being studied and represented. Their inside knowledge of the setting brings a truth to the telling of the stories. The writing teams, by bringing the diverse voices of various other actors into the portraiture process, can further enhance this truth.Various service-learning portrait authors indicate that this process has been very helpful to improve their practice. The portraits, completed by stakeholders, provide specific insights into the impact on participants and recommendations for improvement including:

- Improving the way teachers view their students' work;
- Greater alignment of an assessment approach with program goals and purposes;
- Enhanced relationships with community partners;
- Increased capacity to ask critical questions of all stakeholders;

- Expanded scope of the projects through the focus on themes;
- Increased orientation to diversity of participants and their capacities;
- Greater acknowledgement of the political nature of curriculum and service-learning pedagogy;
- Greater listening skills to understand students' concerns and teacher responses;
- Increased appreciation for uncertainty involved in service-learning and willingness to embrace this pedagogy;
- Greater knowledge of the service-learning program, partners' contributions and impacts;
- Greater interaction among program partners; and
- Increased recognition of the positive effects on students, including self-efficacy.

According to one teacher:

When I think about it, it seems that portraiture improved my servicelearning work in ways that reflect the process. It improved the way that I looked at it. It gave me a view of what my students learn that I believe helps me feel more confident in what I tell students about service-learning when they ask questions like "Why do I have to do this?" I really feel that an experiential pedagogy like service-learning demands an interpretive analysis of learning. You can't measure empathy with calipers.

Conclusion

Portraiture is emerging as both an effective and efficient process to help servicelearning advocates in their struggles to apply research to collect, analyze, and communicate information about their work.Portraiture research to study service-learning is organized through the following:

- Agreeing on a central guiding question for research;
- Identifying a small number of dimensions to serve as organizers for data collection and project analysis;
- Identifying a small number of themes from data analysis that guide the writing of a portrait;
- Triangulating data from a variety of sources; and
- Using an outside-in writing strategy that effectively brings the reader into the context of the project.

It also creates a compelling narrative that uses vivid, showing language and includes multiple voices and perspectives. Portraiture is a method that also aligns with the values of service-learning including a focus on reflection and collaboration. In addition, it provides formal opportunities to use information for continuous individual and program improvement.

The challenges of employing portraiture processes (e.g., a different way of writing including multiple voices, triangulation, and finding time for collaborative thinking and writing) are overcome by developing and nurturing collaborative learning communities that bridge disciplines and K-12 and higher education. Portraiture, thus, offers both an opportunity to tell a story through strategic organizing components and to create deep collaborations within and outside educational institutions. Both leading to improved service-learning practice.

18

Respecification of Research Methodology

Introduction

SLA researchers are becoming increasingly sophisticated in such matters. We have not only reached the stage where we are actively exploring what philosophy of science has to say about theory construction; we are also defining the goals of SLA research ever more precisely.

These developments are welcome signs that SLA studies are coming of age. However, this sense of growing maturity is being achieved at some cost to the field. As even a casual reading of the SLA literature will attest, the overwhelming majority of SLA studies are of the logico-deductive, experimental variety. Thus, whether they recognize this or not, most SLA researchers subscribe to a nomothetic epistemology that has, in my opinion, prematurely achieved the status of a dominant orthodoxy.

Although the results of nomothetic science are in many instances impressive, we should not be seduced into accepting the validity of this epistemological position without question. I therefore first present a critique of the current nomothetic orthodoxy in SLA research from an ethnomethodological perspective and then demonstrate how Conversation Analysis may be used to motivate the theoretical position that conversation is the sociocultural context of second-language learning.

Current Orthodoxy in Sla Research

Let me begin with a summary of some technical terms. Ochsner differentiates between nomothetic and hermeneutic scientific traditions by noting that the former is concerned with explaining and predicting how natural phenomena work, whereas the latter focuses on understanding and interpreting how these phenomena are organized. More specifically, nomothetic science (the Greek prefix nomo means "lawful") assumes the existence of a single, discoverable reality that causally obeys the laws of nature. In contrast, hermeneutics (meaning "the art of interpretation") assumes that multiple realities exist and that human events in particular can be interpreted only according to their outcomes. In terms of research methodology, an experimental, quantitative methodology is associated with the nomothetic tradition, and a naturalistic, qualitative methodology is associated with the hermeneutic tradition.

As I noted earlier, the dominant paradigm in SLA research today is that of nomothetic science. The value of this tradition has been forcefully, even relentlessly, articulated by Mike Long and various colleagues and collaborators. Specifically addressing issues of theory construction, Larsen-Freeman and Long differentiated between two types of theories in nomothetic science. These are causal-process theories and setsof-laws theories. They noted that sets-of-laws theories consist of collections of (often) unrelated generalizations or laws regarding SLA that are based on observed and tested relationships between variables. The problem with this type of research, according to the authors, is that it does not provide an explanation for the processes being studied; it merely establishes that they are in need of explanation. On the other hand, causal-process theories consist of definitions and operationalizations of abstract theoretical constructs, existence statements, and deterministic and/or probabilistic statements, which are mathematically tested to explain how and why SLA occurs. LarsenFreeman and Long therefore argued that causal-process theories are the most desirable type of theory from a theory construction perspective because they lead to predictions and generalizations of great explanatory power.

A few writers, principally Schumann, supported by Candlin, Guiora and van Lier, have valiantly attempted to stem the nomothetic tide. But the debate has unfortunately been somewhat lopsided. For the most part, these have been voices crying in the applied linguistic wilderness.

Various statements by Crookes, Larsen-Freeman and Long give a flavor of the confidence with which the nomothetic cause is being advanced in SLA studies. Thus, Crookes stated: "It may be that SL production research is at the point where the field is ready to move from primarily descriptive research to greater use of experimental investigations of a more obviously hypothesis-testing, theory-developing nature". Similarly, although acknowledging the utility and necessity of descriptive studies as a means of establishing baseline data, Larsen-Freeman and Long labeled these studies as limited and maintained that only a causal-process approach to theory construction can explain SLA.

I disagree with these statements for two reasons. First, although nomothetic science does not preclude descriptive studies, these statements have the undesirable (if unintentional) effect of severely undercutting the viability of hermeneutics in SLA studies by pinning a negative (and incorrect) label ("limited") on qualitative research. And second, these statements gloss over the fact that a nomothetic epistemology is itself open to serious criticism, a fact that its proponents rarely mention, much less address in any serious fashion.

Before I develop this latter point, I should make it clear that I am not interested in reopening the argument whether qualitative and quantitative approaches to SLA research are mutually exclusive. There is, in fact, considerable agreement, among SLA researchers on both sides of the methodological divide, that qualitative and quantitative studies are in reality complementary ways of creating new knowledge. I wholeheartedly endorse this assessment. What I wish to do in this chapter is reexamine the relative value that we currently describe to understanding versus explaining SLA phenomena and question whether explanation can be achieved only through a causal-process approach to SLA theorizing.

What are the weaknesses of a causal-process approach to SLA? I address this question from the perspective of ethnomethodology, a radical sociology in the hermeneutic tradition proposed by the sociologist Harold Garfinkel, who defined ethnomethodology as "the investigation of the rational properties of indexical expressions and other practical actions as contingent ongoing accomplishments of organized artful practices of everyday life".

The ethnomethodological critique of nomothetic science focuses crucially on experimentalists' rejection of ordinary language and day-to-day experience as valid ways of knowing and organizing the world, both these ways of accessing knowledge are viewed by experimentalists as too value-laden and subjective to be useful tools for science, which must above all else be valuefree and objective. In order to go beyond the perceived inadequacies of the lay talk of ordinary social actors and the "shallow" explanations of social phenomena that a dependence on ordinary language generates, experimentalists have developed a highly technical language to describe their subject matter and to provide "deeper" explanations that are cast in terms of underlying causes and effects. Thus, they attempt to define and operationalize abstract theoretical constructs and develop logico-deductive hypotheses about a given phenomenon (such as SLA), which they then set out to falsify using the pure, value-free language of mathematics. But in their efforts to develop this objective, value-free language, experimentalists are confronted with the contradiction that the technical language and causative explanations of social science cannot be anything but parasitic upon the ordinary language of social actors and their lay explanations of everyday experience.

More specifically, I wish to develop the following theses: The operationalization of constructs and the technical definitions that experimentalists develop are contaminated by the notion of reasonable agreement concerning the defining characteristics of a given phenomenon. Furthermore, experimentalists depend on lay talk as a component of any technical definition and/or depend on highly metaphorical language to develop their arguments. In addition, the degree to which a discipline has been mathematized (i.e., the extent to which it routinely uses inferential statistics to test predicted interactions between variables) is not necessarily an indication of maturity. Not only can the use of some statistical procedures result in unnecessarily opaque discourse whose actual conclusions may in the end be comparatively meager, but the supposed objectivity of such discourse also frequently camouflages the many practical decisions, judgments, and subjective interpretations that inform this attempt to objectivize the language of science. Therefore, there can be no absolute guarantee that an abstract, mathematical explanation of a phenomenon is necessarily superior to a hermeneutic explanation that is constructed in terms of lay participants' real-time understanding of the same phenomenon.

Let me now illustrate what I mean by critiquing some undeniably good examples of recent experimental SLA research. This research has been selected to show that, notwithstanding its careful research design and attention to detail, it is nonetheless vulnerable to the criticisms outlined previously.

In line with the position developed by Long, Long and Porter and Porter used the qualitative work on conversational repair in Schegloff, Jefferson, and Sacks to generate their own operational definition of repair as a prelude to quantification and experimentation. Briefly, Long and Porter defined repair as a composite variable consisting of six subcategories including confirmation checks, clarification requests, comprehension checks, verifications of meaning, definition requests, and expressions of lexical uncertainty. They used this new definition of repair to test hypotheses about the relative importance of different types of input and interaction that native and nonnative speakers provide to each other in taskcentered talk. These hypotheses were inspired by Long hypothesis that negotiated comprehensible input is the necessary and sufficient cause of language learning.

The first problem that Long and Porter came up against was that their operationalization of the construct of repair was based on the notion of reasonable agreement. That is, they accepted that Schegloff et al.'s treatment of repair was an accurate and trustworthy account of how participants actually achieve repair. Note that I am not denying the high quality of Schegloff et al.'s work here (which would be foolish, because it constitutes a foundation for the analysis presented in the second part of this chapter). What I am pointing out is that, in terms of their own epistemology, the supposedly objective research enterprise described by Long and Porter in their various papers is founded on the quicksand of opinion, however well informed this opinion may be. The ostensibly scientific definition of the composite variable of repair that they propose cannot escape being contaminated by the so-called imprecisions of everyday language, because our understanding of notions like comprehension checks and clarification requests (as shown by the italicized turns in the following extracts) must necessarily depend ultimately on examples of ordinary talk extracted from transcripts of the participants' original conversations:

Comprehension check
L: To sin- uh . . . to sink
N: Do you know what that is?
L: To go uh-
N: To go under . . .

Definition request
L: . . . what is the meaning of research?
N: Um, study? You study a problem and find an answer.

With respect to the question of camouflage in this particular research, notice that the statistical analyses reported later to test the hypotheses of the study depend crucially on such categories as comprehension checks and definition requests being objectively distinct. But what Porter's analysis glosses over is that, from a participant's intersubjective perspective, these categories have little or no psychological validity. They are in fact superficial artifices of the analyst that distort the pragmatic intent of the participants. More specifically, there is no real-world justification for treating these two categories as discrete illocutionary acts. The interlocutors in both extracts orient to (a) a need to resolve some trouble in their conversation, and (b) a resolution by means of some definitional work on the lexical items that are problematic. Arguably, therefore, the single category of defining, in which the meaning that the participants themselves attach to what they are doing is intersubjectively constructed over several turns, seems better motivated by the data than the two categories proposed by Porter. The analyst's subjective and unwarranted decision to treat these categories as discrete entities therefore inevitably taints the subsequent statistical analysis.

I wish to emphasize that these kinds of problems are not peculiar to the particular research I have just reviewed. For example, with respect to the issue of how important it is to mathematize a discipline if it is to have anything worthwhile to say, the work of Bayley (this volume, chapter 9) also illustrates some of the problems faced by researchers who work in the nomothetic tradition rather well.

Bayley explained the interlanguage variation exhibited by Mandarin Chinese speakers of English as a second language with respect to their use of the phonetic form of the past tense and their use of grammatical aspect by using the method of maximum likelihood estimation, a form of multivariate statistical analysis. This is expressed by the following mathematical formula:

The exact meaning (or, rather, the lack of meaning to perhaps the majority of his readers) of this supposedly objective but hardly very transparent equation required Bayley to devote about a quarter of his chapter to explaining what all this actually means. Yet, in order to explain this highly abstract communication, Bayley had to explain himself through language!

The persistent reader was rewarded with the conclusion that "variation in interlanguage tense marking is indeed systematically conditioned by a range of linguistic, social, and developmental factors" (which are then outlined in greater detail). I leave it to readers to decide whether their investment of time and energy into an understanding of the statistical procedure was worth the conclusions that Bayley reached.

Finally, the question of metaphor in "objective" research is highly problematic for the nomothetic tradition (and indeed for researchers who work in the more logical-deductive tradition that informs much formal linguistic research). Consider the following citation from Bley-Vroman and Chaudron, in which the authors set out their ideas on how language is stored in the brain:

In keeping with nearly all present thinking on language processing, we assume that, in the native speaker, the language processor automatically and obligatorily produces representations of the input and does not itself require the use of shortterm memory. To borrow the evocative allusion of Fodor, parsing is not "sicklied o'er with the pale cast of thought". In the conception of current generative linguistics, the language processor is "encapsulated" in a language module. Parsing thus cannot affect imitation accuracy directly by "filling up" short-term memory. It is important to be clear about this matter. The claim is not that the parser has no memory store: No doubt it has at least some sort of "look-ahead buffer". Rather, whatever the store used by the parser, it is not the same short-term store that is used by a subject in remembering what was said in order to repeat it.

What is remarkable about this extract is that it draws on no less than three different metaphors in one paragraph to clarify the authors' position. These metaphors are identified explicitly by the use of quotation marks. First, there is the Shakespearean metaphor, which is used throughout the chapter to provide one explanation of how short-term memory may work. Second, there is the formalist metaphor of generative linguistics, which suggests that the language processor (whatever that is, neurobiologically) is "encapsulated" in something called a language module (again, whatever this might be, from a neurobiological perspective). And third, there are the artificial intelligence/computer science metaphors of "filling up" memory banks and putative "look-ahead buffers."

The reader may wonder which of these three metaphors is the most important in these authors' discussion. Furthermore, it is instructive to consider that if this chapter had been written in the 17th century, we most likely would have been presented with a metaphor involving language as a well-regulated mechanism that could be explained by analogy with the chronometer (the dominant metaphor of the day, used by Newton and others to explain the universe). Thus, a fundamental epistemological question for researchers working in this kind of tradition is: Does the use of such metaphors serve to clarify the phenomenon of SLA or does it serve merely to obfuscate it?

Experimental researchers interested in developing causative theories of SLA may reply that these kinds of issues are merely technical problems that should not sidetrack us from the real business of SLA research, which is to provide causative explanations of SLA. Furthermore, so the argument runs, many of these objections can be met by developing better coding procedures.

The development of better coding procedures is indeed always a possibility. However, the elaboration per se of better analytical categories does not circumvent the basic problem of "objective" technical definitions being dependent on "subjective" lay talk and/

or on the inescapable use of metaphor. But even if we accept the technocratic argument that these deeper epistemological matters can be set aside temporarily in the interests of scientific progress (an argument that, of course, I do not accept), it is by no means an irrefutable, objective fact that only nomothetic science can explain SLA phenomena.

The categories that constitute Porter's composite variable of repair by themselves tell us next to nothing about the fundamental properties of second-language learning. For example, we do not know whether, by repairing their speech, the learners in the two extracts actually understood, much less learned, what the words to sink or research mean. Thus, the use of quantified data cannot tell us whether a particular conversational mechanism (such as turn-taking or repair) is actually available as a resource for second-language learning; it merely tells us how often this mechanism occurs in a conversation and whether this frequency of occurrence is statistically significant. Thus, SLA researchers are left in the peculiar position of positing that negotiated comprehensible input is an important variable in SLA, without really knowing on the basis of empirical evidence what successful input (i.e., input that results in demonstrable learning) actually looks like in context. Ironically, therefore, the kind of predictive explanation that researchers working in the nomothetic tradition seek to construct seems to be quite limited in its ability to capture the essence of the phenomena I have just been discussing.

In contrast, the originality of the ethnomethodological respecification of social science (and therefore of SLA studies) offered by Giddens and others is that this respecification (a) problematizes the methodological assumptions in traditional social science about the process of theory construction as intersubjectively achieved phenomena that are worthy of analysis in their own right; and (b) embraces ordinary language as the indispensable medium for analyzing participants' constructions of their everyday experience, whether this analysis is done by participants or by analysts. Thus, as Benson and Hughes put it, ethnomethodology is an attempt to make the world investigable in the participants' own terms. Consequently, from an ethnomethodological perspective, the scientific rigor of a study is not evaluated in terms of the sophistication of the statistical techniques that might be employed, because ethnomethodologists rarely use such techniques. Rather, a study is rigorous to the extent that it explains the intersubjective achievement in which participants understand the locally recognizable and locally adequate turns-at-talk that they engage in to organize their world.

At the risk of being accused of setting up a straw man and/or of being redundant, I predict that many experimentalists will raise the familiar objections: (a) such a program of research is useful only to describe baseline SLA phenomena but, cannot explain SLA for the reason given in (b); (b) ethnomethodologists do not attempt to make a priori predictions that can be falsified experimentally; and (c) ethnomethodologists do not work with large groups of subjects, which is the only methodology that can explain SLA phenomena in such a way that the results can be generalized from the subjects tested to a broader population of learners.

It should be obvious by now that I believe that objections of this kind entirely miss the point of the arguments developed in this chapter. Perhaps an example from anatomy will demonstrate the fallacy of such arguments. It would be a very strange version of anatomy indeed that insisted that the function of the human heart as a pump could be reliably explained only by dissecting a large number of hearts to check whether the pumping hypothesis was true of a statistically significant sample of hearts, so that this fact could be generalized to the entire population of human beings. Dissecting a single cadaver is sufficient to demonstrate (i.e., explain) that the heart does indeed function as a pump. Similarly, researchers interested in the "anatomy" of conversation (i.e., its structure) can make valid generalizations from single cases to the broader population because, as Benson and Hughes argued, "the point of working with 'actual occurrences,' single instances, single events, is to see them as the products of 'machinery' that constituted members' cultural competence enabling them to do what they do, produce the activities and scenes of everyday life the explication, say, of some segment of talk in terms of the 'mechanism' by which that talk was produced there and then, is an explication of some part of culture". Thus, although the explanation is of a different type, it is no less powerful and generalizable in its own terms than is predictive explanation.

Conversation-Analytic Explication of Spoken Definitions

I now demonstrate how Conversation Analysis (CA), a manifestation of ethnomethodology that has already been successfully used in SLA research, can be used to provide an interpretive explanation of the mechanisms that enable language learners to use spoken definitions as a resource for language learning. Four basic assumptions govern CA work: (a) conversation has structure; (b) conversation is its own autonomous context—that is, the meaning of a particular utterance is shaped by what immediately precedes it and also by what immediately follows it; (c) there is no a priori justification for believing that any detail of conversation, however minute, is disorderly, accidental, or irrelevant; and (d) the study of conversation requires naturally occurring data.

Because the rules of evidence used by conversation analysts are not as well understood as those used by experimental researchers, let me briefly review what counts as evidence in CA and the kinds of claims made by conversation analysts. The methodology of CA is qualitative and subject to the usual evaluation criteria for qualitative research. Beyond this, however, the methodology of CA attempts to explicate the lay knowledge of conversationalists by "unpacking" examples that demonstrate the participants' orientations to the conversations they construct in real time. Such examples provide the primary evidence for the asserted existence of particular conversational mechanisms identified by analysts; a case is convincing to the extent that it is directly motivated by the conversational data presented for analysis. Thus, CA makes no appeal to ethnographic knowledge to make an argument. Furthermore, conversation analysts do not develop arguments about the structure of conversation on the basis of quantitative analyses of frequency data, because such analyses cannot tell us anything about the underlying structure of conversation per se. Instead, conversation analysts seek to demonstrate that conversation could not be conversation if such universal interactional resources for constructing meaning as turntaking, repair, or preference rules did not exist.

In order to demonstrate the existence of such phenomena, conversation analysts use prototypical examples that give discursive form to the phenomenon being analyzed. But such examples are not by themselves sufficient to make a convincing argument. Analysts must be able to corroborate their claims by pointing to a convergence of different types of textual evidence or by showing that a single structure identified by the analyst plays a role in different types of cases. Note that the use of convergent evidence, like the use of related data, is a particularly important resource in countering the charge that an analysis is merely an artifact of the examples collected and chosen for presentation to readers. Thus, for example, a preceding preinvitation turn shows that reading the following turn as an invitation is contextually warranted. Finally, analyses must be subject to critical falsification. That is, analysts must demonstrate that potential counterexamples and different accounts for the same data set have been anticipated and that other researchers can replicate findings with different transcripts. Let us now move on to an analysis of classroom data that demonstrates how CA might be used to motivate an ethnomethodological respecification of SLA studies.

The Database

The complete database for this project consists of 14 lower-intermediate to upper-intermediate English as a Second Language (ESL) classes at a large research university located in the Midwest of the United States. These classes were video- and audiotaped during spring semester, 1990. Each class lasted 50minutes. Currently, the conversations of 3 teachers and 33 learners (11 in Class 1, 10 in Class 2, and 12 in Class 3) interacting in ordinary classrooms" have been fully transcribed, using transcription conventions that are based on those developed by Jefferson (1978) and van Lier (1988) (see Appendix). The data analyzed in this chapter come from Class 2 only.

Data Collection Procedures

Two video cameras were used to film the participants, who were visually identified by a number pinned to their clothing (i.e., L1, L2 L3, etc.); the video signals were fed into an electronic switcher operated by an assistant. Camera I (the main camera) recorded learners interacting in groups or whole class acuvities, and Camera 2 filmed teacher-fronted activities and/or presentations by students using the blackboard or overhead projector. These video recordings were used primarily to check visually who was speaking to whom when this information could not be determined from the audio data.

The audio recordings are the primary sources of data. Each participant was issued a numbered Walkman-sized stereo cassette recorder and a lapel microphone. The number on each recorder (and on each cassette) corresponded to the number pinned to a participant's clothing. This set-up allowed the analyst to identify participants visually on the videotape and aurally on their audiotapes. The portability of this equipment also enabled teachers and students to move around the class without having to worry about problems like tripping over cables. The availability of multiple audio recordings meant that such technically significant information as the difference between pauses and inhaled or exhaled breaths, the specific number of laughter tokens, the precise onset and resolution of overlaps, and the content of muttered commentaries could be distinguished and therefore transcribed with a high degree of confidence. Transcripts for each group and teacher in every class were produced on the basis of these multiple recordings; in the case of Class 2, this yielded a total of six transcripts for the lesson (four parallel transcripts for the four groups, one teacher's transcript, and one transcript consisting of collections of definitions excerpted from the class interaction).

The Tasks

The tasks learners had to complete in Class 2 involved an open-ended fourway exchange of information. Students first read and discussed in four small groups, one of four thematically-related magazine articles on the greenhouse effect. A representative or representatives from each group then presented the information contained in each reading with an overhead projector in an oral, whole-class activity. The end product was some written work, which was done in a later class that was not recorded. Approximately 30 minutes (which included 5 to 10 minutes of silent reading, depending on the group) were allocated to small group discussion and about 20 minutes were given over to three oral presentations. The first seven excerpts cited here were produced collaboratively by Group 3 during the group work phase, and Excerpt 8 was produced by L10 (an erstwhile member of Group 3) as part of the oral report to the whole class.

The Data

Excerpt 1: Group Work Phase

1. L10: < hh >hhhh what is th- what is the (+) coral (+) what's ((whis-
2. per)) (+) I don't know (h)
3. L11: just- look at it (+) as a (+) an m- material that's all
4. (+)
5. L9?: uhm don't worry about it
6. (+)

Excerpt 2: Group Work Phase

1. L10: excuse me what is c-o-r-a-l ((L10 spells out the word))
2. (+)
3. T: can 1: (+) open //(h)// < h > (+ +) get an idea (+) see where's that
4. L10: //(h)//
5. L10: < h > I don't know whether the-
6. (+)
7. T: corals (+) does anyone know? (+) where you find corals?
8. L9: corals (+) u- underwater //you mean? under the-//
9. T: //uh huh,//
10. (+)

A Definition of Spoken Definitions

For the purposes of the analysis of the larger corpus from which these data were taken, the defining characteristics of spoken definitions, were determined not on the basis of a priori categories but on the basis of an analysis of the interaction in all three fully transcribed classes. Thus, spoken definitions are not defined here as linguistic products or as logical forms. Rather, they are defined as any turn(s)-at-talk that are hearable by participants as explanations of lexical items or phrases whose meaning is actually or potentially unclear. More specifically, participants achieve definitions by simultaneously orienting to the resources of turn-taking and repair available to them as conversationalists and using a range of vocabulary elaboration strategies to resolve the problem they are confronted with. These strategies (which may be used singly or in combination) include the use of iconic, nonverbal means of defining, such as pointing, acting, drawing, and showing pictures. They also may be explicit verbal strategies such as simplification, synonymy, antonymy, classification, approximation, exemplification, comparison, and translation. Finally, these explicit strategies are complemented by such implicit verbal elaboration strategies as apposition, parallelism, and paraphrase.

Identify the Conversational Structure of Spoken Definitions

The data were first examined to establish the prototypical conversational structure of definitions. Prototypical definitions are achieved as sequences that consist of a question-and-answer adjacency pair, followed by an evaluation turn in which participants indicate whether they have understood the definition. In the question turn(s) of the adjacency pair, participants predominantly use wh-questions such as what does X mean, what's the meaning of X, what is X, (or interlingual variations thereof to initiate definitions; however, a number of other forms (such as yes/no questions or plain X with rising intonation) are also found. In the answering turn(s), participants define problematic terms using the kinds of elaboration strategies identified by Chaudron. And in the third and final commenting turn(s), participants typically use change-of-state tokens like oh (ok), which assert understanding and which may close the sequence.

In order to guard against inadvertent analyst bias, the data were also checked (a) to see if participants achieved definitions in ways that did not conform to this prototypical pattern, and (b) to confirm that participants did indeed orient to sequences that superficially conformed to the prototypical pattern as bona fide definitions. As the teacher's talk in Excerpt 3 (lines 1-10) demonstrates, Excerpt 8 includes talk (at lines 4-9) that is intended by L10 to be heard as a definition, even though it is not done as a sequence and does not display the three-part structure I have just alluded to. And with respect to the issue of talk that superficially resembles prototypical definitions, untaped classroom observations and field notes from a fourth class that is not fully transcribed at the present time indicate that sequences that begin with a What is X turn followed by the prototypical answering and commenting turns need not necessarily count as definitions of unknown terms. More specifically, a learner in this fourth class (which was discussing euthanasia) rhetorically asked, "What is death?" His interlocutor initially oriented to this question as a request to define this word and began to provide a definition in his answering turn. But it immediately became clear, when the first student interrupted this definition-in-progress with his own answering turn, that he asked this question so that he could develop his own views on this subject, not because he did not know the meaning of death. The final commenting turn of the second student confirmed the rhetorical nature of this definition, because he indicated that he understood that the first learner was not in fact asking for help in understanding the meaning of death.

On the basis of these procedures, a total of 82 attempted and/ or completed spoken definitions have been identified in the three classes that constitute the current database in the larger corpus. The eight definitions cited in the data section are representative of the range of definition types used in the database as a whole.

Analysis

The first question we might ask ourselves is what conversational resources L10 draws on in Excerpts 1-8, first to understand what coral means, and ultimately to explain this word to her fellow students. The definitions in Excerpts 1-7 are not planned. They are locally occasioned (i.e., they are constructed in real time by interlocutors who use the resource of turn-taking to develop a definition sequence cooperatively). And they are also done as repairs. Following Schegloff and other writers, repair consists of any work participants engage in to clear up conversational trouble as it occurs. This work usually involves a switch in the focus of the discourse and is often signaled by the presence of such lexical devices as well, you know, I mean and by repetitions and/or reordering of syntactic units; furthermore, nonlexical devices such as silences, pauses, false starts, cut-offs, lengthenings, emphatic stress, hesitation markers such as uh or uhm, gestures, and other paralinguistic phenomena are also frequently present. Finally, participants may modulate repairs by laughing or by using modal verbs or question forms to make themselves sound more tentative, and therefore less challenging, to their interlocutors. The greater the number of these microlevel signals of repair found in a stretch of talk, the stronger the evidence that participants are repairing the interaction.

Notice that if we look at the first 24 lines of Excerpt 5, we can find several of the technical signals of repair mentioned earlier. More specifically, there is a switch in the focus of the discourse at line 1 (where L10 is reading from the article to herself) from reading for information to asking about the meaning of coral at line 3. Interturn silences occur at lines 2 and 4; interturn pauses are found at lines 10, 12, 19, and 21; and intraturn pauses occur at lines 7, 9, 11, 13, and 24. We also find multiple instances of various hesitation markers at lines 7, 8, 11, 13, and 18; cut-offs at lines 6, 11, and 22; and syllable lengthenings at lines 7, 11, 13, and 18. Furthermore, L9 constructs her turns at lines 5, 20, and 23 as questions. Finally, notice that repetition occurs not only at lines 13, 14, and 17 but also across excerpts in L10's repeated requests for an explanation of what coral means. Thus, there can be no doubt that these participants are repairing their talk in this excerpt (as in the other excerpts cited).

But how can we demonstrate that repaired conversations are actually a resource for language learning? More specifically, what evidence can we use to show that the conversational resources of turn-taking and repair not only help L10 to understand what coral means but also promote some kind of learning, as opposed to mere short-term, localized understanding?

First, let us discard the kind of evidence that we should not rely on to answer these questions. Notice that L10 repeatedly uses the change-of-state token oh in Excerpts 2 and 3 and actually closes these sequences with the combined tokens oh ok at lines 25 (in Excerpt 2) and 18 (in Excerpt 3).

Because the teacher does not pursue this matter any further, we have reason to believe that he or she interprets L10's use of these tokens (particularly at line 25 of excerpt 2, where she says, "Oh ok oh I see thank you") as evidence that L10 has understood what coral means. But such a reading (on the part of either the teacher or the analyst) of what L10 means by these final tokens would be erroneous, because L10 subsequently initiates two more sequences on the same word. I suggest that in Excerpt 2, L10 is only indicating that she understands that corals are found at the bottom of the sea, and in Excerpt 3, that a definition of what coral means must be provided in the subsequent whole-class activity. But for the reasons already outlined, L10 cannot have fully understood what coral means by the end of Excerpt 3. These "appropriate" answers therefore do not constitute sufficient evidence of understanding.

What evidence, then, should we rely on to demonstrate localized understanding and perhaps even learning? The most important evidence that we can point to in this regard occurs in the marked turns of excerpt 5 (lines 18, 23-30, 32, 35, 38-39). At line 23, in response to L10's question at line 18 asking whether coral is food for fish, L9 replies that coral is like stone. This information seems to trigger a breakthrough in understanding for L10. More specifically, L10 vehemently asserts at line 24 that she has understood (which indicates at least that L10 is rather confident that she has indeed understood this word and is willing to expose herself to a potential loss of face if she turns out to be wrong). At line 25, she independently provides the extra information that coral is very beautiful, which L9 corroborates at line 27. At lines 27, 29, and 30, L9 provides more descriptive information about coral, which L10 overlaps with further assertions that she has understood, at lines 28 and 32. In addition, in the last part of her turn at line 32 and also at line 35, L10 again goes further by providing a translation of this word into Chinese. Because L9 is not a Chinese speaker, she does not understand these translations; consequently, L10 translates the Chinese term back into English by saying "coral" at line 38. The correctness of this translation is corroborated by L11 (who is also a Chinese speaker), who overlaps L10 at line 39 by also saying "coral." We may therefore conclude that L10 has indeed understood what coral means.

We now need to demonstrate that these sequences actually contribute to learning that goes beyond a mere understanding of coral in its immediate local context in the interaction. Finding evidence of this kind in data that are transcribed from a single lesson is difficult, because learning is not necessarily public and occurs over extended periods of time. Fortunately, however, the data in Excerpt 8, which L10 produced during her oral report to the rest of the class some 10 minutes after the end of Excerpt 5, provides the kind of internal textual evidence we need. These data include L10's definition for her peers of the word coral, which, as we have just seen, she had only just learned. As we have already noted, we can be sure that the highlighted parts of Excerpt 8 are intended by L10 to be understood as a definition, because the teacher had requested Group 3 to give a definition of coral in Excerpt 3. To the extent that this definition is conversationally adequate, therefore, the evidence in Excerpt 8 suggests that L10 has actually learned this word and uses this new knowledge for her own purposes in a different part of the conversation.

Notice, too, that the more planned definition found in Excerpt 8 is also done as a repair (in this regard, note the same kinds of technical signals of repair I have already remarked on, distributed throughout this excerpt). More specifically, L10 borrows the highlighted parts of Excerpts 2, 3, 5, 6, and 7 and recombines these elements to produce her own original definition of coral in excerpt 8.23 Thus, "at the bottom of the sea" first occurs at lines 18 and 22 of Excerpt 2; this phrase reappears at lines 13, 15, and 17 of Excerpt 5 and again at line 5 of Excerpt 8. "Coral reefs" is borrowed from line 13 of Excerpt 3 and also reappears at line 5 of Excerpt 8; and the remaining components of the definition found in Excerpt 8 ("fossil" in lines 4 and 5, "habitat" in lines 6 and 8, and "home" in line 9) are borrowed from Excerpt 6 (lines 1, 2, and 7-8) and Excerpt 7 (lines 4, 8, and 9).

Finally, notice that the definition that L10 produces in lines 4-9 of Excerpt 8 is a planned definition (see also Crookes, 1989). That is, it contains many of the elements of logical definitions, which are often constructed as three- part statements like the following: An A is a B, which does C. Thus, coral would fit in the A part of this statement, the information classifying coral as a type of fossil found at the bottom of the sea would fit in the B part of the statement, and the information about coral being an important habitat or home for fish would fit into the C part of the statement. This more formal and complex definition also provides internal textual evidence that L10 has actually learned the meaning of coral.

Conclusion

I have demonstrated two things in the preceding paragraphs. In the first part of this chapter, I showed that the nomothetic characterization of descriptive studies as limited and non-theory-generating need not be unquestioningly accepted. Interpretive explanations, inspired by hermeneutics, of ordinary data have considerable theoretical power, which may be generalized beyond the single events on which they are based. And in the second part, I applied CA to explain how the mechanisms of turn-taking and repair may be used as resources for successful second-language learning.

If these proposals for respecifying SLA studies have any merit, our notions of what constitutes the most valuable kind of research will have to be reassessed. This does not mean that I believe that research in the nomothetic tradition has no value. As I indicated at the beginning of this chapter, I acknowledge that qualitative and quantitative research represent complementary paths to new knowledge about the phenomenon of SLA and that the results of nomothetic research are in many ways impressive. But it does mean that researchers will have to reevaluate whether the current dominance of the nomothetic tradition is entirely beneficial to the field. At a time when epistemology and theory construction are high on the SLA research agenda, I believe that an ethnomethodological respecification of the process of SLA research is of the essence because it simultaneously problematizes the way in which we try to theorize SLA and provides a distinctive methodology for analyzing this complex phenomenon. Thus, in my opinion, the value of ethnomethodology lies in the fact that it provides the field with opportunities for critically reevaluating its dominant epistemology and also for reassessing the criteria by which it measures its level of success as a scientific endeavor. These are matters that a maturing discipline cannot afford to ignore.

19

Research Methodology of Construction and Validation

Introduction

There are many reasons for the prestige and influence that external tests hold on the general testing scene. One is the power of external tests to affect the lives of individuals; another is the lack of training in testing methods on the part of both teachers and researchers; yet another is that external tests are promoted by testing companies with economic interests. The focus of this chapter is the role of language tests within the context of SLA research. Before addressing the specific contribution of language testing to SLA research, it is important to note that the external testing context differs from the SLA research context in a number of ways. Thus, testing is used in SLA research to provide evidence for theories or research questions, but tests are used in the external context to arrive at decisions about individuals' futures. Consequently, testing in research does not have a direct impact on test takers' lives, whereas results obtained from external tests do. Also, in many SLA studies, tests are not the only devices used for collecting data; rather, multiple procedures such as questionnaires, observations, and interviews are employed. In most external testing contexts, tests are the only procedures used for obtaining information on the subjects' language ability.

In spite of these differences, it is clear that language tests (LT) can contribute to SLA theories and research in a number of ways: (a) defining and identifying means of measuring language ability (the dependent variable in SLA research), (b) improving the quality of the data collection instruments used in SLA research, and (c) identifying and testing hypotheses for SLA research. On the other hand, there are also a number of ways in which SLA research and theory can contribute to language testing: (a) identifying areas to be tested and perspectives for analyzing the language samples, (b) proposing a variety of tasks useful in the collection of language data (not just tests), and (c) alerting language testers as to potential differences in performance due to the first language (LI) of the respondents. Each of these contributions is now discussed in detail.

Contribution of Lt to Sla

Much of the work in LT in the past two decades has been devoted to defining language ability, under the rationale that if there is clear identification of the structure of language, it will be possible to design tests to match such descriptions. In the early work of Oller, language was viewed as a unitary factor underlying language behavior competence, based on the learner's pragmatic expectancy of grammar operationalized through integrative tests such as cloze and dictation. Canale and Swain hypothesized that language competence comprises four competencies linguistic, sociolinguistic, discourse, and pragmatic implying that a valid language measure needs to include these components.

More recently, Bachman offered his model of language ability, concentrating on organizational and pragmatic competencies. In this model, organizational competence involves grammatical and textual competencies, and organizational competence involves illocutionary and sociolingistic competencies.

The main contribution of the different models to SLA theory and research is in providing a framework for measuring the dependent variable, that is, language ability. After all, SLA researchers must test their hypotheses about SLA (regarding, for example, the acquisition processes, factors interacting with and affecting SLA, strategies used by learners in SLA) in relation to language ability. These models can thus provide information on what constitutes language ability and how it can be validly measured. For example, given current models, it would be unwise for SLA researchers to measure the dependent variable of language via a cloze test, whereas 15 years ago it would have been acceptable. Today, it is clear that to measure language in SLA one must focus on a number of components linguistic, sociolinguistic, discourse, and pragmatic, to use the Canale and Swain model. Alternatively, the focus must be on organizational (grammatical and textual) and pragmatic (illocutionary and sociolinguistic) competence, as in Bachman's model.

However, the contribution of LT to SLA research in this area of measuring language ability is still limited, because many of these models have not yet been validated empirically. It is not known, for example, whether the different components are independent of one another and what is the relationship between them in testing situations. Some work in this area has been done by Harley, Cummins, Swain and Allen, in which they examined whether grammatical, discourse, and SL competence can be distinguished empirically. Factor analysis failed to confirm the hypothesized three-trait structure of proficiency. In other studies there was support for the existence of separate grammatical and discourse components, whereas evidence for the existence of a separate sociolinguistic competence was not as strong. The Bachman model has not been validated empirically, although it is based on a previous study by Bachman and Palmer showing that language ability consists of one factor plus a number of unique abilities.

But there is yet another problem that limits the contribution of LT to SLA research. Testers rely on tests as the exclusive procedures for validating their models and as the only way of obtaining data. But language ability is a broad and complex construct that cannot be fully measured by tests. Thus, much as language testers would like to contribute to the definition of language ability, as long as they continue to obtain their data exclusively from tests, their contribution to SLA research and theory will be limited. Only when language testers begin to explore the use of other assessment procedures, especially those that are less testlike and more ethnographic (for example, observation or analysis of natural occurring documents) will they be in a position to contribute more substantially to SLA theory and research by providing more valid information about language ability and ways of assessing it.

Related to this problem of reliance on tests is another problem that originates from a conflict existing between the construct of language and the procedure of test analysis. Most current techniques for analyzing testing data, such as Item Response Theories (IRT) and latent trait models, are based on the assumption of unidimensionality. However, because language is clearly not a unidimensional construct, a serious conflict and a mismatch exist between the domains of LT and SLA. Specifically, how can LT analyses contribute to SLA research when they are based on different assumptions?

This is clearly a problem that has not yet been resolved and is a point of ample discussion in the field of language testing. One perspective on this issue is provided by Henning, who attempted to resolve the problem by arguing that the effort to equate psychometric reality with psychological reality is mistaken. Henning argued that the two must be viewed as representing separate and distinct realities a psychological reality and a psychometric one. These can be better referred to as a psychometric reality and a language (or second language) reality. Thus, testers should try to identify not what knowing a language means but rather what knowing a language means in testing situations. According to this approach, the contribution of LT to SLA will lie in providing information on the performance of test takers in testing situations and not in language in general. Performance on tests can therefore be considered a subset of general language performance. For example, if the SLA researcher is studying the area of communicative strategies, the use of such strategies in SL tests may be considered to be one subset of more general use of such strategies. Any results are therefore not necessarily generalizable to nontesting situations. Thus, the contribution of language testing to SLA lies in defining the dependent variable, though at this point the definition applies only to testlike situations.

Improving the Quality of SLA Data Collection Instruments Used in SLA Research. It was mentioned earlier that the results of external tests have a major impact on the lives of the test takers. Due to this responsibility, external tests should be of high quality and must pass strict quality criteria. These requirements (for example, that external tests be reliable and valid, that items and tasks be pretested and piloted before the actual administration, that bad items be revised or removed, that cultural and contextual biases be avoided), as imposed by the field of psychometrics, could be adopted by SLA research to improve research instruments.

Although tests in SLA research do not have a direct impact on the test takers' lives, they do have an indirect impact insofar as they contribute to an increased understanding of the theory of SLA, as well as to practical conclusions and implications. Thus, the inappropriateness of tests in research and the lack of quality criteria for instruments are likely to lead to a misunderstanding of SLA phenomena and to mistaken conclusions regarding new programs, new teaching methods, and new curricula.

SLA researchers often use tasks and not tests, but here quality criteria are equally important. Several SLA studies that examined communicative strategies reached conclusions that could be challenged because they had no testretest or parallel form reliability information. Test-retest reliability provides information on whether similar results would be obtained had the tests been administered on a different occasion, and parallel form reliability shows whether the use of a similar version of the instrument will result in the same data. Similar criticism applies to work on variation, introspection, and pragmatics. The type of reliability (for example, internal consistency, test-retest, or parallel forms) depends, of course, on the specific instrument used. Ethnographic procedures should not be exempt from scrutiny as to quality control. Seliger and Shohamy outlined specific ways of examining quality criteria in relation to the specific research questions and type of data collection procedures used.

Instruments used in SLA research need to be tested for their validity as well. Evidence of construct validity needs to be obtained in order to show that the instruments measure the construct in light of current theories. This type of validity is different from the pragmatic validity that is required of external tests. Pragmatic validity is related to real life as it questions whether the test predicts well (predictive validity) or whether it correlates with another test and can therefore serve as a substitute (concurrent or criterion validity).

The impact that tests have on the lives of individuals is not very relevant for tests used in SLA research. These tests are generally one-shot events in which control over all the variables of the study may affect the validity of the results. However, an area that is gaining importance in external testing is that of fairness and ethics in testing; this aspect is currently being viewed as a new type of validity. This type of validity is certainly relevant to the SLA researcher as well, because it applies to the protection of the subjects of research studies.

In reading SLA research, however, too often it is found that quality criteria were not applied. Specifically lacking is information about the process of test development and about the different types of reliability and validity. It is apparent that many of the tests used are inappropriate for the specific research questions being studied and that often tests designed for making decisions about individuals are used for answering research questions. It often seems that the researchers simply had easy access to certain tests and used them without giving serious consideration as to their appropriateness for the specific research questions.

One study that illustrates the consequences of using instruments of doubtful quality was reported by Rosansky. She provided convincing evidence that the Bilingual Syntax Measure (BSM) tests in the morpheme acquisition studies that led to a whole new policy for limited English speakers were based on instruments that had no reliability or validity. She demonstrated how major decisions were based on studies that used inappropriate and inaccurate tests and that led to invalid theoretical conclusions and implications and to inappropriate language teaching programs. She cautioned, "Continued use of the BSM as a research tool, with its questionable validity, leaves many otherwise well-designed research studies subject to serious criticism at their very core the data base. Continued placement of children in bilingual programs on the basis of the BSM, with its limited sample of items and fuzzy proficiency level assignments, is risky". By applying some of the procedures used by language testers, SLA researchers are likely to obtain data that are more reliable and valid.

Related to the issue of the data collection instruments is that of the ample research available to language testers about language tests and the language testing process. In LT research, as distinguished from LT development, researchers examine questions concerning the testing process, the effect of testing methods, or the effect of contextual variables on test takers' scores. One illustrative example involves the effect of the method of testing on test scores. Results of certain studies show that the method of testing, that is, the procedure used for collecting the data, the type of instrument, or even the type of questions (multiple-choice versus open-ended) affect the scores obtained on language tests. Similar studies showed that familiarity with topic, genre and a variety of other contextual variables affect the test taker's scores.

Interestingly, the work of Tarone on elicited versus spontaneous tasks, which indicated that task and context have an effect on the language samples obtained, is a method effect study. Yet one wonders if Tarone's conclusions can be interpreted as an indication of variation or of testing method effect. Here, again, LT research can be instrumental in interpreting findings. In the testing literature there are procedures for finding out whether differences are a result of the method of eliciting the data regarding the trait (that is, method) or the language (that is, the trait). This is a very important area in which language testers can contribute to SLA research by virtue of their own research and experience in applying different validation methods such as multitrait multimethod in a number of major studies.

Thus, language testing can contribute to improved data collection procedures in SLA research by applying psychometric criteria and by applying the results obtained in LT research, especially in the area of different elicitation tasks.

Identifying and Testing Hypotheses for SLA Research

Advances in testing using procedures such as Differential Item Functioning (DIF) and latent trait may have an effect on SLA research. Through the DIF procedure, for example, it is possible to find out that certain items on tests function differently for certain groups of test takers. This procedure is especially powerful in tests such as the TOEFL, where it is possible to observe that certain ethnic groups, for example, behave differently than do other groups. Information of this sort can be valuable for second-language researchers in constructing hypotheses from language data. Pollitt reported recently on a study in which a group with a certain L1 performed differently on the Cambridge test than did other test takers. In analyzing the specific items, he identified those that discriminated against this group because of idiosyncracies in their LI. The fact that specific psychometric techniques such as DIF are capable of identifying different linguistic behaviors is important because it can provide SLA researchers with a variety of new hypotheses in SLA.

Furthermore, language testers, especially those in large testing agencies, often have vast amounts of data. These data are a powerful resource for confirming and testing hypotheses, regarding, for instance, the success on tests of test takers who have different language learning backgrounds (that is, formal vs. informal), the possibility of a natural developmental process in acquiring a language, or the question whether teaching makes a difference.

Contribution of Sla to Lt

Identifying Areas to Be Tested and Perspectives for Analyzing Language Samples

The major contribution of SLA research to LT is in identifying the construct of language acquisition that the language tester needs to consider in the construction of second-language tests. There are endless examples of this: The most striking ones are those involving analysis of reading comprehension (RC) or the writing processes. The fact that RC involves different types of schema, that it is an interactive process, and that different strategies play a role in language processing would make it imperative that language testers incorporate this information into their tests. An awareness on the part of testers of how writing is a process that requires revision would serve to remind them that they cannot administer a one-shot-type test, but rather must use a test in which test takers have the opportunity to revise their writing samples before the final assessment is made.

Unfortunately, a large number of testers do not utilize this information and as a result, the tests do not have construct validity. In a recent article on discourse analysis and language testing, it was pointed out that language testers have overlooked the vast work done in discourse analysis. As a prominent example, the American Council of the Teaching of Foreign Language guidelines did not consider the work in SLA; rather, they were based on a view of language that was unitary, hierarchical, and homogeneous, and therefore detached from current understanding of language and especially from findings concerning language variation. Similar claims can be made regarding the TOEFL and other tests. Clearly, those working on the development of tests for decision making are often not aware of and do not apply the findings of SLA research.

Proposing a Variety of Tasks, not Just Tests

SLA researchers have long been collecting data using different types of procedures and have not limited themselves to tests. Language testers could begin to expand their repertoire of procedures for collecting language data beyond the traditional test approach. This is an area where language testers can benefit from the experience of language researchers and begin to use procedures such as judgment tests, observation of natural language use, documents, and self-assessments.

Alerting Language Testers to Potential Differences in Performance Due to LI

On the basis of their findings, SLA researchers can forewarn the language tester as to possible problem areas. If SLA research has concluded that the Ll makes a difference in SLA, then the language tester cannot treat test takers from different Ll backgrounds in the same way. If different learners process language differently, attempts should be made to give different tasks to different learners. The evidence that the type of elicitation task has a significant impact on the language elicited should be of equal interest to language testers and to SLA researchers.

Conclusions

In this chapter, an attempt was made to point out ways in which language testing can contribute to SLA research and SLA research can contribute to LT. It was shown that although language testers and SLA researchers have different purposes, there are many areas where they can contribute to one another. If testers use creative tasks invented by SLA researchers they may enrich the pool of testing tasks and improve both test quality and the accuracy of decisions based on these tools. At the same time, SLA researchers should know which tools to use to obtain reliable and valid research results.

It is also important for SLA researchers to demand that language testers pay attention to their research findings. By the same token, those working in SLA research could turn to language testers to ensure that their instruments, whether tests or other elicitation tasks, are of high quality. At the same time, SLA researchers can help to interpret language test results on the basis of their research and can alert testers as to where problems may be expected to occur.

It is clear that researchers who collect language data and testers who make decisions about the language of individuals must begin to pay more attention to one another, thus making it possible for researchers to arrive at more valid theories and for testers to make sounder decisions about the future of individuals.

It is also important for test users to demand that language testers have [illegible] to [illegible] research [illegible] [illegible]. A research could turn to language test [illegible] that [illegible] [illegible] [illegible]. A [illegible] research can help [illegible] language test [illegible] [illegible] and [illegible] as [illegible] problems may be [illegible].

It [illegible] language [illegible] about [illegible] [illegible] more attention to one another, making it possible for researchers to [illegible] and test users to make sounder decisions about the [illegible].

Bibliography

A Student Handbook (3rd edition). Morristown: General Learning Press.

ADAMS, R. and J. PREISS (eds.) 1960. Human Organization Research: Field

AGAR, Michael H. 1980. The Professional Stranger: An Informal Introduction to

AGAR, Michael H. 1982. Towards an Ethnographic Language. American Anthropologist

ANTA (Australian National Training Authority), 1994 Towards a Skilled Australia: a national strategy for vocational education and training, ANTA, Brisbane Anthropological Association.

Baker, Carolyn D. and Freebody, Peter, 1987 "'Constituting the Child in Beginning School Reading Books'", British Journal of Sociology of Education vol. 8, no. 1, pp. 55-76

Baker, Carolyn D. and Keogh, Jayne, 1995 "'Accounting for Achievement in TeacherParent Interviews'", Human Studies vol. 18, nos 2/3, pp. 263-300

Boundaries and Grounds of a Field Science. Berkeley: University of California

BURGESS, Robert G. (ed.) 1982. Field Research: A Sourcebook and Field Manual.

BUTLER, B. and D. TURNER (eds.) 1987. Children and Anthropological Research. New

CARRITHERS, Michael. 1996. Fieldwork. In Barnard, Alan and Jonathan Spencer

Carson Richard T., Jordan J. Louviere, Don A. Anderson, Phipps Arabie, David S. Bunch , David A. Hensher, Richard M.

Johnson, Warren F. Kuhfeld, Dan Steinberg , Joffre Sait, Harry Timmermans, and James B. Wiley. "Experimental Analysis of Choice". Marketing Letters 5, no. 4 (1994), pp. 35613567.

COLE, J. (ed.) 1982. Anthropology for the Eighties: Introductory Readings. New

CRANE, Julia G. and Michael V. ANGROSINO. 1992. Field Projects in Anthropology:

Dobber David, and Ian G. Horgan. "A Comparison of Techniques Used and Journals Taken by Marketing Researchers in Britain and the USA". Service Industries Journal 8, no. 3 (1988), pp. 277-285.

EMBER, Carol R. and Melvin EMBER. 2000. Cross-Cultural Research Methods. Oxford:

EMERSON, R.M. (ed.) 1988. Contemporary Field Research: A Collection of Readings.

EVANS-PRITCHARD, Evans E. 1951. Fieldwork and the Empirical Tradition. In: E.E.

EVANS-PRITCHARD, Evans E. 1965. The Comparative Method in Social Anthropology.

FETTERMAN, David M. 1989. Ethnography: Step by Step. Newbury: Sage.

FLICK, Uwe. 1998. An Introduction to Qualitative Research. London: Sage.

FLINN, J. et al. (eds.) 1997. Fieldwork and Families: Constructing New Modelsfor Ethnographic Research. Honoluiu: University of Hawaii Press.

GLASER, Barney G. and Anselm L. STRAUSS 1967. The Discovery of Grounded Theory:

HAINES, D., RUTHERFORD, D. and P. THOMAS. 1981. The Case for Exploratory

HAMMERSLEY, Martyn and Paul ATKINSON. 1994. Ethnography: Principles in Practice

HILL, C. 1974. Graduate Education in Anthropology: Conflicting Role Identity in

HIRSCHKIND, L. 1991. Redefining the "Field" in Fieldwork. Ethnology 30:237-49.

HOCKINGS, Paul (ed.) 1975. Principles in Visual Anthropology. The Hague: Mouton

Honour of Roger Keesing. Canberra Anthropology (special volume) 20(1&2).

Introduction and Casebook. Altamira Press.

JACKSON, A. (ed.) 1987. Anthropology at Home. London: Tavistock Publications.

JACKSON, Bruce. 1987. Fieldwork. Urbana: University of Illinois Press.

JOHNSON, J.C. 1990. Selecting Ethnographic Informants. Newbury Park: Sage.

KIRSCHNER, S. 1987. "Then What Have I to Do With Thee?": On Identity, Fieldwork,

KLOOS, P. 1969. Role Conflicts in Social Fieldwork. Current Anthropology

LUNDBERG, C. 1968. A Transactional Conception of Fieldwork. Human Organization

MALINOWSKI, Bronislaw. 1922. Argonauts of the Western Pacific. London:

Naumann Earl, Donald W. Jackson, and William G. Wolfe. "Examining the Practices of United States and Japanese Market Research Firms". California Management Review 36, no. 4 (1994), pp. 49-69.

NORDSTROM, Carolyn and A. ROBBEN 1995. Fieldwork Under Fire: Contemporary

OBERG, K. 1960. Cultural Shock: Adjustment to New Cultural Environments.

PAGE, H. 1988. Dialogic Principles of Interactive Learning in the Ethnographic

PUNCH, Keith F. 1998. Introduction to Social Research: Quantitative and

Qualitative Approaches. London: Sage.

RASMUSSEN, Susan J. 1996. The Tent as Cultural Symbol and Field Site: Social and

RICHARDSON, Miles. 1975. Anthropologist - the Myth Teller. American Ethnologist

ROSE, D. 1990. Living the Ethnographic Life. Newbury Park: Sage.

Routledge.

SANJEK, Roger (ed.). 1990. Fieldnotes: The Making of Anthropology. Ithaca:

SANJEK, Roger. 1996. Ethnography. In Barnard, Alan and Jonathan Spencer (eds.),

STRAUSS, Anselm L. 1987. Qualitative Analysis for Social Scientists. Cambridge:

STRAUSS, Anselm L. and Juliet CORBIN. 1998. Basics of Qualitative Research:

Structure of Inquiry. Cambridge: Cambridge University Press.

Student Anthropologists. Ann Arbor: University of Michigan Press.

Studies of Violence and Survival. Berkeley: University of California Press.

Symbolic Space, "Topos", and Authority in a Tuareg Community. Anthropological

Techniques and Procedures for Developing Grounded Theory (Second Edition).

The Anthropological Experience. San Francisco: Chandler. the Field: Problems and Challenges in Sociological Investigation. Delhi: Oxford the Hermeneutic Method. New York: State University of New York Press.

WACASTER, C. and W. FIRESTONE. 1978. The Promise and Problems of Long-Term,

WEBB, Eugene J., D.T. CAMPBELL, R.D. SCHWARTZ, and L. SECHREST. 1966.

WOLCOTT, Harry F. 1999. Ethnography: A Way of Seeing. Oxford: AltaMira Press.

Worlds. Houndmills: Macmillan.

Index

A

B

C

D

S

T

U

V

W

Y

Z